# THE
# PILOT'S GUIDE TO
# AFFORDABLE
# CLASSICS

### BILL CLARKE

**TAB** TAB BOOKS Inc.
Blue Ridge Summit, PA

To Ralph H. Mosher, friend and pilot, who lived his 75 years to the fullest.

**Other TAB Books by the Author**

No. 2372   *The Illustrated Buyer's Guide to Used Airplanes*
No. 2412   *The Cessna 170 and 172*
No. 2422   *The Cessna 150 and 152*
No. 2432   *The Piper Indians*
No. 2442   *Cold Weather Flying*

FIRST EDITION
THIRD PRINTING

Printed in the United States of America

Library of Congress Cataloging in Publication Data

Clarke, Bill (Charles W.)
The pilot's guide to affordable classics.

Includes index.
1. Used aircraft—Purchasing.   2. Airplanes—
Conservation and restoration.   I. Title.
TL685.1.C545   1986      629.133′34      85-27700
ISBN 0-8306-0292-5 (pbk.)

TAB BOOKS Inc. offers software for
sale. For information and a catalog,
please contact TAB Software Department,
Blue Ridge Summit, PA 17294-0850.

Questions regarding the content of this book
should be addressed to:

Reader Inquiry Branch
TAB BOOKS Inc.
Blue Ridge Summit, PA 17294-0214

# Contents

# Acknowledgments

There have been so many years since the "classics" were built that it has become quite difficult to obtain accurate information about these fine airplanes that are now a part of flying history. Needless to say I asked for, and received, much assistance. The following is a list of those people/firms/clubs I owe thanks to:

Michael Sellers, of Univair, for data, reprints, and diagrams.

Lorretta Kelly, of Cessna, for background information and pictures.

Ray Stits for expert re-covering and refinishing instructions.

AVCO Lycoming for their "Key Reprints," charts, and photos.

Continental Teledyne for pictures, charts, and storage information.

Sensenich Corp. for photos and applications information.

Narco, King, David Clark Co., and R.S.T. for photos and info on avionics.

Blue River Aircraft for their airframe covering information and photos.

Wag-Aero for information and photos.

Marion Pyles, Air Pix Aviation Photography, for providing photos.

The men and women who operate the various owners clubs. They are experts on their planes, and always ready to share their experience.

# Introduction

At some time or another anyone who has ever flown will entertain thoughts of owning his own airplane. But, like everything else, it costs money, and like everything else, these costs have elevated over the years.

In 1984 even a Cessna 152 had a price tag in the vicinity of $40,000, and four-place planes were starting at $60,000 when equipped with only modest avionics. If the high costs aren't enough, each year finds more complexities on new airplanes. The result is that many of us who yearn for simple and inexpensive flight have been placed outside the new airplane market.

But there is an alternative.

*The Pilot's Guide to Affordable Classics* calls attention to a delightful alternative to the high-priced and complex flight found today—an alternative that includes a little history, loads of fun, inexpensive flight, and real pride in ownership.

In this book we will discuss what "classic" flying means and list the airplanes that are considered classics. We will consider where and how to find a good used classic airplane, and, more importantly, how to keep from getting "stung" in the process of purchasing it.

All too often the search for a used airplane involves vague ads, notes on bulletin boards, and even word of mouth. These ads describe, briefly, an airplane that's for sale, normally by the use of more-or-less standardly employed "airplane language." You will learn to read this language and understand these ads.

Although the prospective buyer may have a basic idea of what the advertised airplane looks like, he should have a source to review for further information about the airplane, its equipment, and value. Here you will find complete descriptions of all the commonly found classic airplanes, including specifications, pictures, and items to watch out for when purchasing. A price guide, based upon the current market, is included.

An easy-to-follow pre-purchase inspection plan is explained, followed with a walk-through of all the purchase paperwork, with examples of the necessary forms.

Complete discussions are made with regards to older airplane engines and how they cope with the new low-lead fuels. Avionics are approached from a no-nonsense angle, and cost-saving advice is given about their needs and purchase.

Then go on to learn how to perform preventive maintenance on these planes, as well as how to recover tube-and-fabric airplanes. There is a complete chapter included about polishing and painting a metal airplane.

All the "where-to-goes" for help, parts, and advice are included, including information on owners/operators clubs and addresses of the FAA offices.

In summary, *The Pilot's Guide to Affordable Classics* was written to aid the potential classic aircraft purchaser, by assisting in economical decision making and allowing the sidestepping of many pitfalls found in aircraft purchasing and ownership.

# Chapter 1

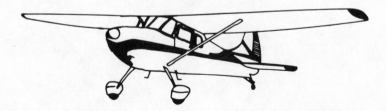

# What Is a Classic?

Ah, to smell an old hangar on a hot summer afternoon—the smells of avgas, oil, dust, hot fabric. To once again hear the wind blowing past the old hangar, making the timbers creak and the doors rattle—now that would surely be heaven. But alas, the old times are gone forever—or are they?

I remember when I was a kid, I learned to fly in an Aeronca 7AC (Fig. 1-1). It was a two-seat plane that had no nosewheel. A good little ship she was; had 65 horsepower up front, and used about four gallons of "av" gas an hour (sometimes this was Amoco white gas). There was no electric system to complicate the plane, and the panel was so simple that I still rejoice when I think of it (Fig. 1-2).

I learned to fly when you navigated with a compass and looked for landmarks. It was called pilotage. I used the rivers, railroads, mountains, and highways as my waypoints. My best chart was an ESSO road map. Now I get in a "new" plane and see all those radios and gadgets and think how it used to be when you flew low and slow. I saw the world go by with my own eyes, not the invisible

eyes of some magical black box (Fig. 1-3).

But alas, the old times are gone forever—or are they?

Don't get me wrong; there is a place for all the modernization of aviation. After all, isn't everyone going at a faster pace now than they were 30 years ago? Maybe that's why today's pilots fly high and need all those luxurious gadgets in their airplanes, modern paved facilities, and those expensive aircraft service centers to keep it all working. After all, aren't these the essentials of flying—or are they?

To me there is nothing like taking an old "Cub" up on a cool evening for a proper end to a busy day. to pass over the hills, through the valleys, maybe over a small lake, to be so close to the earth that I can smell the sweet green grass. *That's* flying.

The planes and type of flying that I refer to are "classic"—flying the machines made during the great airplane boom of the postwar (World War II) era until the end of 1955. The planes manufactured during this period represent inexpensive flying, practical solid design, and a "touch with flying" that cannot be duplicated by today's "spamcan"

1

Fig. 1-1. An Aeronca 7AC awaiting its pilot on a warm summer day. Note the plane is tied down on grass.

Fig. 1-2. The simple panel of an Aeronca 7AC. It's really all you need.

Fig. 1-3. This Cessna is "loaded" with black boxes, and can go anywhere, anytime. (courtesy Cessna)

Fig. 1-4. The Piper Archer is a real fine plane for going from one place to another, but its "spamcan" design lacks the "classic appeal."

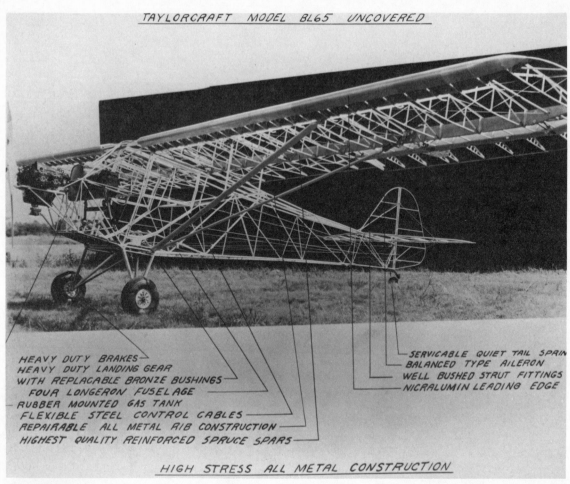

TAYLORCRAFT MODEL BL65 UNCOVERED

HEAVY DUTY BRAKES
HEAVY DUTY LANDING GEAR
WITH REPLACABLE BRONZE BUSHINGS
FOUR LONGERON FUSELAGE
RUBBER MOUNTED GAS TANK
FLEXIBLE STEEL CONTROL CABLES
REPAIRABLE ALL METAL RIB CONSTRUCTION
HIGHEST QUALITY REINFORCED SPRUCE SPARS

SERVICABLE QUIET TAIL SPRIN
BALANCED TYPE AILERON
WELL BUSHED STRUT FITTINGS
NICRALUMIN LEADING EDGE

HIGH STRESS ALL METAL CONSTRUCTION

Fig. 1-5. Without cover, this is the inside of a Taylorcraft. All tube-and-fabric planes are similar in design. (courtesy the Taylorcraft Club)

Fig. 1-6. Notice the tailwheel on this Aeronca 11AC Chief. With only a few exceptions, conventional gear is the rule on classics.

Fig. 1-7. Although a classic, this Luscombe 8 is of all-metal construction.

Fig. 1-8. Tricycle landing gear and metal construction make the Ercoupe appealing to many classic owners. (courtesy Marion Pyles, Air Pix Aviation Photography)

Fig. 1-9. Not appearing until the early '50s, the Piper Tri-Pacer is one of the most affordable four-place family airplanes on today's market.

**THIS DOCUMENT MUST BE KEPT IN THE AIRPLANE AT ALL TIMES**

C.A.A. Approved
February 4, 1948

PIPER AIRCRAFT CORPORATION
Lock Haven, Pennsylvania

**Piper PA-15**
Normal Category

C.A.A. Identification No. ..........................................

## AIRPLANE FLIGHT MANUAL

### I. Limitations

The following limitations must be observed in the operation of this airplane:

| | | | |
|---|---|---|---|
| ENGINE | Lycoming O-145-B2. | | |
| ENGINE LIMITS | For All Operations—2550 RPM. | | |
| FUEL | 80 Minimum Octane Aviation Fuel. | | |
| Propeller | Fixed Pitch Wood 70" Maximum Diameter. | | |
| | 68.5" Minimum Diameter. | | |
| | Static Limits: | Maximum 2320 RPM. | |
| | | **Minimum 2160 RPM.** | |
| POWER INSTRUMENTS | Oil Temperature | Unsafe if indicator exceeds **RED** line (220°F.). | |
| | Oil Pressure: | Unsafe if indicator exceeds **RED** line (85 lbs. maximum) or below the **RED** line (25 lbs. minimum). **Normal** flight operation GREEN arc (65 lbs.—85 lbs.). **Caution or idling** YELLOW arc (25 lbs.—65 lbs.). | |
| | Tachometer: | **RED** line at rated engine speed. **DO NOT EXCEED.** | |
| AIRSPEED LIMITS (True Indicated Airspeed) | | | Normal Category |
| | Never Exceed | | 126 MPH |
| | Maximum Cruising Speed | | 100 MPH |
| | Maneuvering Speed | | 87 MPH |
| FLIGHT LOAD FACTORS | | | |
| | Maximum Positive Load Factor | | 3.8 |
| | Maximum Negative Load Factor (No Inverted Maneuvers Approved) | | |
| MAXIMUM WEIGHT | 1100 lbs. Take-Off and Landing. | | |
| C. G. RANGE | | | |
| (Aft W.L.E.) | 12.5" to 19.0" | | |
| (% M.A.C.) | 19.6% to 30.2% | | |
| MAXIMUM BAGGAGE ALLOWED: | 40 lbs. | | |

NOTE: **It is the responsibility of the airplane owner and the pilot to insure that the airplane is properly loaded.**

LEVELING MEANS: Plumb from upper door channel to center punch mark on front seat cross tube.

AIRSPEED INSTRUMENT MARKINGS AND THEIR SIGNIFICANCE

(a) Radial **RED** line (126) marks the never exceed speed which is the maximum safe airspeed.

(b) **YELLOW** arc (100-126) on indicator denotes range of speed in which operations should be

Fig. 1-10. This is the first page of the flight manual for the Piper PA-15.

conducted with caution and only in smooth air.

(c) **GREEN** arc (45-100) denotes normal operating speed range.

**2. Procedures**

(a) Carburetor heat **shall** be used during all ground operations such as engine warm-up, taxiing, etc.

(b) All other operations are normal.

**3. Performance Information**

The following performance figures were obtained during Civil Aeronautics Administration type tests and may be realized under conditions indicated with the airplane and engine in good condition and with average piloting technique.

All performance is given for the Lycoming O-145-B2 engine installation, fixed-pitch propeller, 1100 pounds weight, with no wind and on level, paved runways.

In using the following data allowance for actual conditions must be made.

| ITEM | ALT. | OUTSIDE AIR TEMPERATURE | | | | | |
|---|---|---|---|---|---|---|---|
| | | 0°F | 20°F | 40°F | 60°F | 80°F | 100°F |
| **Take-Off Distance (In Feet)** | Sea Level | 1273 | 1369 | 1470 | 1572 | 1680 | 1799 |
| Distance to Take-Off and climb 50 ft. at full throttle MPH 63 T.I.A.S. | 3000 | 1815 | 1964 | 2122 | 2302 | 2486 | 2699 |
| | 5000 | 2374 | 2599 | 2860 | 3130 | 3407 | 3755 |
| | 7000 | 3325 | 3695 | 4140 | 4675 | 5205 | 5855 |
| **Landing Distance (In Feet)** | Sea Level | 1224 | 1243 | 1261 | 1280 | 1297 | 1316 |
| Distance required to land over 50 ft. obstacle and stop Approach at 63 MPH T.I.A.S. | 3000 | 1273 | 1293 | 1315 | 1335 | 1356 | 1378 |
| | 5000 | 1310 | 1332 | 1356 | 1376 | 1399 | 1422 |
| | 7000 | 1350 | 1373 | 1398 | 1425 | 1447 | 1471 |
| **Normal Rate of Climb** | Sea Level | 555 | 530 | 508 | 490 | 472 | 456 |
| In feet per minute Airspeed MPH 65 T.I.A.S. | 3000 | 427 | 408 | 390 | 370 | 353 | 337 |
| | 5000 | 345 | 325 | 305 | 290 | 272 | 255 |
| | 7000 | 260 | 245 | 225 | 208 | 190 | 175 |

| Angle of Bank | | 0 | 10 | 20 | 30 | 40 | 50 | 60 |
|---|---|---|---|---|---|---|---|---|
| Stalling Speeds (MPH T.I.A.S.) Power Off | | 48 | 49 | 50 | 52 | 55 | 60 | 69 |

Approved by: *Charles F. Dycusson*

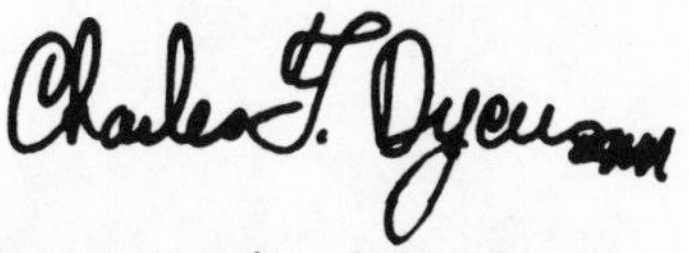

Director, Aircraft and Components Service, Civil Aero. Administration

Fig. 1-11. Here is the second—and last—page. Compare this two-page manual to the 50 or better pages found in the typical late-model Piper or Cessna.

airplanes (Fig. 1-4).

Many of these fine classic airplanes are still flying today, and can be seen at the "rural" airports. Some of these airports have grass strips instead of the paved runways so often found today. You're unlikely to see many classics at the typical modern suburban airport unless there happens to be an airshow there the day you go looking.

Most of these planes are of tube-and-fabric design (Fig. 1-5), two-seat, and have conventional landing gear (Fig. 1-6). These include the Aeronca Champs and Chiefs, Piper Cubs, and Taylorcrafts. There were metal planes such as the Cessna 120/140 series and the Luscombe 8s (Fig. 1-7), and even the Ercoupe with its tricycle gear (Fig. 1-8).

For the family man there were the Cessna 170s, Luscombe Sedans, Piper Pacers/Tri-Pacers, and the Stinson 108 series (Fig. 1-9).

All of these airplanes today represent a little bit of history, but not so much that ownership is prohibitively expensive—in fact, quite the contrary. These classic airplanes may well be the last vestage of affordable flying.

Compared to today's standards, the classics are inexpensive to purchase and uncomplicated to operate (Figs. 1-10, 1-11). Additionally, they're easy to maintain, when contrasted with today's complex systems oriented craft; they don't have retractable landing gear, autopilots, turbochargers, etc.

# Chapter 2

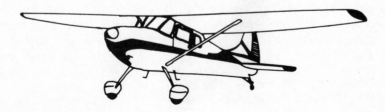

# Buying Your Classic

Finding a good used airplane can be very difficult, especially if you're looking for one particular make and model. You could have an airplane broker do the search for you, but the individual usually does all his own searching. After all that's part of the fun of airplane ownership—the search. Besides, look at all the pleasure of going to many airports looking for that elusive one-of-a-kind airplane—the one you want.

## THE SEARCH

The search can begin—and end—with the local FBO (Fixed Base Operator). However, most current FBOs are more likely to be concerned with newer airplanes. Check the bulletin boards at the local airport(s). Ask around while you're there, and walk around looking for airplanes with For Sale signs in the windows.

The best airports for classics will be uncontrolled grass strips. These fields will normally be well away from any major metropolitan area, and will often appear run-down and out of date—that

is, out of date by "spamcan" standards.

The local newspaper will sometimes have airplanes listed in the classified ads; however, it will pay to expand your search. The wider the search, the larger the selection. A few national publications of interest are:

*Trade-A-Plane*
Crossville
Tenn 38555

*Aircraft Bulletin*
Box 186
Brookfield, CT 06084

*Air Show*
45 West Broadway, Suite 6
Eugene, OR 97401
For further information, call *Air Show*: (800) 247-9005.

Other listings may sometimes be found in the various flight-oriented magazines (*AOPA Pilot, Sport Aviation, Plane & Pilot, Private Pilot*, etc.).

If you have decided on a particular make and model, then I suggest you join the appropriate owners club and read the classified ads in their newsletters (information about these clubs is included in the chapters about the individual makes).

Most ads of airplanes for sale make use of various more-or-less standard abbreviations. These abbreviations describe the airplane. Also in the ads will be a telephone number, but seldom a location where the airplane is located. The clue here is the area code.

Here's a sample ad:

49 C170,2309TT,605 SMOH,Nov ANN,
KX170 NAV/COM,ELT,polished, Ceconite
wings,NDH. Asking $10,900.
800-555-1234

Translated, this ad reads: For sale, a 1949 Cessna 170 airplane with 2309 total hours on the airframe and an engine with 605 hours since a major overhaul. The next annual inspection is due in November. The plane is equipped with a King KX170 Nav/Com, has an Emergency Locator Transmitter, is polished aluminum and has Ceconite covered wings. Best of all, the airplane has no history of damage. The price is $10,900, and the seller will bargain, as most do. Last is the telephone number.

As you can see, there sure was a lot of information inside those four little lines.

Here are two lists that can help you when reading airplane ads:

## Abbreviations

| | |
|---|---|
| AD | Airworthiness Directive |
| ADF | Automatic Direction Finder |
| AF | airframe |
| AF&E | airframe and engine |
| AI | Aircraft Inspector |
| ALC | alcohol |
| ALT | altimeter |
| ANN | annual inspection |
| ANNUAL | annual inspection |
| AP | autopilot |
| ASI | airspeed indicator |
| ATP | Airline Transport Pilot |
| ATR | Airline Transport Rating |
| A/C | air conditioning |
| A&E | airframe and engine |
| A/P | autopilot |
| BAT | battery |
| B&W | black and white |
| CAT | carburator air temperature |
| CFI | Cert. Flight Instructor |
| CFII | Cert. Flight Instrument Instructor |
| CHT | cylinder head temperature |
| COMM | communications radio |
| CS | constant speed propeller |
| C/S | constant speed propeller |
| C/W | complied with |
| DBL | double |
| DG | directional gyro |
| DME | Distance Measuring Equipment |
| FAC | factory |
| FBO | Fixed Base Operator |
| FD | flight director |
| FGP | full gyro panel |
| FWF | firewall forward |
| G | gravity |
| GAL | gallons |
| GPH | gallons per hour |
| GS | glideslope |
| HD | heavy duty |
| HP | horsepower |
| HSI | horizontal situation indicator |
| HVY | heavy |
| IFR | Instrument Flight Rules |
| ILS | Instrument Landing System |
| INS | Instrument Navigation System |
| INSP | inspection |
| INST | instrument |
| KTS | knots |
| L | left |
| LDG | landing |
| LE | left engine |
| LED | light emitting diode |
| LH | left-hand |
| LIC | license |
| LOC | localizer |
| LSMOH | left eng. since major overhaul |
| LTS | lights |
| L&R | left and right |

| | | | | |
|---|---|---|---|---|
| MB | marker beacon | | SMOHR | since major overhaul right eng. |
| MBR | marker beacon | | SMOHRE | since major overhaul right eng. |
| MGTW | maximum gross takeoff weight | | SNEW | since new |
| MP | manifold pressure | | SPOH | since propeller overhaul |
| MPH | miles per hour | | STC | Supplemental Type Certificate |
| MOD | modification | | STOH | since top overhaul |
| MTOW | maximum takeoff weight | | STOL | short takeoff and landing |
| NAV | navigation | | TAS | true airspeed |
| NAV/COM | navigation/communication radio | | TBO | time between overhaul |
| NDH | no damage history | | TC | turbocharged |
| OAT | outside air temperature | | TLX | telex |
| OX | oxygen | | TNSP | transponder |
| O2 | oxygen | | TNSPNDR | transponder |
| PAC | package | | TSN | time since new |
| PAX | passenger | | TSO | Technical Service Order |
| PKG | package | | TT | total time |
| PMA | parts manufacture approval | | TTAF | total time airframe |
| PROP | propeller | | TTA&E | total time airframe and engine |
| PSGR | passenger | | TTE | total time engine |
| PSI | pounds per square inch | | TTLE | total time left engine |
| R | right | | TTRE | total time right engine |
| RADALT | radar altimeter | | TTSN | total time since new |
| RC | rate of climb | | TXP | transponder |
| RE | right engine | | T&B | turn and bank |
| REMAN | remanufactured | | VAC | vacuum |
| RH | right-hand | | VFR | Visual Flight Rules |
| RMFD | remanufactured | | VHF | very high frequency |
| RMFG | remanufactured | | VOR | visual omnirange |
| RNAV | area navigation | | XC | cross-country |
| ROC | rate of climb | | XMTR | transmitter |
| RSMOH | right eng. since major overhaul | | XPDR | transponder |
| SAFOH | since airframe overhaul | | XPNDR | transponder |
| SCMOH | since chrome major overhaul | | YD | yaw damper |
| SEL | single engine land | | 3LMB | three-light marker beacon |
| SFACNEW | since factory new | | 3BL | three-blade propeller |
| SFN | since factory new | | 3BLP | three-blade propeller |
| SFNE | since factory new engine | | | |
| SFREM | since factory remanufacture | | | |
| SFREMAN | since factory remanufacture | | **Area Codes** | |
| SFRMFG | since factory remanufacture | | | |
| SHSO | since hot section overhaul | | 201 | NJ north |
| SMEL | single/multi engine land | | 202 | Washington, DC |
| SMELS | single/multi engine land/sea | | 203 | CT |
| SMOH | since major overhaul | | 205 | AL |
| SMOHL | since major overhaul left eng. | | 206 | WA west |
| SMOHLE | since major overhaul left eng. | | 207 | ME |
| | | | 208 | ID |

11

| | | | |
|---|---|---|---|
| 209 | CA Fresno | 516 | NY Long Island |
| 212 | NY City | 517 | MI central |
| 213 | CA Los Angeles | 518 | NY northeast |
| 214 | TX Dallas | 601 | MS |
| 215 | PA east | 602 | AZ |
| 216 | OH northeast | 603 | NH |
| 217 | IL central | 605 | SD |
| 218 | MN north | 606 | KY east |
| 219 | IN north | 607 | NY south central |
| 301 | MD | 608 | WI southwest |
| 302 | DE | 609 | NJ south |
| 303 | CO | 612 | MN central |
| 304 | WV | 614 | OH southeast |
| 305 | FL southeast | 615 | TN east |
| 307 | WY | 616 | MI west |
| 308 | NE west | 617 | MA east |
| 312 | IL northeast | 618 | IL south |
| 313 | MI east | 619 | CA southeast |
| 314 | MO east | 701 | ND |
| 315 | NY north central | 702 | NV |
| 316 | KS south | 703 | VA north & west |
| 317 | IN central | 704 | NC west |
| 318 | LA west | 712 | IA west |
| 319 | IA east | 713 | TX Houston |
| 401 | RI | 714 | CA southwest |
| 402 | NE east | 715 | WI north |
| 404 | GA north | 716 | NY west |
| 405 | OK west | 717 | PA central |
| 406 | MT | 801 | UT |
| 409 | TX southeast | 802 | VT |
| 412 | PA southwest | 803 | SC |
| 413 | MA west | 804 | VA southeast |
| 414 | WI west | 805 | CA west central |
| 415 | CA San Francisco | 806 | TX northwest |
| 417 | MO southwest | 808 | HAWAII |
| 419 | OH northwest | 812 | IN south |
| 501 | AR | 813 | FL southwest |
| 502 | KY west | 814 | PA northwest & central |
| 503 | OR | 815 | IL north central |
| 504 | LA east | 816 | MO northwest |
| 505 | NM | 817 | TX north central |
| 507 | MN south | 901 | TN west |
| 509 | WA east | 904 | FL north |
| 512 | TX south central | 906 | MI northwest |
| 513 | OH southwest | 907 | ALASKA |
| 515 | IA central | 912 | GA south |

| | |
|---|---|
| 913 | KS north |
| 914 | NY southeast |
| 915 | TX southwest |
| 916 | CA northwest |
| 918 | OK northeast |
| 919 | NC east |

## INSPECTIONS BEFORE YOU BUY

After you locate an airplane with purchase in mind, you'll have to inspect it. The object of the pre-purchase inspection is to determine if the airplane you are looking at is really worth consideration as a possible purchase. I consider the pre-purchase inspection of a used airplane as the most important single step in the process of buying. If the inspection is not completed in an orderly, well-planned manner, you could end up purchasing someone else's troubles, and be spending a lot more money than planned. Due to their age, this is particularly true with classics.

The very first item of inspection is a question that I always ask the seller: "Why are you selling your airplane?" Fortunately, most people are honest, and you'll usually get a truthful answer. Very often the owner is moving up to a larger plane, is wanting to start another rebuild/restoration project, or perhaps has other commitments (i.e.: spouse says sell, or perhaps the present owner can no longer afford the plane). Ask the seller if he knows of any problems or defects with the airplane. Again, the owner will probably be honest; however, there could be things he doesn't know about. Remember: *Buyer beware.*

### Definitions

**airworthy**—The airplane must conform to the original type certificate, or those STCs (Supplemental Type Certificates) issued for a particular airplane. In addition, the airplane must be in safe operating condition relative to wear and deterioration.

**annual inspection**—All small airplanes not in commercial use must be inspected annually by an FAA certified Airframe & Powerplane mechanic who holds an IA (Inspection Authorization), by an FAA certified repair station, or by the airplane's manufacturer. This is a complete inspection of the airframe, powerplant, and all subassemblies. The object of the annual is to make the airplane safe to fly. This inspection is required every twelve months; without it, you don't fly.

**preflight inspection**—The preflight is a thorough inspection, by the pilot, of an aircraft prior to flight. The purpose is to determine if the aircraft is indeed airworthy. The pilot makes this decision by looking for discrepancies while inspecting the exterior, interior, and engine of the airplane. The preflight is required by FARs, and as with all inspection requirements, it shows that safety is of great importance (Fig. 2-1).

**preventive maintenance**—FAR Part 43 lists a number of maintenance operations that a certificated pilot may perform on an airplane he/she owns, provided the airplane is not flown in commercial service. (These maintenance operations are described elsewhere in this book.)

**repairs and alterations**—There are two classes of repairs and/or alterations: *major* and *minor*. Major repairs/alterations must be approved for a return to service by an FAA certified Airframe & Powerplant mechanic holding an IA authorization, repair station, or by the FAA. Minor repairs/alterations may be returned to service by an FAA certified Airframe & Powerplant mechanic, or any of the above.

**Airworthiness Directives**—Airworthiness Directives (ADs) are covered under FAR Part 39, and must be complied with. An AD can be a simple one time inspection, a periodic inspection (i.e., every 50 hours of operation), or a major modification to the airframe/engine of a particular airplane or group of airplanes (make/model). Notice of an AD will be placed in the Federal Register and sent by mail to registered owners of the aircraft concerned. In an emergency, the information will be sent by telegram to registered owners. Either way, its purpose is to assure the integrity of your flying machine and your safety.

# SERVICE  MEMO

Service Memo No. 65

## SAFETY PRECAUTIONS

Operational carelessness is increasing at an alarming rate and has become a matter of great concern to the aircraft manufacturers as well as the Civil Aeronautics authorities. The modern airplanes which are being built today are far superior to those of yesteryear in that they require less maintenance and almost reach the everyday dependability of the automobile. These two factors alone are primarily responsible for the apparent indifferent attitide toward basic operational safety precautions.

The Service Department would like to put particular emphasis on the following safety procedure instructions which must become an integral part of the aircraft owner's operational routine and/or preflight inspection.

Before each flight, visually inspect the airplane, and/or determine that:

1. The tires are satisfactorily inflated and not excessively worn.
2. The landing gear oleos and shock struts operate within limits.
3. The propellers are free of detrimental nicks.
4. The ground area under propeller is free of loose stones, cinders, etc.
5. The cowling and inspection opening covers are secure.
6. There is no external damage or operational interference to the control surfaces, wings or fuselage.
7. The windshield is clean and free of defects.
8. There is no snow, ice or frost on the wings or control surfaces.
9. The tow-bar and control locks are detached and properly stowed.
10. The fuel tanks are full or are at a safe level of proper fuel.
11. The fuel tank caps are tight.
12. The fuel system vents are open.
13. The fuel strainers and fuel lines are free of water and sediment by draining all fuel strainers once a day. (See Manual for location.)
14. The fuel tanks and carburetor bowls are free of water and sediment by draining sumps once a week.
15. There are no obvious fuel or oil leaks.
16. The engine oil is at proper level.
17. The brakes are working properly.
18. The radio equipment is in order.
19. There is adequate carburetor heat.
20. The weather is satisfactory for the type of flying you expect to do.

End.

## PIPER AIRCRAFT CORPORATION, LOCK HAVEN, PA.. U. S. A.

Fig. 2-1. Typical preflight requirements. (courtesy Univair)

## FOUR STEPS OF INSPECTION

Now let's examine the proper way to inspect a potential purchase. There are four steps to a pre-purchase inspection:

1. The walk-around inspection.
2. The logbook check.
3. The test flight.
4. The mechanic's inspection.

### Step One: Walk-Around Inspection

The walk-around is really a very thorough preflight. It's divided into three logical parts.

**1. Cabin:** The first part of the walk-around is to check that all required paperwork is with the airplane. This includes the Airworthiness Certificate, Aircraft Registration Certificate, flight manual or operating limitations, and logbooks (airframe, engine, and propeller). If the airplane is equipped with communications equipment, look for an FCC (Federal Communications Commission) station license.

While you're inside the airplane looking for the paperwork, notice the general condition of the interior. Does it appear clean, or has it just been scrubbed after a long period of inattention? Look in the corners, just as you would if you were buying a used car. The care given the interior can be a good indication of what care was given to the remainder of the airplane. However, beware of cosmetic fixes. Often an older airplane will have a new interior, tires, and wax job, but hidden under this skin of beauty lurks a monster with red eyes just waiting for the unwary buyer. This is the reason, in a later step, I recommend you have a mechanic check the plane over also.

Look out the windows. Are they clear, unyellowed, and uncrazed?

**2. Airframe:** While continuing with the walk-around, look for the following:

Is the paint in good condition, or is some of it laying on the ground under the airplane? Paint jobs are expensive, yet necessary for the protection of the metal/fabric surfaces.

Dents, wrinkles, or tears of the metal or fabric skin may indicate prior damage or just careless handling. Each discrepancy must be examined very carefully.

If the airframe or flying surfaces are covered with fabric that is considered "lifetime" you should consider how much time has passed since recovery. The covering should be removed after 12 to 15 years to see what's going on underneath—at least to inspect and varnish the spars.

Look for signs of rust on the tail section. This is quite common among taildraggers, as moisture seeks low spots, and the tailwheel area of a conventional geared airplane is a low spot. One sign is rust discoloration of the fabric. A complete check, including the removal of inspection plates, is recommended.

Corrosion or rust on surfaces, or on control systems, should be cause for alarm. Corrosion is to aluminum what rust is to iron. It's destructive. Any corrosion or rust should be brought to the attention of a mechanic for his judgement.

The landing gear should be checked for evidence of being sprung. Check the tires for signs of unusual wear that might indicate other structural damage. Also look at the oleo struts for signs of fluid leakage.

Move all the control surfaces, and check each for damage. They should be free in movement. Pay close attention to control surface hinges when looking for rust. When the controls are centered, the surfaces should also be centered. If they are not, a problem in the rigging of the airplane may exist.

**3. Engine:** When checking the engine, search for signs of oil leakage. Do this by looking at the engine, inside the cowl, and on the firewall. If the leaks are bad enough, there'll be oil dripping to the ground. Naturally the seller has probably cleaned away all the old oil drips; however, oil leaves stains. Look for these stains.

Check all hoses and lines for signs of deterioration or chafing. Also check all connections for tightness and signs of leakage.

Check control linkages and cables for obvious damage and ease of movement.

Check the battery box and battery for corrosion. On some classics you won't have this problem, as there is no electrical system.

Check the propeller for damage such as nicks, cracks, or gouges. These often small defects cause stress areas on the prop. Any visible damage to a propeller must be checked by a mechanic, as inflight catastrophic blade separation is not fun. Also check the prop for movement that would indicate looseness at the hub.

Check the exhaust pipes for rigidity, then reach inside them and rub your finger along the inside wall. If your finger comes back perfectly clean, someone has washed the inside of the pipes, possibly to remove the oily deposits that form there when an engine is burning a lot of oil. Black oily goo indicates problems for your mechanic to check. A light grey dusty coating indicates proper operation. Also check for exhaust stains on the belly of the plane to the rear of the stacks. This area has probably been washed, but look anyway. If you find black oily goo, see your mechanic.

## Step Two: Logbook Check

If you are satisfied with what you've seen up to this point, then go back to the cabin and have a seat. Pull out the logbooks and start reading them.

The owner of an aircraft is required to keep aircraft maintenance records that contain a description of the work performed on the aircraft, the date the work was completed, and the signature and FAA certificate number of the person approving the aircraft for return to service. The owner's aircraft records must contain additional information required by FAR Section 91.173.

A. There must be records of maintenance, alterations and inspections (annual or otherwise). These records may be discarded when the work is repeated or superseded by other work, or one year after the work is performed.

B. There must also be records of:
    (1) The total time in service of the airframe.
    (2) The current status of life-limited parts of each airframe, engine, propeller, and appliance.

(3) The time since the last overhaul of all items included on the aircraft which are required to be overhauled on a specific time basis.
(4) The identification of the current inspection status of the aircraft including the time since the last required inspection.
(5) The current status of applicable ADs including the method of compliance, AD number, revision date.
(6) A list of the current major alterations to each airframe, engine, propeller, and appliance.

These records must be retained by the owner/operator and must be transferred with the aircraft when ownership changes.

Be sure you're looking at the proper logs for the aircraft, and that they are the original logs. Sometimes logbooks get "lost" and are replaced with new ones. The new logs may be lacking very important information, or could be outright frauds. Be on your guard if the original logs are not available, although this is not uncommon among airplanes 30 to 40 years old.

Start with the airframe log, and look in the back for the AD compliance section. Check that it's up-to-date, and that any required periodic inspections have been made. Now go back to the most recent entry; it probably is an annual inspection. The annual inspection will be a statement that reads:

> July 27, 1984    Total Time: 2435 hrs.
> I certify that this aircraft has been inspected in accordance with an annual inspection and was determined to be in airworthy condition.
>                signed here
>                IA # 0000000

From this point back to the first entry in the logbook you'll be looking for similar entries, always keeping track of the total time for continuity purposes, and to indicate the regularity of usage (i.e., number of hours flown between inspections). Also you will be looking for indications of major repairs and modifications. This will be signaled by the phrase, "Form 337 filed." A copy of this form may be with the logs, and will tell what work was done. The work should be described in the logbook. Be sure there is a current weight and balance sheet with the logbook.

The engine log will be quite similar in nature to the airframe log, and will contain information from the annual. Total time will be given, and possibly an indication of time since a major overhaul (you may have to use your basic math skills here).

Pay particular attention to the numbers that indicate the results of a differential compression check. These numbers give a good indication of the overall health of the engine. Each is given as a fraction, with the lower number always being 80. The 80 indicates the air pressure that was utilized for the check. 80 PSI (pounds per square inch) is the industry standard. The upper number is the air pressure that the combustion chamber was able to maintain while being tested; 80 would be perfect, but it isn't attainable. The figure will always be less. The reason for the lower reading is the air pressure loss that results from loose, worn, or broken rings; scored or cracked cylinder walls; or burned, stuck, or poorly seated valves. There are methods mechanics use to determine which of the above is the cause and, of course, repair the damage. Normally repairs made to an engine to remedy any of the above faults equate to large dollar amounts.

Normal readings would be no less then 70/80, and should be uniform (within 2 or 3 PSI) for all cylinders. A discrepancy between cylinders could indicate the need of a top overhaul of one or more cylinders. The FAA says that a loss in excess of 25 percent is cause for further investigation. That would be a reading of 60/80. I think that a reading such as this indicates a very tired engine in need of much work.

By the way, the results of the latest compression check for each cylinder should be written on the valve cover of that cylinder. Look for them.

Read the information from the last oil change. It may contain a statement about debris found on the oil screen. However, oil changes are often performed by owners, and may or may not be recorded in the log. If they are recorded, how regular were they? I prefer every 25 hours, but 50 is acceptable.

Oil is cheap insurance for long engine life.

If the engine has been top overhauled or majored, there will be a description of the work performed, a date, and the total time on the engine when the work was accomplished. If this is not the original engine for this aircraft, then there will be an indication in the logbook giving a date when it was installed.

Check to see if the ADs have been complied with, and the appropriate entries made.

## Step Three: Test Flight

The test flight is only a short flight to determine that the airplane "feels" right to you. It is not meant to be a rip-snort'n, slam-bang, shakeout ride. Remember, you are looking at a classic, not a hot rod.

I suggest that either the owner or a competent flight instructor accompany you. (The latter may be difficult to find, as there are increasingly fewer instructors competent in taildraggers.) This will eliminate problems of currency, ratings, etc., with the FAA and the owner's insurance company.

After starting the engine, pay particular attention to the gauges. Do they jump to life, or are they sluggish? Are they indicating as should be expected? Watch these gauges again during the takeoff and climbout. Do the numbers match those called for in the operations manual?

More than likely the only gauge you will be looking at is the oil pressure gauge, and possibly the airspeed.

Pay attention to the gyro instruments, if there are any installed, and be sure they are stable.

Check the ventilation and heating system for proper operation (usually ventilation will be no problem in these old birds, but heat may well be nonexistant).

Do a few turns, stalls, and some level flight. Does the airplane perform as expected? Can it be trimmed for hands-off flight?

Return to the airport for a couple of landings. Check for proper brake operation, and for tailwheel or nosewheel vibration/shimmy.

After returning to the parking ramp, open the engine compartment and look again for oil leaks.

Also check along the belly for indications of oil leakage and blow-by (black oily goo).

## Step Four: Mechanic's Inspection

If you are still satisfied with the airplane and want to pursue the matter further, then have it inspected by an A&P or AI. This will cost you a few dollars; however, it could save you thousands. The average for a pre-purchase inspection is three to four hours labor, at shop rates. (I know one shop that does the job for $25—and does a good job at that.)

The mechanic's inspection will include a search of ADs and SDRs, a complete check of the logs, and an overall check of the plane. A compression check and a borescope examination must be made. If the plane is fabric-covered, then have that tested also.

## Points of Advice

Use your own mechanic for the pre-purchase inspection, not someone who may have an interest in the sale of the plane (i.e., employee of the seller).

Have the plane checked even if an annual was just done, unless you know and trust the AI who did the inspection.

You may be able to make a deal with the owner over the cost of the mechanic's inspection, particularly if an annual is due.

I said this in *The Illustrated Buyer's Guide to Used Airplanes* (TAB book No. 2372), and I think it is probably the most important piece of advice I can give you: If an airplane seller refuses you anything that has been mentioned in this chapter, then thank him for his time (and that's optional), walk away, and look elsewhere. Do not let a seller control the situation. Your money, safety, and possibly your very life are at stake. Airplanes are not hot sellers, and there is rarely a line forming to make a purchase. *You* are the buyer and *you* have the final word.

## PURCHASING PAPERWORK

The day has finally arrived. You're going to take the big step, and purchase an airplane.

Assuming that you have completely inspected your prospective purchase and found it acceptable at an agreeable price, you're ready to sit down and complete the paperwork that will lead to ownership.

## Title Search

The first step in purchasing an airplane is to be sure that the craft has a clear title. A clear title means there are no encumbrances (such as liens, mortgages, or other claims) against the aircraft. This is done by a title search.

A title search is accomplished by checking the aircraft's individual records at the Mike Monroney Aeronautical Center in Oklahoma City, Oklahoma. These records include title information, chain of ownership, Major Repair/Alteration (Form 337) information, and other data pertinent to your particular airplane. The FAA files this information by N-number.

Just because an airplane is 30 or 40 years old doesn't mean it can't have a lien or two against it.

The title search may be done by you, your attorney, or other representative selected by you.

Since most of us would find it rather inconvenient to travel to Oklahoma City to do the search ourselves, it is advisable to contract with a third party specializing in this service to do our bidding for us.

One such organization is the AOPA (Aircraft Owners and Pilots Association). This group has an Oklahoma City office just for this purpose. There are other businesses that provide similar services.

## What You Must Get

The following documents must be given to you with your airplane:

1. Bill of Sale.
2. Airworthiness Certificate (Fig. 2-2).
3. Logbooks.
   a. Airframe.
   b. Engine.
   c. Propeller.
4. Equipment List (including weight and balance data).

**UNITED STATES OF AMERICA**
**DEPARTMENT OF TRANSPORTATION—FEDERAL AVIATION ADMINISTRATION**
## STANDARD AIRWORTHINESS CERTIFICATE

| 1. NATIONALITY AND REGISTRATION MARKS | 2. MANUFACTURER AND MODEL | 3. AIRCRAFT SERIAL NUMBER | 4. CATEGORY |
|---|---|---|---|
| N 12345 | Douglas    DC-6A | 43210 | Transport |

5. AUTHORITY AND BASIS FOR ISSUANCE

This airworthiness certificate is issued pursuant to the Federal Aviation Act of 1958 and certifies that, as of the date of issuance, the aircraft to which issued has been inspected and found to conform to the type certificate therefor, to be in condition for safe operation, and has been shown to meet the requirements of the applicable comprehensive and detailed airworthiness code as provided by Annex 8 to the Convention on International Civil Aviation, except as noted herein.
Exceptions:

   NONE

6. TERMS AND CONDITIONS

Unless sooner surrendered, suspended, revoked, or a termination date is otherwise established by the Administrator, this airworthiness certificate is effective as long as the maintenance, preventative maintenance, and alterations are performed in accordance with Parts 21, 43, and 91 of the Federal Aviation Regulations, as appropriate, and the aircraft is registered in the United States.

| DATE OF ISSUANCE | FAA REPRESENTATIVE      R. R. White | DESIGNATION NUMBER |
|---|---|---|
| 12/20/68 | R. R. White | ACE EMDO 30 4346 |

Any alteration, reproduction, or misuse of this certificate may be punishable by a fine not exceeding $1,000, or imprisonment not exceeding 3 years, or both. THIS CERTIFICATE MUST BE DISPLAYED IN THE AIRCRAFT IN ACCORDANCE WITH APPLICABLE FEDERAL AVIATION REGULATIONS.

**FAA Form 8100-2** (7-67)  FORMERLY FAA FORM 1362                    GPO 1967—O-270 931

Fig. 2-2. FAA Form 8100-2, Standard Airworthiness Certificate. It must be displayed in the aircraft.

5. Operating Limitations and/or Flight Manual.

## Forms to Be Completed

AC Form 8050-2, Bill of Sale, is the standard means of recording transfer of title (Fig. 2-3).

AC Form 8050-1, Aircraft Registration, is filed with the Bill of Sale, or its equivalent. The pink copy of the registration is retained by you, and will remain in the airplane until the new registration is issued by the FAA (Fig. 2-4).

If you are purchasing the airplane under a Contract of Conditional Sale, then that contract must accompany the registration application in lieu of the AC Form 8050-2.

AC 8050-41, Release of Lien, must be filed by the seller if he still owes money on the airplane (Fig. 2-5).

AC 8050-64, Assignment of Special Registration Number, will be issued upon written request (Fig. 2-6). All N-numbers consist of the prefix N, and are followed by: one to five numbers, one to four numbers and a letter suffix, or one to three numbers and a two-letter suffix. This is similar to obtaining personalized license plates for your automobiles.

FCC (Federal Communications Commission) Form 404, Application for Aircraft Radio Station License (Fig. 2-7) must be completed if you have any radio equipment (capable of transmitting). The application tears in two; after completion, one portion will be mailed to the FCC, the other will remain in your airplane as temporary authorization until the new license is sent to you.

Most forms you send to the FAA or FCC will result in the issuance of a document to you. Be patient; it all takes time (Fig. 2-8).

## Special Flight Permits

A special flight permit, often called a ferry per-

UNITED STATES OF AMERICA
DEPARTMENT OF TRANSPORTATION FEDERAL AVIATION ADMINISTRATION

# AIRCRAFT BILL OF SALE

FORM APPROVED
OMB No 2120-0029
EXP. DATE 10/31/84

FOR AND IN CONSIDERATION OF $ THE UNDERSIGNED OWNER(S) OF THE FULL LEGAL AND BENEFICIAL TITLE OF THE AIRCRAFT DESCRIBED AS FOLLOWS:

UNITED STATES REGISTRATION NUMBER **N 110592**

AIRCRAFT MANUFACTURER & MODEL
*Gates Learjet 35 B*

AIRCRAFT SERIAL No.
*11765-20176-1562998 BZL*

DOES THIS 23 DAY OF Aug 19 89 HEREBY SELL, GRANT, TRANSFER AND DELIVER ALL RIGHTS, TITLE, AND INTERESTS IN AND TO SUCH AIRCRAFT UNTO:

Do Not Write In This Block
FOR FAA USE ONLY

**PURCHASER**

NAME AND ADDRESS
(IF INDIVIDUAL(S), GIVE LAST NAME, FIRST NAME, AND MIDDLE INITIAL.)

*Couch, Kenneth P.*
*2912 So. Federal Blvd.*
*APT. # 102 A*
*Denver, Colorado.*
*80236*

DEALER CERTIFICATE NUMBER *765*

AND TO 1 EXECUTORS, ADMINISTRATORS, AND ASSIGNS TO HAVE AND TO HOLD SINGULARLY THE SAID AIRCRAFT FOREVER, AND WARRANTS THE TITLE THEREOF.

IN TESTIMONY WHEREOF HAVE SET HAND AND SEAL THIS DAY OF 19

| | NAME (S) OF SELLER (TYPED OR PRINTED) | SIGNATURE (S) (IN INK) (IF EXECUTED FOR CO-OWNERSHIP, ALL MUST SIGN.) | TITLE (TYPED OR PRINTED) |
|---|---|---|---|
| **SELLER** | K J. Olsen | *K. J. Olsen* | |
| | | | |
| | | | |
| | | | |

ACKNOWLEDGMENT (NOT REQUIRED FOR PURPOSES OF FAA RECORDING: HOWEVER, MAY BE REQUIRED BY LOCAL LAW FOR VALIDITY OF THE INSTRUMENT.)

ORIGINAL: TO FAA

AC FORM 8050-2 (9-82) (0052-00-629-0002)

Fig. 2-3. FAA Form 8050-2, Aircraft Bill of Sale.

FORM APPROVED
OMB NO. 2120-0029
EXP. DATE 10/31/84

**UNITED STATES OF AMERICA DEPARTMENT OF TRANSPORTATION**
**FEDERAL AVIATION ADMINISTRATION-MIKE MONRONEY AERONAUTICAL CENTER**
**AIRCRAFT REGISTRATION APPLICATION**

CERT. ISSUE DATE

UNITED STATES
REGISTRATION NUMBER  **N**

AIRCRAFT MANUFACTURER & MODEL

AIRCRAFT SERIAL No.

FOR FAA USE ONLY

TYPE OF REGISTRATION (Check one box)

☐ 1. Individual  ☐ 2. Partnership  ☐ 3. Corporation  ☐ 4. Co-owner  ☐ 5. Gov't.  ☐ 8. Foreign-owned Corporation

NAME OF APPLICANT (Person(s) shown on evidence of ownership. If individual, give last name, first name, and middle initial.)

TELEPHONE NUMBER:  (        )                    —

ADDRESS (Permanent mailing address for first applicant listed.)

Number and street: _____

Rural Route: _____  P.O. Box: _____

| CITY | STATE | ZIP CODE |
| --- | --- | --- |
|  |  |  |

☐  **CHECK HERE IF YOU ARE ONLY REPORTING A CHANGE OF ADDRESS**

**ATTENTION! Read the following statement before signing this application.**

A false or dishonest answer to any question in this application may be grounds for punishment by fine and / or imprisonment (U.S. Code, Title 18, Sec. 1001).

## CERTIFICATION

I/WE CERTIFY:

(1) That the above aircraft is owned by the undersigned applicant, who is a citizen (including corporations) of the United States.

(For voting trust, give name of trustee: _____ ), or:

CHECK ONE AS APPROPRIATE:

a. ☐ A resident alien, with alien registration (Form 1-151 or Form 1-551) No. _____

b. ☐ A foreign-owned corporation organized and doing business under the laws of (state or possession) _____ , and said aircraft is based and primarily used in the United States. Records of flight hours are available for inspection at _____

(2) That the aircraft is not registered under the laws of any foreign country; and
(3) That legal evidence of ownership is attached or has been filed with the Federal Aviation Administration.

NOTE: If executed for co-ownership all applicants must sign. Use reverse side if necessary.

TYPE OR PRINT NAME BELOW SIGNATURE

| EACH PART OF THIS APPLICATION MUST BE SIGNED IN INK. | SIGNATURE | TITLE | DATE |
| --- | --- | --- | --- |
|  | SIGNATURE | TITLE | DATE |
|  | SIGNATURE | TITLE | DATE |

NOTE:  Pending receipt of the Certificate of Aircraft Registration, the aircraft may be operated for a period not in excess of 90 days, during which time the PINK copy of this application must be carried in the aircraft.

AC FORM 8050-1 (1-83) (0052-00-628-9005)

Fig. 2-4. FAA Form 8050-1, Aircraft Registration Application.

**THIS FORM SERVES TWO PURPOSES**

PART I acknowledges the recording of a security conveyance covering the collateral shown.
PART II is a suggested form of release which may be used to release the collateral from the terms of the conveyance.

**PART I – CONVEYANCE RECORDATION NOTICE**

NAME (last name first) OF DEBTOR

NAME and ADDRESS OF SECURED PARTY/ASSIGNEE

NAME OF SECURED PARTY'S ASSIGNOR (if assigned)

Do Not Write In This Block
FOR FAA USE ONLY

| FAA REGISTRA-TION NUMBER | AIRCRAFT SERIAL NUMBER | AIRCRAFT MFR. (BUILDER) and MODEL |
| --- | --- | --- |
| | | |

| ENGINE MFR. and MODEL | ENGINE SERIAL NUMBER(S) |
| --- | --- |
| | |

| PROPELLER MFR. and MODEL | PROPELLER SERIAL NUMBER(S) |
| --- | --- |
| | |

THE SECURITY CONVEYANCE DATED_____COVERING THE ABOVE COLLATERAL WAS RECORDED BY THE FAA AIRCRAFT REG-ISTRY ON_____ AS CONVEYANCE NUMBER_____.

FAA CONVEYANCE EXAMINER

**PART II – RELEASE** – (This suggested release form may be executed by the secured party and returned to the FAA Aircraft Registry when terms of the conveyance have been satisfied. See below for additional information.)

THE UNDERSIGNED HEREBY CERTIFIES AND ACKNOWLEDGES THAT HE IS THE TRUE AND LAWFUL HOLDER OF THE NOTE OR OTHER EVIDENCE OF INDEBTEDNESS SECURED BY THE CONVEYANCE REFERRED TO HEREIN ON THE ABOVE-DESCRIBED COLLATERAL AND THAT THE SAME COLLATERAL IS HEREBY RELEASED FROM THE TERMS OF THE CONVEYANCE. ANY TITLE RETAINED IN THE COLLATERAL BY THE CONVEYANCE IS HEREBY SOLD, GRANTED, TRANS-FERRED, AND ASSIGNED TO THE PARTY WHO EXECUTED THE CONVEYANCE, OR TO THE ASSIGNEE OF SAID PARTY IF THE CONVEYANCE SHALL HAVE BEEN ASSIGNED: PROVIDED, THAT NO EXPRESS WARRANTY IS GIVEN NOR IMPLIED BY REASON OF EXECUTION OR DELIVERY OF THIS RELEASE.

This form is only intended to be a suggested form of release, which meets the recording requirements of the Federal Aviation Act of 1958, and the regulations issued thereunder. In addition to these requirements, the form used by the security holder should be drafted in accordance with the pertinent provisions of local statutes and other applicable federal statutes. This form may be reproduced. There is no fee for recording a release. Send to FAA Aircraft Registry, P. O. Box 25504, Oklahoma City, Oklahoma 73125.

ACKNOWLEDGEMENT (If Required By Applicable Local Law):

DATE OF RELEASE: ..................................................................

.......................................................................................
(Name of security holder)

SIGNATURE (in ink) ...............................................................

TITLE ..................................................................................

(A person signing for a corporation must be a corporate officer or hold a managerial position and must show his title. A person signing for another should see Parts 47 and 49 of the Federal Aviation Regulations (14 CFR).

Fig. 2-5. FAA 8050-41, Conveyance Recordation Notice and Release.

**DEPARTMENT OF TRANSPORTATION —** Federal Aviation Administration

**ASSIGNMENT OF SPECIAL REGISTRATION NUMBERS**

Special Registration Number

N 7316

Aircraft Make and Model   BIG DEAL, BA-OH

Present Registration Number

Serial Number   00021

N 123BJ

1000 WHITEHOUSE ROAD
OKLAHOMA CITY, OKLAHOMA 73100

Issue Date   July 31, 1980

This is your authority to change the United States registration number on the above described aircraft to the special registration number shown.

Carry duplicate of this form in the aircraft together with the old registration certificate as interim authority to operate the aircraft pending receipt of revised certificate of registration. Obtain a revised certificate of airworthiness from your nearest Flight Standards field office.

The latest FAA Form 8130-6 on file is dated

The airworthiness classification and category

FOLD

SIGN AND RETURN THE ORIGINAL of this form to the FAA Aircraft Registry, within 5 days after placing the special registration number on the aircraft. A revised certificate will then be issued. Unless this authority is used and this office so notified, the authority for use of the special number will expire on

CERTIFICATION: I certify that the special registration number was placed on the aircraft described above.

Signature of Owner: *Marion N. Williams*

Title of Owner:

Date Placed on Aircraft:   August 1, 1980

RETURN FORM TO:

FAA Aircraft Registry
P. O. Box 25504
Oklahoma City, Oklahoma 73125

BELOW THIS POINT FOR FAA USE ONLY

1. ☐ FP   NAME
2. ☐ NF
ADDRESS

CITY          FC        ZIP          EMP CODE       DATE

AC Form 8050-64 (11-77)

Fig. 2-6. FAA Form 8050-64, Assignment of Special Registration Numbers. Special registration numbers are similar in nature to vanity plates on automobiles.

mit, is an authorization to operate an aircraft that may not currently meet applicable airworthiness requirements, but is safe for a specific flight. For the classic purchaser/owner this might include a plane that has marginal fabric covering, damage to the metal skin, a poor engine, or malfunctioning instruments.

Before the permit is issued, an FAA inspector may personally inspect the aircraft, or require it to be inspected by a licensed mechanic, to determine its safety for the intended flight. This inspection must be recorded in the logbook.

The special flight permit is issued to allow the aircraft to be flown to a base where repairs, alterations, or maintenance can be performed. It is issued for one-time use.

For further information about special flight permits, contact your nearest GADO.

## Insurance

Insure your airplane from the moment you sign on the dotted line. No one can afford to take risks.

There are two types of insurance: *Liability* protects you in instances of claims against you resulting from your operation of the airplane (i.e., bodily injury or property damage). If someone is injured or killed as a result of your flying, *you will be sued. Hull insurance* protects your investment from the elements of nature, fire, theft, vandalism, or other loss. Your lending institution will require it.

A check of any of the various aviation publications will produce telephone numbers for several aviation underwriters. Check with more than one company, as services, coverage, and rates do differ. Also, the AOPA and the EAA both have companies they recommend; check with them.

Stay clear of policies that have exclusions, or

FCC Form 404
March 1982

UNITED STATES OF AMERICA
**FEDERAL COMMUNICATIONS COMMISSION**
**APPLICATION FOR AIRCRAFT RADIO STATION LICENSE**

Approved by OMB
3060-0040
Expires 10/31/84

**A.** Read instructions before completing.

**B.** Use typewriter or print clearly in ink.

**C.** Sign and date application.

**D.** Mail this form to Federal Communications Commission, P.O. Box 1030, Gettysburg, PA. 17325.

**DO NOT WRITE IN THIS BLOCK**

**1.** FAA Registration or FCC Control Number *(If known)*

**N**

**2.** Is application for a fleet license? *If yes, give number of aircraft in fleet.*

No ☐   Yes ☐   No. of aircraft

**3.** Type of Applicant *(Check one)*

☐ (I) Individual   ☐ (P) Partnership   ☐ (A) Association   ☐ (C) Corporation

☐ (D) Individual with Business Name   ☐ (G) Governmental Entity

**4A.** Name of Individual *(Last, First, Middle Initial)*

**4B.** Name *(If other than individual)*

**4C.** Names of Partners *(Last, First, Middle Initial)* *(Answer only if you checked partnership in item 3)*

**5.** Mailing Address of Applicant *(Number and Street, City, State, ZIP Code)*

**6.** Will the applicant own the radio equipment? *If no, give name of owner.*   Yes ☐ No ☐

Name

**7.** Does the applicant own the aircraft on which the radio equipment is to be installed? *If no, give name of owner.*   Yes ☐ No ☐

Name

**8.** If not the owner of the radio equipment, is applicant a party to a lease or other agreement under which control will be exercised in the same manner as if the applicant owned the equipment?   Yes ☐ No ☐

**9.** Frequencies requested *(Check all you will use under this license)*

**A.** Do not check both private aircraft and air carrier

☐ (A) Private Aircraft   ☐ (C) Air Carrier   ☐ (S) Public Service   ☐ 121.5 & 243 MHz only   *(For emergency locator transmitter)*

**B1.** Specify frequencies by rule number(s) if you check here.

☐ (E) Aeronautical Enroute ➡ Rule Number(s)

**B2.** Answer only if you checked item 9B1, aeronautical enroute frequencies.

Will a valid agreement with licensees of aeronautical enroute stations be in effect as required by the rules?   Yes ☐ No ☐

**C.** You must submit additional information, if you check here. *(See instructions)*

☐ (A) Instructional   ☐ (T) Flight Test HF   ☐ (V) Flight Test VF   ☐ (O) Other *(specify)*

**10** Categories of transmitters *(Check all transmitters to be used)*

| | | | | | |
|---|---|---|---|---|---|
| A | Emergency Locator (121.5 & 243 MHz) | | H | Radar (9300 to 9500 MHz) |
| B | VHF Communications (118 to 136 MHz) | | I | Radar (15,400 to 15,700 MHz) |
| C | Distance Measuring Equipment (DME) (960 to 1215 MHz) | | J | Doppler Radar (8750 to 8850 MHz) |
| D | Transponder (1090 MHz) | | K | Doppler Radar (13,250 to 13,400 MHz) |
| E | Radio Altimeter (1600 to 1660 MHz)   *(See instruction)* | | L | High Frequency Communication (2–25 MHz) |
| F | Radio Altimeter (4200 to 4400 MHz) | | M | Marine Transmitter for Public Service |
| G | Radar (5350 to 5470 MHz) | | N | Other |

**11.** Answer space for any required statements *(Use reverse side if more space is needed)*

**READ CAREFULLY BEFORE SIGNING**

Certification: 1) The applicant waives any claim to the use of any particular frequency or of the ether because of previous use of same, whether by license or otherwise. 2) The applicant accepts full responsibility for the operation and control of the requested station license in accordance with applicable law and rules of the FCC. 3) The applicant will have unlimited access to the radio equipment and will take effective measures to prevent its use by unauthorized persons. 4) Neither applicant nor any member thereof is a foreign government or representative thereof.

**WILLFUL FALSE STATEMENTS MADE ON THIS FORM OR ATTACHMENTS ARE PUNISHABLE BY FINE AND IMPRISONMENT, U.S. CODE: TITLE 18, SECTION 1001.**

SIGNATURE of individual, partner, or authorized person on behalf of a governmental entity, or an officer of a corporation or association.

DATE

Fig. 2-7. FCC Form 404, Application for Aircraft Radio Station License.

UNITED STATES OF AMERICA
DEPARTMENT OF TRANSPORTATION — FEDERAL AVIATION ADMINISTRATION
CERTIFICATE OF AIRCRAFT REGISTRATION

This certificate must be in the aircraft when operated.

NATIONALITY AND REGISTRATION MARKS N 123BJ

AIRCRAFT SERIAL NO. 00021

MANUFACTURER AND MANUFACTURER'S DESIGNATION OF AIRCRAFT

BIG DEAL BA-OH

ISSUED TO

MARION W. WILLIAMS
1000 WHITE HOUSE ROAD
OKLAHOMA CITY, OKLAHOMA 73100

INDIV

This certificate is issued for registration purposes only and is not a certificate of title. The Federal Aviation Administration does not determine rights of ownership as between private persons.

It is certified that the above described aircraft has been entered on the register of the Federal Aviation Administration, United States of America, in accordance with the Convention on International Civil Aviation dated December 7, 1944, and with the Federal Aviation Act of 1958, and regulations issued thereunder.

DATE OF ISSUE 7/25/80

Administrator

AC Form 8050-3 (5-77)

(CUT ON DOTTED LINE)

DEPARTMENT OF TRANSPORTATION
FEDERAL AVIATION ADMINISTRATION
AERONAUTICAL CENTER
P. O. BOX 25504
OKLAHOMA CITY, OKLAHOMA 73125

OFFICIAL BUSINESS
PENALTY FOR PRIVATE USE, $300

U.S. MAIL

POSTAGE AND FEES PAID
FEDERAL AVIATION ADMINISTRATION
DOT 515

TO:

**RETAIN THIS INFORMATION FOR FUTURE REFERENCE**

CHANGE OF ADDRESS

Federal Aviation Regulations require that the registered owner of the aircraft shall report in writing within 30 days any change in permanent mailing address. A revised Certificate of Registration will be issued without charge. The Application for Registration AC Form 8050-1 may be used to report a change of address.

REPLACEMENT OF CERTIFICATE

If this certificate is lost, destroyed, or mutilated, a replacement may be obtained at the written request of the holder. Send your request and $2.00 (check or money order made payable to Federal Aviation Administration) to:

FAA Aircraft Registry
P. O. Box 25504
Oklahoma City, Oklahoma 73125

NOTE: All correspondence should include the registration "N" number, manufacturer, model, and serial number of the aircraft.

EFFECT OF REGISTRATION

Section 501(f) of the Federal Aviation Act of 1958 (49 U.S.C. 1401) provides: ". . . Registration shall not be evidence of ownership of aircraft in any proceeding in which such ownership by a particular person is, or may be, in issue."

NOTICE: Instruments affecting interests in aircraft are received by the FAA Aircraft Registry for recording. These are public records open for inspection in Room 123 of the Aviation Records Building, Aeronautical Center, Oklahoma City, Oklahoma. Persons needing information as to recorded instruments may make a personal search of the records or avail themselves of the services of an agent or attorney.

THIS CERTIFICATE MUST BE SIGNED AND RETURNED BY THE REGISTERED OWNER WHEN IT IS NO LONGER IN EFFECT FOR ONE OF THE FOLLOWING REASONS:

a. ☐ Registration is cancelled at the request of the owner. (Also check and/or complete Block, b, c, d, e, f, or g).

b. ☐ The aircraft is totally destroyed or scrapped.

c. ☐ United States citizenship has been lost.

d. ☐ Thirty days have elapsed since the death of the registered owner (estate representative should sign).

e. ☐ The certificate is revoked because of noncompliance with FAR 47.44.

f. ☐ The aircraft is to be registered under the laws of a foreign country:

(NAME OF FOREIGN COUNTRY)

g. ☐ The ownership of the aircraft is transferred to:

(NAME)

(ADDRESS)

(CITY, STATE, ZIP)

(SIGNATURE) (TITLE) (DATE)

This certificate must be returned to:
FAA AIRCRAFT REGISTRY, P. O. BOX 25504, OKLAHOMA CITY, OKLAHOMA 73125

Fig. 2-8. FAA Form 8050-3, Certificate of Aircraft Registration. The registration must be in the aircraft during operation.

other specific rules involving maximum preset values for replacement parts. The industry buzzword for this is "components parts endorsement."

## CLUBS

Whenever people have a common interest to bond them together, some form of social organization will usually be developed. Such is the case with owners clubs and classic airplanes.

The typical airplane club is formed with the idea in mind to get as many owners of a particular make/model of airplane together, either physically or by newsletter.

Most classic clubs have at least one fly-in each year. Some will have several in different areas of the country. A few of the larger organizations have several geographical divisions, with local activities directed at specific regions. These fly-ins will usually result in much handshaking, making new friends, seeing old ones, and of course the chance to see other planes of similar manufacture to your own. Often there will be exchanges, either formal or otherwise, of technical know-how and "how-to" information. Sometimes there will even be a small flea market, giving the attendee a chance to purchase a hard-to-find part or other nicety for his plane.

Newsletters are a mainstay of the typical club. Bringing social information and technical know-how to the members, these information sheets are possibly the best reason for membership in a classic club. The newsletters range from one-page information sheets to a bimonthly booklet that includes information and pictures about recent club events, service information, safety notices, and even classified ads.

In addition to all this, some clubs maintain good technical libraries that include original blueprints, maintenance manuals, operations manuals, and even FARs (Federal Aviation Regulations). Several clubs even have a photographic history and scrapbook that circulates among the members.

All in all, I feel that as a classic owner you should belong to, and support, the club that supports your particular aircraft. I also feel that if you are not an owner, but are "armchairing," you should belong to these clubs. There is, in most cases, no better method for obtaining information about these fine airplanes. After all, none of these airplanes is still manufactured today, and most of the companies that did manufacture them are only distant memories.

In addition to the clubs specializing in a par-ticular aircraft, there are several other organizations with a broader interest range. Each has a monthly magazine and offers other side benefits (research library, insurance, discount purchases, etc.).

## Aircraft Owners and Pilots Association
421 Aviation Way
Frederick, MD 21701
Phone: (301) 695-2000

## Experimental Aircraft Association
Wittman Field
Oshkosh, WI 54903
Phone: (414) 426-4800

## Seaplane Pilots Association
421 Aviation Way
Frederick, MD 21701
Phone: (301) 695-2000

# Chapter 3

# Aeronca

The Aeronca airplanes were among the most popular trainers of the postwar period. (I learned to fly in one, and that was considerably *after* the war.)

All the Aeronca two-place airplanes are of tube-and-fabric design. This means that the airframe is made of welded steel tubing that is covered with fabric. The wings are also covered with fabric. Although originally covered in grade-A cotton, the examples you'll most likely find today are covered with one of the new synthetic products.

These small airplanes are fun and easy to fly, yet are among the least expensive to operate. Although rather slow by today's standards, they allow one to see what he's flying over.

All the Aeroncas have conventional landing gear, but don't let that scare you. They're honest little airplanes displaying few bad habits.

Based upon the WWII TA Defender and the L3 Liaison plane, there were several planes in the 7 (Champ) series (Figs. 3-1 though 3-8):

**7AC**—had the A-65 Continental 65-hp engine. Although some were built with the Franklin or Lycoming engine, most you see today have the Continental. The 7ACs, often referred to as "airknockers," were produced from 1945 through 1948. All were painted yellow, with red trim. According to historical records, Aeronca once produced 56 Champs in one day. The usual time to build one was 291 man-hours, and the original price was $2999.

**7BCM**—was introduced in 1947, and was powered with the 85-hp Continental engine. This plane was known as the L-16A in the military version.

**7CCM**—with the 90-hp Continental was introduced in 1948. The 7CCM had a slightly larger fin and minor structural changes. The military configuration of this plane was the L-16B.

**7DC**—with the C-85-8F Continental 85-hp engine, it entered production in 1949, and sported a metal propeller.

**7EC**—was the last try for Aeronca. It was like all the other Champs, except it had the Continental C-90-12F engine, an electrical system, and a metal propeller.

Fig. 3-1. This restored Aeronca 7AC Champ looks just as it came from the factory.

Fig. 3-2. This 7 series Aeronca has a custom paint job and wheel pants. (courtesy Marion Pyles, Air Pix Aviation Photography)

Fig. 3-3. The Aeronca 11AC Chief seats two side-by-side.

Fig. 3-4. The frontal appearances of all 7 series Aeroncas are similar.

Fig. 3-5. This 7BCM was built in 1946 and is powered with a Continental C85 engine.

Fig. 3-6. This L-16B is the wartime version of the 7 series. Notice the "greenhouse" that allowed plenty of visibility.

Fig. 3-7. This fine example of the Aeronca 15AC belongs to Dick Welch. Typical of many Sedans, it has spent most of its life on floats. (courtesy Dick Welch)

Fig. 3-8. The Champion 7FC, actually a 7EC on trigear, never achieved the popularity of Cessna or Piper trigear trainers. (courtesy Marion Pyles, Air Pix Aviation Photography)

All told, more than 7,200 Champs were built before production was halted.

In addition to the Champ, there was the 11 series Chief. With a slightly wider body than the Champ, it seated two, side-by-side. The original Chiefs were built prior to the war, and had 50-hp engines. The postwar 11AC Chiefs had the Continental A-65 engine and entered production in 1946. An updated version, the 11CC Super Chief with a Continental C-85-8F and a metal propeller, was introduced in 1947.

Like the 7 series, the Chiefs were constructed of tube and fabric. Overall performance was quite similar to the Champ series. 1,962 Chiefs were produced between 1946 and 1949.

If a four-placer interests you, then perhaps you should consider the Aeronca Sedan, model 15AC.

The Aeronca Sedan had all-metal wings with a tube-and-fabric fuselage. Only 550 Sedans were built, all between 1948 and 1950. Today there are 262 left, with 69 registered in Alaska. The large number still in use in Alaska is a real testimonial to their worth and strength. Many are on floats; perhaps this is why they are so popular as "bush" planes. Sedans are quite rare on the used market; however, from time to time you may see one or two listed in *Trade-A-Plane*.

The letter S preceding any Aeronca model number indicates a seaplane version.

In 1950 an Aeronca Sedan set an in-the-air endurance record of 42 days. This feat required inflight refueling for airplane and pilots.

As with so many of the postwar era planes, a good design is hard to kill. The Aeronca was one of these. In 1954 the Champion Aircraft Company of Osceola, Wisconsin, was formed. Champion reintroduced the Aeronca 7 series airplanes. The name might have been changed to Champion, but one look and you knew what you were really buying.

Reintroducing the Aeronca 7EC model as the Champion Traveler, the new 7EC was upholstered, carpeted, and had a propeller spinner.

In 1957 a tricycle-geared version was introduced. Called the 7FC Tri-Traveler, 471 were built between 1957 and 1964. There is nothing unusual about these fine little planes—just an "airknocker" with a nosewheel. Unfortunately, their popularity was never that of the Piper or Cessna competition. I personally liked them, and often flew one from an old hayfield.

I realize that this book is supposed to be about "classics," however, I have made a few exceptions for modern airplanes with true classic family trees, which are built by classic methods. The last example of an Aeronca I shall give is just such an exception. The 7ACA appeared in 1971, and was designed to be a "cheap" airplane. The base price was just $4,995. The airplane was a 7 series by looks, and was powered with a Franklin 60 hp two-cylinder engine. Production ended in 1973, as they didn't prove to be very popular. The 7ACA is properly called the Bellanca Champion Champ, as it was built after the Bellanca takeover of Champion Aircraft.

I've seen a few listed in Trade-A-Plane over the years. They remain low in price—at least compared to some of the other classics.

Indicative of how hardy these older designs are, in 1984 a new Champion Aircraft Company was started. For further information write or call:

**Champion Aircraft Co.**
Drawer K
Tomball, TX 77375
Phone: (713) 370-8080

The Aeronca Company is still in business at the original location of Middletown, Ohio. They make subassemblies for many of the current military and airline planes.

## SPECIFICATIONS
### Model: 7AC Champ
Engine

| | |
|---|---|
| Make: | Continental |
| Model: | A-65 |
| hp: | 65 |
| TBO: | 1800 |

Seats: 2 tandem
Speed

| | |
|---|---|
| Max: | 95 mph |
| Cruise: | 86 mph |
| Stall: | 38 mph |

Fuel Capacity: 13 gal
Rate of Climb: 370 fpm
Transitions
    Takeoff: 630 ft
    Landing: 880 ft

Weights
    Gross: 1220 lbs
    Empty: 740 lbs

Dimensions
    Length: 21 ft 6 in
    Height: 7 ft
    Span: 35 ft

**Model: 7BCM Champ**
Engine
    Make: Continental
    Model: C-85
    hp: 85
    TBO: 1800

Seats: 2 tandem
Speed
    Max: 101 mph
    Cruise: 90 mph
    Stall: 42 mph

Fuel Capacity: 19 gal
Rate of Climb: 620 fpm
Transitions
    Takeoff: 500 ft
    Landing: 850 ft

Weights
    Gross: 1300 lbs
    Empty: 80 lbs

Dimensions
    Length: 21 ft 6 in
    Height: 7 ft
    Span: 35 ft

**Model: 7CCM Champ**
Engine
    Make: Continental

Model: C-90
hp: 90
TBO: 1800

Seats: 2 tandem
Speed
    Max: 103 mph
    Cruise: 90 mph
    Stall: 42 mph

Fuel Capacity: 19 gal
Rate of Climb: 650 fpm
Transitions
    Takeoff: 475 ft
    Landing: 850 ft

Weights
    Gross: 1300 lbs
    Empty: 800 lbs

Dimensions
    Length: 21 ft 6 in
    Height: 7 ft 2 in
    Span: 35 ft

**Model: 7DC Champ**
Engine
    Make: Continental
    Model: C-85-8F
    hp: 85
    TBO: 1800

Seats: 2 tandem
Speed
    Max: 101 mph
    Cruise: 90 mph
    Stall: 42 mph

Fuel Capacity: 19 gal
Rate of Climb: 620 fpm
Transitions
    Takeoff: 500 ft
    Landing: 850 ft

Weights
    Gross: 1300 lbs
    Empty: 810 lbs

Dimensions
- Length: 21 ft 6 in
- Height: 7 ft 2 in
- Span: 35 ft

## Model: 7EC Champ
Engine
- Make: Continental
- Model: C-90-12F
- hp: 90
- TBO: 1800

Seats: 2 tandem
Speed
- Max: 103 mph
- Cruise: 90 mph
- Stall: 42 mph

Fuel Capacity: 19 gal
Rate of Climb: 650 fpm
Transitions
- Takeoff: 475 ft
- Landing: 850 ft

Weights
- Gross: 1300 lbs
- Empty: 810 lbs

Dimensions
- Length: 21 ft 6 in
- Height: 7 ft 2 in
- Span: 35 ft

## Model: 11AC Chief
Engine
- Make: Continental
- Model: C-65
- hp: 65
- TBO: 1800

Seats: 2 side-by-side
Speed
- Max: 90 mph
- Cruise: 83 mph
- Stall: 38 mph

Fuel Capacity: 15 gal
Rate of Climb: 360 fpm
Transitions
- Takeoff: 580 ft
- Landing: 880 ft

Weights
- Gross: 1250 lbs
- Empty: 786 lbs

Dimensions
- Length: 20 ft 4 in
- Height: 7 ft
- Span: 36 ft 1 in

## Model: 11CC Super Chief
Engine
- Make: Continental
- Model: C-85 8F (metal prop)
- hp: 85
- TBO: 1800

Seats: 2 side-by-side
Speed
- Max: 102 mph
- Cruise: 95 mph
- Stall: 40 mph

Fuel Capacity: 15 gal
Rate of Climb: 600 fpm
Transitions
- Takeoff: 720 ft
- Landing: 800 ft

Weights
- Gross: 1350 lbs
- Empty: 820 lbs

Dimensions
- Length: 20 ft 7 in
- Height: 7 ft
- Span: 36 ft 1 in

## Model: 15AC Sedan
Engine
- Make: Continental
- Model: C-145

hp:          85
TBO:         1800

Seats: 4
Speed
    Max:        120 mph
    Cruise:     105 mph
    Stall:       53 mph

Fuel Capacity: 36 gal
Rate of Climb: 570 fpm
Transitions
    Takeoff over 50' obs:    1509 ft
    Ground run:               900 ft
    Landing over 50' obs:    1826 ft
    Ground roll:             1300 ft

Weights
    Gross:       2050 lbs
    Empty:       1180 lbs

Dimensions
    Length:      25 ft 3 in
    Height:       7 ft 4 in
    Span:        37 ft 5 in

## Model: 7EC/FC Traveler/Tri-Traveler
Engine
    Make:        Continental
    Model:       C-90-12F
    hp:          90
    TBO:         1800

Seats: 2 tandem
Speed
    Max:        115 mph
    Cruise:     105 mph
    Stall:       44 mph

Fuel Capacity: 24 gal
Rate of Climb: 700 fpm
Transitions
    Takeoff over 50' obs:    890 ft
    Ground run:              630 ft
    Landing over 50' obs:    755 ft
    Ground roll:             400 ft

Weights
    Gross:       1450 lbs
    Empty:        860 lbs

Dimensions
    Length:      21 ft 6 in
    Height:       7 ft 2 in
    Span:        35 ft 2 in

## Model: 7ACA
Engine
    Make:        Franklin
    Model:       2A-120
    hp:          60
    TBO:         1800

Seats: 2 tandem
Speed
    Max:         98 mph
    Cruise:      86 mph
    Stall:       44 mph

Fuel Capacity: 13 gal
Rate of Climb: 400 fpm
Transitions
    Takeoff over 50' obs:    850 ft
    Ground run:              525 ft
    Landing over 50' obs:    755 ft
    Ground roll:             400 ft

Weights
    Gross:       1200 lbs
    Empty:        750 lbs

Dimensions
    Length:      21 ft 11 in
    Height:       7 ft
    Span:        35 ft  1 in

## ADs

Most of the following ADs are old and probably have long ago been complied with; however, you should still check for compliance:

**47-20-2** requries the replacement of the landing gear oleo piston on some 7 and 11 series aircraft.

**47-30-1** requires the replacement of the lift strut wing fittings on some 7 and 11 series Aeroncas.

**48-4-2** calls for an inspection of the wing ribs on 7 and 11 series planes.

**48-38-1** changes the oil cooler installation on some model 15 Sedans.

**49-11-2** requires reinforcement of the wing attachment fittings on all Aeronca airplanes.

**49-15-1** calls for the reworking of the seat anchors on 11 series aircraft.

**61-16-1** requires a periodic inspection of the lift strut fittings on 15 Sedans.

**68-20-5** requires inspection of the fuel cells on the model 15 Sedans.

## STCs AND PARTS

Wagner Aerial Service (Box 3, 401 1st St. East, Clark, SD 57225) sells interesting STCs for those Aeronca owners desiring more power and the addition of an electrical system. They also have a good supply of parts. Parts for Aeroncas are also available from Univair. Used parts also abound in the *Trade-A-Plane* ads.

**STC SA302NW** is available for the 15 Sedan. It allows the installation of a Lycoming 180-hp engine, Hartzell C/S prop, and a two piece fiberglass cowling. A claimed takeoff run of 150 feet at gross is made on wheels, and 400 feet on floats. It is available from Monahan Aircraft Inc. (2311 East Lake Sammamish Pl SE, Issaquah, WA 98027).

Fuel tanks are available from Monahans also. These will take care of **AD 68-20-5.**

## CLUBS

There are several clubs supporting the Aeronca airplanes.

## Aeronca Club

The Aeronca Club claims to be the oldest of the Aeronca clubs in existence. They are affiliated with the Antique Aircraft Association in Hales Corners, Wisconsin, and are members of both organizations. Emphasis is on restoration and research. Membership services include:

☐ Maintain a current detailed Aeronca roster including model, engine, year, NC, and serial numbers and miscellaneous information supplied by the owners.

☐ Publish newsletters that contain fly-in information, maintenance and safety tips, free classifieds and news from members.

☐ Make copies of technical information available from their technical library, which consists mainly of service-related materials.

☐ Sponser the annual Aeronca Fly-In over the July 4th weekend at Antique Airfield in Blakesburg, Iowa.

☐ Work actively with the other Aeronca clubs to promote Aeronca activities in general.

The dues are $3.00 per year. Patches are $3.00 each. For further information contact:

**Aeronca Club**
c/o Augie and Pat Wegner
1432 28th Court
Kenosha, WI 53140

## Aeronca Aviators Club

The Aeronca Aviators Club was started about four years ago. The club provides information on parts, service, and maintenance. They have a newsletter with a question-and-answer column.

For further information about the Aeronca Aviators Club contact:

**Aeronca Aviators Club**
511 Terrace Lake Rd.
Columbus, IN 47201

## Aeronca Lovers' Club

The Aeronca Lovers' Club is four years old, and was started by Buzz Wagner, a well-known expert on Aeroncas who gives forums annually at Oshkosh. The club has a quarterly newsletter for the exchange of information pertaining to maintenance and general Aeronca news.

Membership is $15 yearly. For further information about the Aeronca Lovers' Club, contact:

**Aeronca Lovers Club**
Box 3
401 1st St. E
Clark, SD 57225

## Aeronca Sedan Club

The Aeronca Sedan Club is over eight years old now, and was originated by Dick Welsh. There are about 300 members, and about that number of Sedans still flying. A newsletter is used for the exchange of Sedan-related information including STCs, where to get parts, and classified ads.

The club has many complete drawings for use by rebuilders, and there is a club scrapbook with pictures of most of the existing Sedans in it.

For further information about the Aeronca Sedan Club, contact:

**Aeronca Sedan Club**
2311 East Lake Sammamish Pl.
Issaquah, WA 98027

In addition to the individual clubs, there is a national fly-in held each year at Middletown, Ohio, which encompasses all the Aeronca Clubs. This fly-in is usually held in early June.

# Chapter 4

# Cessna

The Cessna classic two-placers first appeared in 1946 as the model 120. The 120 was a metal-fuselage craft with fabric-covered high wings. Naturally, it was a taildragger. The seating, as in all the Cessna two-placers, was side-by-side. Control wheels graced the instrument panel (Fig. 4-1).

The model 140 was a deluxe version of the 120. An electric system and flaps assisted the pilot, and a plusher cabin comforted the passenger (Fig. 4-2).

Many model 120s have been updated to look like 140s with the addition of extra side windows and electric systems.

The 140A was the final Cessna two-place airplane for almost a decade. It was all-metal and had the Continental C-90 engine. About 500 140As were built (Figs. 4-3, 4-4).

It's interesting to note that the 140A airplane sold new for $3695, and now commands a price more than double that. Production ceased in 1950, after more than 7,000 120/140/140As were manufactured.

The Cessna four-place line of airplanes started

in 1948 with the introduction of the Model 170 (Fig. 4-5).

The first 170s, like the two-place 120s, had metal fuselages and fabric-covered wings. They also had two wing struts on each side. Of course they had conventional landing gear.

In 1949 the 170A appeared with a single lift strut on each side, metal-covered wings, and a new fin (Fig. 4-6).

The last entry in the 170 series was the 170B, with the large flaps we have all become used to on Cessnas (Fig. 4-7).

In 1957 the day had come for Cessna, as with Piper and their Pacer series, to end production of old-style conventional-geared airplanes. The demand for the "easy drive-it" airplane saw sales lagging with the 170 and gaining with the 172. Basically the 172 is a 170 with a nosewheel and a different rudder. There were 5,136 170-series airplanes built.

A good 170 will take you just about anywhere, and do it economically. They are considered, based

Fig. 4-1. 1946 Cessna 120. (courtesy Cessna)

Fig. 4-2. 1946 Cessna 140. Notice the additional rear window. Many 120s have been modified to look like 140s by addition of this window. (courtesy Cessna)

Fig. 4-3. 1950 Cessna 140A. The wing struts have been replaced with a single unit and a leading edge landing light has been added. (courtesy Cessna)

Fig. 4-4. Instrument panel of a 1949 Cessna 140A. (courtesy Cessna)

upon the period of production, classics. However, due to their metal construction, are just as modern as today. As I said before, they are the basis for the Cessna model 172, which is possibly the all-time favorite four-place airplane. A good 170 will cost better than $10,000 today.

## SPECIFICATIONS
### Model: 120 and 140
Engine

| | |
|---|---|
| Make: | Continental |
| Model: | C-85 |
| hp: | 85 |
| TBO: | 1800 |

Seats: 2 side-by-side
Speed

| | |
|---|---|
| Max: | 125 mph |
| Cruise: | 105 mph |
| Stall: | 49 mph (w/o flaps) |
| Stall: | 45 mph (with flaps) |

Fuel Capacity: 25 gal
Rate of Climb: 640 fpm
Transitions

| | |
|---|---|
| Takeoff over 50′ obs: | 1850 ft |
| Ground run: | 650 ft |
| Landing over 50′ obs: | 1530 ft |
| Ground roll: | 460 ft |

Fig. 4-5. 1948 Cessna 170. (courtesy Cessna)

Fig. 4-6. 1950 Cessna 170A. Notice the single wing strut. (courtesy Cessna)

Fig. 4-7. 1956 Cessna 170B. This was the end of the line for the 170s. Put a nosewheel on it, and you have a 172. (courtesy Cessna)

Weights
    Gross:        1450 lbs
    Empty:        800 lbs

Dimensions
    Length:       20 ft 9 in
    Height:       6 ft 3 in
    Span:         32 ft 8 in (120)
    Span:         33 ft 3 in (140)

## Model: 140-A
Engine
    Make:         Continental
    Model:        C-90
    hp:           90
    TBO:          1800

Seats: 2 side-by-side
Speed
    Max:          125 mph
    Cruise:       105 mph
    Stall:        45 mph

Fuel Capacity: 25 gal
Rate of Climb: 640 fpm
Transitions
    Takeoff over 50' obs:    1850 ft
    Ground run:              680 ft
    Landing over 50' obs:    1530 ft
    Ground roll:             460 ft

Weights
    Gross:        1500 lbs
    Empty:        850 lbs

Dimensions
    Length:       20 ft 9 in
    Height:       6 ft 3 in
    Span:         33 ft 3 in

## Model: 170 (all)
Engine
    Make:         Continental
    Model:        C-145-2

hp:           145
TBO:          1800

Seats: 4
Speed
    Max:          140 mph
    Cruise:       120 mph
    Stall:        52 mph

Fuel Capacity: 42 gal
Rate of Climb: 690 fpm
Transitions
    Takeoff over 50' obs:    1820 ft
    Ground run:              700 ft
    Landing over 50' obs:    1145 ft
    Ground roll:             500 ft

Weights
    Gross:        2200 lbs
    Empty:        1260 lbs

Dimensions
    Length:       25 ft
    Height:       6 ft 5 in
    Span:         36 ft

## ADs

The following ADs, although old, should be checked for compliance in the logbooks:

**47-50-2:** Reinforce fuselage bulkhead on all model 120/140 airplanes through SN 14289.

**50-31-1:** Reinforce fin spar on 120/140 series planes from SN 8001 to 15035.

## STCs AND PARTS

Cessna is extremely supportive of all their products, and these classics are no exception. Parts are available for the 120/140/170 airplanes directly from them, or through their many dealers. Many 150 parts fit the 120/140s and 172 parts often fit the 170s. Additionally, there are many suppliers of parts that advertise in *Trade-A-Plane*.

Some of the two-placers have been modified by the addition of the Continental 0-200 engine, which is a completely bolt-in job, requiring no other modifications. Also, the Cessna 150 seats have found new homes in some 120/140 planes.

## INSPECTION TIPS

These aircraft are all prone to damage in the gear boxes caused by rough landings. Be sure to inspect this area carefully, or have it inspected by a knowledgeable person such as your mechanic.

Another place to look for indications of rough handling is the lower door posts at the wing attach points. Wrinkling here indicates the need for further investigation.

## CLUBS

There are several clubs that support Cessna products.

### International Cessna 170 Club

The International Cessna 170 Club was officially formed in order to keep the 170 flying as inexpensively and as easily as possible. The purpose is to furnish information about service, parts, and flying techniques to its members. In addition, general aviation gossip, insurance and safety data, as well as other "non-essential" information is exchanged.

The club issues a quarterly magazine, the *170 News*. It contains photos, news items, want ads, articles, and letters. They also put out a newsletter 11 times a year. Included in the newsletter are want ads (free to members).

The club has an annual convention in the summer which is advertised as a "week of family fun with a little education thrown in." There are also regional get-togethers.

For further information about the International Cessna 170 Club contact:

**International Cessna 170 Club**
Route 2, Box 274
Hartville, MO 65667
Phone: (417) 741-6557

### International Cessna 120/140 Association

For further information about the International Cessna 120/140 Association, contact:

**International Cessna 120/140 Association**
Box 92
Richardson, TX 75080
Phone: (817) 497-4757

### West Coast 120/140 Club

For further information about the West Coast 120/140 Club, contact:

**West Coast 120/140 Club**
Box 5298
San Mateo, CA 94402

# Chapter 5

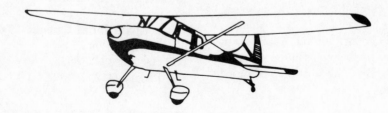

# Ercoupe

The Ercoupe airplanes are considered among the most foolproof craft ever built. They were originally designed with only a control wheel for all directional maneuvering. The wheel operated the ailerons and rudder via control interconnections and even steered the nosewheel. No pilot coordination was required to make turns. In addition to the coordination effect, the controls were limited in the amount of travel, thereby limiting the stalls that could be entered. The original airplane was designed to be spin-proof. After all, how can you spin if you can't get into uncoordinated flight during a stall? This fact led to some limited pilot licenses back in the late '40s, as the feeling prevailed, at that time, that an Ercoupe was not a complete airplane; therefore, its pilots were not complete pilots.

The Ercoupe was the dream child of Fred Weick, who later designed the Piper Cherokee. The first year of manufacture was 1940, and the planes were produced by Engineering Research Corp. (ERCO) of Riverdale, Maryland. Like so many of the classic airplanes, the Ercoupe's history is full of bumps.

Here is a breakdown of the various models and manufacturers:

**415C**—Produced prior to WWII, and powered with a 65-hp engine. There were 113 model 415Cs built before the war haulted production. After the war, production was restarted. As a matter of record, during nine months in 1946 over 4000 Ercoupes were built.

**415D**—Introduced in 1947, the D had a Continental C-75-12 (12 means electric start).

**415E**—Appeared in 1948, and again the power was increased, this time to 85-hp with the Continental C-85-12. The 415E sold new for $3995.

**415G**—Same as the E model, but with rudder pedals installed. It was introduced in 1949, and was the last ERCO craft to be built.

In 1950 Universal Aircraft purchased the production rights. Universal built no airplanes, but did supply necessary parts to the owners of Ercoupes. They still do.

1956 saw the Forney Aircraft Company of Fort

Collins, Colorado, as the owner of the production rights. Fornair produced the F1 Ercoupe until 1960. The F-1 was all metal, and powered by the Continental C-90-12 engine.

Alon Inc., of McPhearson, Kansas, purchased the Ercoupe production rights in the middle 1960s after Forney gave up. The new A-2 was a 90-hp craft that offered an option of three controls or two controls (rudder pedals being the option). Also, the canopy was converted to a sliding operation. The price of the A2 was $7825.

Alon gave up in 1967 and sold the production rights to Mooney Aircraft of Kerrville, Texas. Mooney produced the A-2 as their A-2A. Then in 1968 Mooney saw fit to completely redesign the Ercoupe. The new model was the M-10 Cadet. It didn't sell well, and was quickly discontinued.

Interestingly, the Ercoupe was designed to be very safe. Stalls were very minimal, and spins were impossible. In fact, it is placarded "This Airplane Characteristically Incapable of Spinning." When Mooney introduced the Cadet the stalls and spins were put back in. Also gone was the twin tail.

In 1970 the last remnants of Ercoupe went the way of so many other good things in life. Production ceased—probably for all time.

Of the more than 5000 Ercoupes (including Forney, Alon, and Mooney) there is still a large number of these fine little planes flying, no doubt due to their small thirst for gasoline, low prices, and low taxation of pilot skills (Figs. 5-1, 5-2).

The first Ercoupe models had metal fuselages and fabric-covered wings; the later versions were of all-metal design. They all had tricycle landing gear. One feature that has always made them popular is the fighter-like canopy that can be opened during flight. Another is the unique way crosswind landings are handled.

Cross-wind operations are rather different in the Ercoupe than in other aircraft (Figs. 5-3 through 5-8). The trailing beam main gear takes the shock of the crabbed landing, then makes the correction. This is not as novel as you may think. The Boeing 707 lands the same way, being unable to drop a wing during crosswind landings due to low engine-to-ground clearance. Landings can be made with up to a 30 degree crab angle. Try *that* in a taildragger, sports fans!

While we're talking about simplicity, here is the Cockpit Checklist (Courtesy of Univair):

Fig. 5-1. This Ercoupe model 415 is typical of the "coupes" you will see. Notice the fighter-like appearance of the cabin/low wing combination.

Fig. 5-2. The side windows on the 415 Ercoupe slide down for entry. You can leave them down while flying.

**Starting:**
1. Amount of gas and oil
2. Both fuel valves—On.
3. Mixture—Full Rich.
4. Carburetor Heat—Off.
5. Prime two to six strokes—Lock plunger.
6. Throttle—Crack one-eighth inch.
7. Ignition on—Pull starter.
8. Warm up—700 to 900 rpm.

**Before Takeoff:**
1. Carburetor Heat—Off.
2. Oil Temperature—90 degrees minimum.
3. Oil Pressure—35 lbs/sq in.
4. Full throttle—(2050 rpm).
5. Ignition check—Max 75 rpm drop.

**Flight:**
1. Oil Pressure—30 to 40 lb/sq in.
2. Oil Temperature—100 to 220 degrees.
3. Adjust mixture for best rpm.

**Landing:**
1. Mixture—Full rich.
2. Open throttle periodically during glide.

Before purchasing an Ercoupe, be sure to have a mechanic who is very familiar with the ways of Ercoupes check the plane well. These airplanes are nearing 40 years of age, and there will always be some metal deterioration (corrosion); you will do well to have an expert pass judgement before you are financially committed.

## SPECIFICATIONS
**Model: 415C**

Engine

|  |  |
|---|---|
| Make: | Continental |
| Model: | A-65-8 |
| hp: | 65 |
| TBO: | 1800 |

Seats: 2 side-by-side
Speed
   $V_{ne}$:       144 mph
   Cruise:   108 mph
   Stall:     56 mph
Fuel Capacity: 14 gal

Rate of Climb: 550 fpm
Transitions
   Takeoff over 50' obs:   2375 ft
   Ground run:          590 ft
   Landing over 50' obs:   1750 ft
   Ground roll:           750 ft

## CROSS WIND TAKE-OFF IN AN ERCOUPE

In taking off cross wind, it is advisable to keep the control wheel well forward, which holds the nose wheel firmly on the ground and gives good steering control. Some excess in forward speed should be gained to allow the airplane to take off very definitely, and at the moment of breaking contact with the ground, the control wheel should be straightened laterally to neutral position. The airplane may weathercock into the wind just after it leaves the ground, but this need cause no concern, as it is merely adjusting itself to true flight with respect to the air, and a straight course of travel is maintained without difficulty. The pilot should not hesitate to make slight turns near the ground in order to maintain the desired path and avoid being drifted off course by the wind.

**START AT BOTTOM AND READ UP**

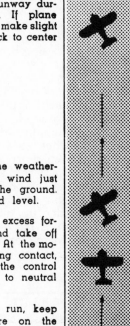

**4.** A straight course of flight is maintained on the center line of runway during the climb. If plane drifts sideways, make slight turns to get back to center of runway.

**3.** The airplane weathercocks into the wind just after leaving the ground. Wings are held level.

**2.** Gain some excess forward speed and take off very definitely. At the moment of breaking contact, straighten the control wheel laterally to neutral position.

**1.** On ground run, keep forward pressure on the control wheel and some right control necessary to overcome weathervaning. (Tendency to head into the wind.)

**WIND FROM LEFT**

Fig. 5-3. Crosswind takeoff. (courtesy Univair)

## CROSS WIND LANDING IN AN ERCOUPE

START AT BOTTOM AND READ UP

In the approach to a cross wind landing, the airplane will be pointing up wind sufficiently to **keep** the flight path in line with the runway rather than attempt to drop the windward wing as is done in the three control plane. The glide should be continued in this crabbing attitude down until contact is made with the ground. At the moment of contact the airplane should be given its head, and the grip on control wheel relaxed. This allows the nose wheel to caster and line up with the direction of motion of the airplane along the ground. Immediately thereafter ease the control wheel forward slowly and roll down the runway. Prompt application of the brakes or setting the brakes on about half way during the glide approach brings the nose down and completes the change in heading more quickly.

**5.** During ground run steer like a car.

**4.** On ground plane will change heading to line up with path along runway.

**3.** Make contact **decisively** at low speed with plane still crabbed, but **relax grip on control wheel** to allow nose to caster and ease forward on control wheel slowly.

**2.** If plane drifts sideways, make slight turns to get back to center line of runway.

**1.** Finish turn with ERCOUPE on extended centerline of runway and headed or crabbed into wind just enough to keep its flight path (not heading) on extended centerline.

**WIND FROM LEFT**

**PATH OF SHIP**

Fig. 5-4. Crosswind landing. (courtesy Univair)

Weights
  Gross:    1260 lbs
  Empty:     800 lbs

Dimensions
  Length:   20 ft  9 in

Height:   5 ft 11 in
Span:     30 ft

**Model: 415D**
Engine
  Make:     Continental

Fig. 5-5. The trailing beam landing gear that allows the unique crosswind operations.

Fig. 5-6. Single fork nosewheel on a 415.

Fig. 5-7. Dual fork nosewheel.

Model:      C-75-12F
hp:         75
TBO:        1800

Seats: 2 side-by-side
Speed
   $V_{ne}$:        144 mph
   Cruise:     114 mph
   Stall:       56 mph

Fuel Capacity: 24 gal
Rate of Climb: 560 fpm
Transitions
   Takeoff over 50' obs:    2250 ft
   Ground run:               570 ft
   Landing over 50' obs:    1750 ft
   Ground roll:              750 ft

Weights
   Gross:    1400 lbs
   Empty:     815 lbs

Dimensions
   Length:    20 ft  9 in
   Height:     5 ft 11 in
   Span:      30 ft

**Model:  415E/G**
Engine
   Make:     Continental
   Model:    C-85-12F
   hp:       85
   TBO:      1800

Seats: 2 side-by-side
Speed
   $V_{ne}$:        144 mph
   Cruise:     118 mph
   Stall:       56 mph

Fuel Capacity: 24 gal
Rate of Climb: 560 fpm

Transitions
| | |
|---|---|
| Takeoff over 50' obs: | 2100 ft |
| Ground run: | 520 ft |
| Landing over 50' obs: | 1750 ft |
| Ground roll: | 750 ft |

Weights
| | |
|---|---|
| Gross: | 1400 lbs |
| Empty: | 830 lbs |

Dimensions
| | |
|---|---|
| Length: | 20 ft  9 in |
| Height: | 5 ft 11 in |
| Span: | 30 ft |

**Model: Fornair F-1** (serial numbers start at 5600)

Engine
| | |
|---|---|
| Make: | Continental |
| Model: | C-90-12F |
| hp: | 90 |
| TBO: | 1800 |

Speed
| | |
|---|---|
| $V_{ne}$: | 144 mph |
| Cruise: | 120 mph |
| Stall: | 56 mph |

Fuel Capacity: 24 gal
Rate of Climb: 600 fpm
Transitions
| | |
|---|---|
| Takeoff over 50' obs: | 2100 ft |
| Ground run: | 500 ft |
| Landing over 50' obs: | 1750 ft |
| Ground roll: | 600 ft |

Weights
| | |
|---|---|
| Gross: | 1400 lbs |
| Empty: | 890 lbs |

Dimensions
| | |
|---|---|
| Length: | 20 ft  9 in |
| Height: | 5 ft 11 in |
| Span: | 30 ft |

Fig. 5-8. Notice how the nosegear is part of the engine mount. Rough landings can damage the mount and/or the firewall.

**Model:** **Alon A-2** (serial numbers A-2 thru A-245)

**Mooney A2-A** (serial numbers B-246 thru B-298)

Engine
  Make:       Continental
  Model:      C-90-16F
  hp:         90
  TBO:        1800

Seats: 2 side-by-side
Speed
  Max:        128 mph
  Cruise:     124 mph
  Stall:       56 mph

Fuel Capacity: 24 gal
Rate of Climb: 640 fpm
Transitions
  Takeoff over 50' obs:    2100 ft
  Ground run:               540 ft
  Landing over 50' obs:    1750 ft
  Ground roll:              650 ft

Weights
  Gross:      1450 lbs
  Empty:       930 lbs

Dimensions
  Length:     20 ft  2 in
  Height:      5 ft 11 in
  Span:       30 ft

**Model:** **Mooney M-10** (serial numbers start at 690001)
**Name:** **Cadet**
Engine
  Make:       Continental
  Model:      C-90
  hp:         90
  TBO:        1800

Seats: 2 side-by-side
Speed
  $V_{ne}$:       144 mph
  Cruise:     110 mph
  Stall:       46 mph

Fuel Capacity: 24 gal
Rate of Climb: 835 fpm
Transitions
  Takeoff over 50' obs:    1953 ft
  Ground run:               534 ft
  Landing over 50' obs:    1016 ft
  Ground roll:              431 ft

Weights
  Gross:      1450 lbs
  Empty:       950 lbs

Dimensions
  Length:     20 ft 8 in
  Height:      7 ft 8 in
  Span:       33 ft

## ADs

The Ercoupes had many ADs issued against them in their early years, and even a few late ones. Not all are listed here, so be sure to have your mechanic check the logs for you.

**46-23-03** requires a test/inspection of the control wheel to determine integrity of the control wheel and aileron control system on model 415 serial number 113 thru 1306.

**46-38-02:** inspect and modify the Aileron control horn on 415 models serial number 113 thru 2706 (with some exceptions).

**46-49-1** requires the replacement of the nosewheel on early 415-C Ercoupes.

**47-20-5** requires the reinforcement of the belly skin on many 415 Ercoupe models serial number 800 thru 2037.

**47-20-6** calls for the reinforcement of the aileron skin on most 415 models.

**47-42-20** requires an inspection/replacement of the control column shaft. This applies to 415 models with serial numbers between 1033 and 1327.

**59-5-4:** reinforcement of the rear spar is required on early 415-Cs.

**52-02-02** requires inspection of aileron hinges and the aileron balance assembly on all 415 series planes.

## RUDDER PEDAL CONTROL KIT

The rudders are completely disengaged from the aileron system and therefore independent of the lateral controls, allowing the airplane to be flown in slips, and misuse of the rudder pedals can be demonstrated in flight. It is not necessary to use the rudder pedals in excess of 70 miles per hour, due to the efficiency of the aileron system.

The three-control Ercoupe is an ideal training airplane for pilots intending to fly Navions and Bonanzas since it provides a cheaper, lighter airplane with tricycle landing gear and similar control set up. It has the hand brake system like the Navion; however, the control of the steering on the ground is still with the control wheel. This provides a more natural means of steering since it is like the automobile and provides a more accurate and delicate control than can be provided with rudder pedals. With the three-control Ercoupe, cross-wind landings may be performed in the conventional Ercoupe manner or with a wing low technique developed for older airplanes. Once on the ground, the airplane is stable, and therefore, still handles like an Ercoupe although directional steering may be performed with the rudders down to about 20 miles an hour.

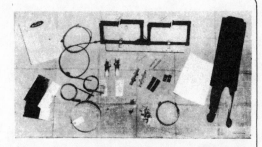

Rudder Pedal Kit consists of foot rest with rudder pedals mounted, cables to connect the rudder pedals to the rudder system with installation parts, hardware and drawings.

The rudder pedals may be installed in approximately eight man hours by the average A & P mechanic. Complete, ready for installation. 4-SK-21

## STROBE LIGHT KITS

SINGLE STROBE BEACON. A direct replacement for bottom fuselage WHELEN HR-DF (Double flash) Strobe. 4-SK-20

SINGLE STROBE BEACON. Provides for the installation of a WHELEN HR-DF Strobe unit in the bottom of the fuselage for aircraft that currently has no strobe or beacon unit. 4-SK-20A

TWO STROBE FUSELAGE MOUNTED SYSTEM. Kit includes a power supply and two WHELEN A470 Strobe Lights, (1 Red, 1 Clear). 4-SK-20B

WING TIP MOUNTED 2 STROBE SYSTEM. WHELEN A413 power supply and two A650 Strobe Lights. (This kit must be used in conjunction with the SK-54 or SK-55 kits which must be purchased separately). 4-SK-20C

THREE STROBE WING AND TAIL MOUNTED SYSTEM. Kit includes power supply, two wing-tip strobes, and one tail strobe. (This kit must be used with the SK-54 or SK-55 and the SK-56 which must be purchased separately). 4-SK-20D

## SPLIT ELEVATOR KIT

The improved control from the split elevator and the safety of a stall warning cushion can be installed on the older Ercoupes, provided the center quadrant trim control is installed. The Ercoupe can be landed five miles per hour slower with the split elevator. (Labor Estimate, 3 Hours) 4-SK-25

## NEW STYLE TAIL CONE

Streamline your Ercoupe with the Alon Tail Cone. Facilitates installation of Tail Mounted Strobe. Gives your Ercoupe that "New Look". 4-SK-56

Fig. 5-9. Here are just a few of the popular updates and conversions available for the Ercoupe. (courtesy Univair)

Fig. 5-10. Ercoupe's classic lines still look good today.

**54-26-02** requires the inspection and replacement of certain control cables on all 415 airplanes.

**55-22-02** requires the inspection and replacement of fuel tanks on all 415 and F-1 aircraft.

**57-02-01** requires a 100 hour inspection of the rudder horn attachments on all 415 and F-1 planes.

**59-05-04** calls for the inspection and replacement of the rear spar center section on all 415 planes.

**59-25-5** requires the reinforcement of the rudder on most 415 Ercoupes.

**67-06-03** requires the inspection and modification of all these types, unless already modified IAW Ercoupe Service Memo #63, of the rudder bell crank assembly.

**70-17-02** calls for the immediate replacement of hardware attaching the rudder pedals on all M10 Cadets.

## STCs AND PARTS

Univair has a rudder pedal kit out for the Ercoupes. It can be installed in about eight hours by an A&P. It allows you the choice of standard crosswind landings, or the "Coupe" method.

Also available is a split rudder kit, claimed to improve safety by allowing the installation of a stall warning cushion. Its use also allows landings five miles per hour slower than is normal.

Fortunately, Univair owns Ercoupe production rights. This will allow the remaining Ercoupes to continue on forever. The Univair people produce all the parts necessary for the maintenance and repair of Ercoupes (Fig. 5-9).

## CLUBS

The Ercoupe Owners Club is made up of persons interested in the history, restoration, and flying of the Ercoupe, and Ercoupe-type airplanes. This includes the Ercoupe, Forney, Alon, and Mooney models (Fig. 5-10).

The club has 11 regions in the U.S. and two in Canada. Each region has social and flying events. The club newsletter is the *Coupe Capers* and is published on a monthly basis.

*Coupe Capers* is a nice combination of general information for the Ercoupe owner, including fly-ins, technical help, letters to the editor (often giving or asking for assistance), classified ads of airplanes, and parts for sale. Also, some of the pages are adorned with commercial advertising of items with special interest to the Ercoupe owner.

Of particular interest is the stressed importance of safety and accident prevention that abounds in the newsletter. Information of past crashes is given in hopes of preventing similar occurrences.

In addition to the club newsletter, some of the club regions produce their own newsletters of primary interest to members residing in that particular geographical area.

The E.O.C. sponsers a national fly-in on an annual basis. The annual dues to the Ercoupe Owners Club are $15.00 U.S. and Canada ($25 foreign). For further information, contact:

**Ercoupe Owners Club**
3557 Roxboro Road
Box 15058
Durham, NC 27704
Phone: (919) 471-9492

# Chapter 6

# Luscombe

Luscombe Silvaire airplanes came into being in 1937. They were designed by Don Luscombe, and were originally powered by engines varying from 50 to 75 hp. As with all small civilian plane production, no Luscombes were built during the war years.

The Luscombe airplanes are neat, all-metal airplanes. There are two series of interest: the 8 series two-place planes, and the 11 series four-place sedans.

The 8 series seated two side-by-side, albiet a bit cozily. They have stick controls, and have two reputations they live up to. First, the Luscombe has one of the strongest airframe and wing structures ever manufactured, as demonstrated by the photograph of a Luscombe with 23 persons perched upon the wings and gear legs. This photo, by the way, can be seen on the Luscombe Association newsletter.

Secondly, over the years many stories have circulated about their poor ground handling characteristics. They're quite untrue, and have no doubt been spread by those who don't really know.

Luscombes are touchy on landings, and their landing gear is rather narrow; however, if the pilot stays on his toes he'll have no problems. (Actually, the same applies to *all* conventional-landing gear airplanes.)

According to National Transportation Safety Board records the two-place Luscombes have an accident rate of 45 incidents per 100,000 hours of operation, and a fatality rate of 5 incidents for the same period of operation. This is mighty high when compared with the Cessna 150 figures of 10 and 1 respectively.

Like most other makes of airplanes, the various models indicated the engine horsepower.

| | | |
|---|---|---|
| **8** : | Continental A-50 | (50 hp) |
| **8A:** | Continental A-65 | (65 hp) |
| **8B:** | Lycoming 0-145-B | (65 hp) |
| **8C:** | Continental A-75 fuel-injected | (75 hp) |
| **8D:** | Continental A-75 | (75 hp) |
| **8E:** | Continental C-85 | (85 hp) |
| **8F:** | Continental C-90 | (90 hp) |

Fig. 6-1. The Luscombe 8 series. Notice the "S" on the engine cowling; it appears on many Luscombes.

Due to their superior handling while in the air, a purchaser is cautioned to carefully inspect for damage caused by overstress from aerobatics.

Luscombes were produced from 1946 through 1949 by the Luscombe Airplane Corp. of Dallas, Texas. In the early '50s, Texas Engineering and Manufacturing Company (TEMCO) produced the Luscombe 8F version. In 1955 Silvaire Aircraft Corp. was formed in Fort Collins, Colorado. Silvaire produced only the 8F. All production stopped in 1960. All in all there were 6,057 series 8 Luscombes manufactured (Figs. 6-1 through 6-5).

Luscombe briefly entered the four-place aircraft field with the family-sized model 11 Sedan

(Figs. 6-6, 6-7). The Sedan was all-metal, had very wide conventional landing gear, and, oddly enough, a rear window (like the modern Cessnas).

The advertising describing the Silvaire Sedan likened the airplane to a large family sedan: Deluxe interior; automotive type walnut grain instrument panel with "Silchrome" trimming; all seats quickly removable; spacious glove compartment; wheel controls; hydraulic "instant action" brakes on the pilot's side; parking brake; 3,716 square inches of window area; spring interconnected rudder and aileron controls; easy opening windows in both doors; hat-throw behind the rear seat; exceptionally large doors; clean-easy pinstripe all-wool

Fig. 6-2. Rear view of a typical Luscombe 8.

Fig. 6-3. This 1946 8A is letter-perfect, right down to the wheel pants.

Fig. 6-4. The front office of a 1946 8A. Notice the sporty curve to the chrome sticks.

Fig. 6-5. This Luscombe 8F is a 1959, built in Ft. Collins, Colorado. Notice the square tail.

upholstery, side panels and kick panels; all-wool rug; foam rubber seat cushions; roomy baggage compartment beneath the rear seat; complete soundproofing around the cabin area; cabin heater and four individual fresh air ventilators; overhead front sunshades; sun visor; no-slip cargo strips; normal flight and engine instruments; ignition lock; wheel type elevator tab control; mixture control; three automotive type individual cigarette lighters and ashtrays (front and rear); metallic bronze deluxe interior trim; hydraulic flap actuating mechanism; front seats individually adjustable; seat backs fold down; balanced controls; electric starter; wood fixed-pitch propeller; full swivel steerable tailwheel; Luscombe landing lights; generator; engine primer; position lights; instrument panel lights; dome light;

Fig. 6-6. The Luscombe Model 11 Sedan was really ahead of its time. Look at the rear window and wasp waist. Unfortunately, few were made.

# ALL METAL WING- 8A, 8E, 8F

Note: "U" Prefixes on part numbers indicate a *FAA-PMA Approved* part.

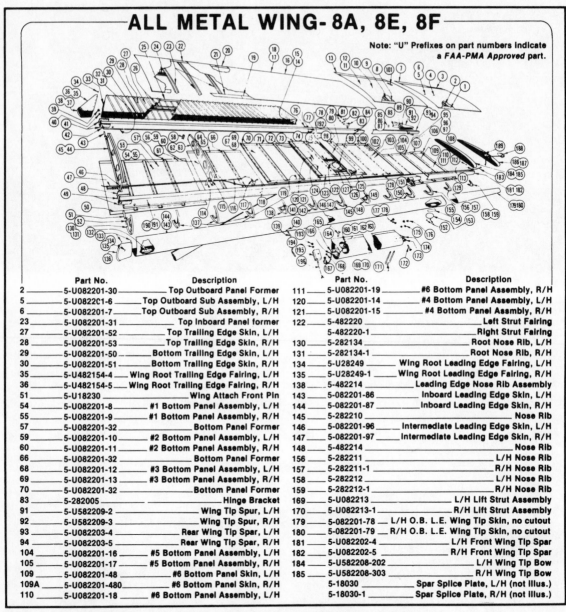

| | Part No. | Description |
|---|---|---|
| 2 | 5-U082201-30 | Top Outboard Panel Former |
| 5 | 5-U0822C1-6 | Top Outboard Sub Assembly, L/H |
| 6 | 5-U082201-7 | Top Outboard Sub Assembly, R/H |
| 23 | 5-U082201-31 | Top Inboard Panel former |
| 27 | 5-U082201-52 | Top Trailing Edge Skin, L/H |
| 28 | 5-U082201-53 | Top Trailing Edge Skin, R/H |
| 29 | 5-U082201-50 | Bottom Trailing Edge Skin, L/H |
| 30 | 5-U082201-51 | Bottom Trailing Edge Skin, R/H |
| 35 | 5-U482154-4 | Wing Root Trailing Edge Fairing, L/H |
| 36 | 5-U482154-5 | Wing Root Trailing Edge Fairing, R/H |
| 51 | 5-U18230 | Wing Attach Front Pin |
| 54 | 5-U082201-8 | #1 Bottom Panel Assembly, L/H |
| 55 | 5-U082201-9 | #1 Bottom Panel Assembly, R/H |
| 57 | 5-U082201-32 | Bottom Panel Former |
| 59 | 5-U082201-10 | #2 Bottom Panel Assembly, L/H |
| 60 | 5-U082201-11 | #2 Bottom Panel Assembly, R/H |
| 66 | 5-U082201-32 | Bottom Panel Former |
| 68 | 5-U082201-12 | #3 Bottom Panel Assembly, L/H |
| 69 | 5-U082201-13 | #3 Bottom Panel Assembly, R/H |
| 70 | 5-U082201-32 | Bottom Panel Former |
| 83 | 5-282005 | Hinge Bracket |
| 91 | 5-U582209-2 | Wing Tip Spur, L/H |
| 92 | 5-U582209-3 | Wing Tip Spur, R/H |
| 93 | 5-U082203-4 | Rear Wing Tip Spar, L/H |
| 94 | 5-U082203-5 | Rear Wing Tip Spar, R/H |
| 104 | 5-U082201-16 | #5 Bottom Panel Assembly, L/H |
| 105 | 5-U082201-17 | #5 Bottom Panel Assembly, R/H |
| 109 | 5-U082201-48 | #6 Bottom Panel Skin, L/H |
| 109A | 5-U082201-480 | #6 Bottom Panel Skin, R/H |
| 110 | 5-U082201-18 | #6 Bottom Panel Assembly, L/H |

| | Part No. | Description |
|---|---|---|
| 111 | 5-U082201-19 | #6 Bottom Panel Assembly, R/H |
| 120 | 5-U082201-14 | #4 Bottom Panel Assembly, L/H |
| 121 | 5-U082201-15 | #4 Bottom Panel Assmbly, R/H |
| 122 | 5-482220 | Left Strut Fairing |
| | 5-482220-1 | Right Strut Fairing |
| 130 | 5-282134 | Root Nose Rib, L/H |
| 131 | 5-282134-1 | Root Nose Rib, R/H |
| 134 | 5-U28249 | Wing Root Leading Edge Fairing, L/H |
| 135 | 5-U28249-1 | Wing Root Leading Edge Fairing, R/H |
| 138 | 5-482214 | Leading Edge Nose Rib Assembly |
| 143 | 5-082201-86 | Inboard Leading Edge Skin, L/H |
| 144 | 5-082201-87 | Inboard Leading Edge Skin, R/H |
| 145 | 5-282210 | Nose Rib |
| 146 | 5-082201-96 | Intermediate Leading Edge Skin, L/H |
| 147 | 5-082201-97 | Intermediate Leading Edge Skin, R/H |
| 148 | 5-482214 | Nose Rib |
| 156 | 5-282211 | L/H Nose Rib |
| 157 | 5-282211-1 | R/H Nose Rib |
| 158 | 5-282212 | L/H Nose Rib |
| 159 | 5-282212-1 | R/H Nose Rib |
| 169 | 5-U082213 | L/H Lift Strut Assembly |
| 170 | 5-U082213-1 | R/H Lift Strut Assembly |
| 179 | 5-082201-78 | L/H O.B. L.E. Wing Tip Skin, no cutout |
| 180 | 5-082201-79 | R/H O.B. L.E. Wing Tip Skin, no cutout |
| 181 | 5-U082202-4 | L/H Front Wing Tip Spar |
| 182 | 5-U082202-5 | R/H Front Wing Tip Spar |
| 184 | 5-U582208-202 | L/H Wing Tip Bow |
| 185 | 5-U582208-303 | R/H Wing Tip Bow |
| | 5-18030 | Spar Splice Plate, L/H (not illus.) |
| | 5-18030-1 | Spar Splice Plate, R/H (not illus.) |

Fig. 6-7. Ever wonder what went into that famous Luscombe wing? (courtesy Univair)

propeller spinner; engine shielding.

Unfortunately, even with all the above, only 80 Sedans were manufactured; fewer survive today. Currently the production rights for the 11 series is owned by Alpha Aviation Service, Majors Field, Box 641, Greenville, TX 75402. Phone: (214)455-9080.

## SPECIFICATIONS

**Model: Luscombe 8**
Engine
    Make:    Continental
    Model:    A-50
    hp:    50 at 1900 rpm

Seats: 2 side-by-side
Speed
    Max:      107 mph
    Cruise:   94 mph
    Stall:    37 mph

Fuel Capacity: 14 gal
Oil Capacity: 4 qts
Weights
    Gross:   1200 lbs
    Empty:   650 lbs
    Load:    550 lbs

Dimensions
    Length:   19 ft 8 in
    Height:   6 ft 1 in
    Span:    34 ft 7 in

### Model: Luscombe 8A,B

Engine
    Make:    Continental or Lycoming
    Model:   A-65 or 0-145-B
    hp:      65 at 2350 rpm
    TBO:    1800

Seats: 2 side-by-side
Speed
    Max:      112 mph
    Cruise:   102 mph
    Stall:    38 mph

Fuel Capacity: 15 gal
Rate of Climb: 550 fpm
Transitions
    Takeoff over 50' obs:   1950 ft
    Ground run:   1050 ft
    Landing over 50' obs:   1540 ft
    Ground roll:   450 ft

Weights
    Gross:   1200 lbs
    Empty:   665 lbs
    Load:    535 lbs

Dimensions
    Length:   19 ft 8 in

Height:    6 ft 1 in
Span:    34 ft 7 in

### Model: Luscombe 8C,D

Engine
    Make:    Continental
    Model:   A-75
    hp:      75 at 2600 rpm

Seats: 2 side-by-side
Speed
    Max:      118 mph
    Cruise:   107 mph
    Stall:    40 mph

Fuel Capacity: 15 gal
Weights
    Gross:   1260 lbs
    Empty:   720 lbs
    Load:    540 lbs

Dimensions
    Length:   19 ft 8 in
    Height:   6 ft 1 in
    Span:    34 ft 7 in

### Model: Luscombe 8E

Engine
    Make:    Continental
    Model:   C-85
    hp:      85 at 2575 rpm
    TBO:    1800

Speed
    Max:      122 mph
    Cruise:   112 mph
    Stall:    48 mph

Fuel Capacity: 25 gal
Rate of Climb: 800 fpm
Transitions
    Takeoff over 50' obs:   1875 ft
    Ground run:   650 ft
    Landing over 50' obs:   1540 ft
    Ground roll:   450 ft

Weights
  Gross:      1400 lbs
  Empty:       810 lbs
  Load:        590 lbs

Dimensions
  Length:    19 ft 8 in
  Height:     6 ft 1 in
  Span:      34 ft 7 in

## Model:  Luscombe 8F

Engine
  Make:      Continental
  Model:     C-90
  hp:        90
  TBO:       1800

Speed
  Max:       128 mph
  Cruise:    120 mph
  Stall:      48 mph

Fuel Capacity: 25 gal
Rate of Climb: 900 fpm
Transitions
  Takeoff over 50' obs:    1850 ft
  Ground run:               550 ft
  Landing over 50' obs:    1540 ft
  Ground roll:              450 ft

Weights
  Gross:     1400 lbs
  Empty:      870 lbs

Dimensions
  Length:    20 ft
  Height:     6 ft 3 in
  Span:      35 ft

## Model:  Luscombe 11 (Sedan)

Engine
  Make:      Continental
  Model:     C-165
  hp:        165
  TBO:       1800

Seats:  4
Speed
  Max:       140 mph
  Cruise:    130 mph
  Stall:      55 mph

Fuel Capacity:  42 gal
Fuel Consumption:    9 gph
Rate of Climb: 900 fpm
Transitions
  Takeoff run:   800 ft
  Landing roll:  500 ft

Gross Weight: 2280 lbs

Dimensions
  Length:    23 ft   6 in
  Height:     6 ft  10 in
  Span:      38 ft

## ADs

The Luscombe airplanes have not suffered greatly from ADs, but there are a few that should concern the owner/purchaser greatly:

**55-24-1** concerns corrosion in the superstructure spars, and involves the drilling of five holes into each of the spars, through which your mechanic checks for internal corrosion at each annual inspection. The AD applies to all series 8 airplanes except the 8F models with serial numbers S-1 and up.

This particular AD cannot be directly corrected as there are no spars currently being manufactured. However, here is an alternate approach to remedy the problem and eliminate this annual AD inspection (Courtesy of the Luscombe Association). The following modification was made on a 337:

1. Removed cabin roof skin (P/N 08011-3).

2. Removed forward spar superstructure (P/N 28018-2) and rear spar superstructure (P/N 28019-2).

3. Constructed new forward and rear spar superstructures from 4130 steel (MIL-S-18729-C) of 0.063" thickness. Cold bent all angles to coincide with existing spar superstructures using

0.250″ radius. All lengths, widths, and dimensions of existing spar superstructures were duplicated, including rivet hole patterns.

4. Primed new spar superstructure with steel metal primer paint (2 coats).

5. Applied zinc chromate tape to areas that come in contact with aluminum parts.

6. Constructed new superstructure skin (cabin roof) leaving out holes required for compliance with AD 55-24-1. Used original rivet hole patterns on .032″ Alclad aluminum 2024-T3.

7. Installed new front spar superstructure to number 2 bulkhead uprights LH and RH using AN470-AD-6 rivets.

8. Install new rear spar superstructure to number 3 bulkhead uprights LH and RH using AN3-4 bolts; AC945 washers; AN365 self-locking nuts.

For the fortunate Luscombe 8 series owner who had no corrosion showing when inspected, here is another permanent fix (Courtesy of the Luscombe Association):

1. Remove the wings, wing attachment fittings, and the superstructure skin (cabin roof), referred to in the AD as the top wing skin. This permits a complete inspection.

2. The spar carry through structures (P/N 28018 and 28019) are inspected and found to be free of any surface corrosion. The spar carry through structures are then cleaned, etched, and painted with Stits Aircraft Coatings brand Epoxy Chromate Metal Primer, in accordance with the manufacturer's instructions.

3. A new superstructure skin (cabin roof) without inspection holes is installed.

As a result of these modifications the FAA allowed discontinuance of the requirements of AD 55-24-01 on both planes.

**79-25-05** pertains to the Luscombe vertical stabilizer forward attach fitting, P/N 28444.

This AD is directed at those round-fin Luscombes having cast aluminum fittings. If you have the square-tip fin, or if your round-tip fin has the steel fitting, the AD does not apply. Obviously then, if you have the round fin, you must pull the fairing to determine the type of fitting. If it turns out to be cast, then the part must be removed from the plane and checked by dye penetrant. Compliance was required within ten hours of operation from 12-17-79. Thereafter, inspection must be made every 100 hours of operation. This subsequent inspection may be made visually, without removing the part from the plane.

Univair Aircraft Corp., can provide an FAA-PMA approved replacement made of 4130 steel that is attached with machine screws instead of rivets. The part number is P/N U-28444.

In reference to this AD, one member of the Luscombe Association wrote (Courtesy of the Luscombe Association): "When I received AD 79-25-05 last winter I thought that this would just be a routine check, probably like many vertical fin, I found a small crack, about 1/4″ long. I was relieved for the AD because I never would have found the crack otherwise. I was even more pleased for the AD when I drilled out the five rivets on the right side and the bracket fell off in my hand. My small 1/4″ crack was actually split all the way up through the five rivets on the left side. To make things worse, the week before I received the AD, I had been practicing spins and loops in the machine. This also puts a little more wood on the fire about the argument of doing aerobatics in old airplanes."

Other less serious ADs that are applicable to Luscombe airplanes are listed here. Most will have been complied with long before this late date; however, they are of interest, and the logs should be checked for their compliance:

**47-10-40** requires a rework of the rudder control arm on certain 8A models only.

**48-49-1** requires the reinforcement of the vertical stabilizer spar on all 8 series airplanes.

**49-40-1** requires a rework of the trim tab control system on 11 series planes.

**49-43-2** requires an inspection of the stabilizer spar on all 8 series airplanes.

**49-45-1** requires a reinforcement of the landing gear bulkhead on 11 Sedans.

**50-37-1** requires a modification be made to the fuel system on 8C aircraft only

**51-10-2** requires an inspection and replacement of frayed control cables in 8 series airplanes.

**51-21-3** requires an inspection of the rudder bellcrank on 11 series airplanes.

**61-3-5** requires an inspection of the fuel lines coming from the wing tanks.

As with all "unofficial" lists of ADs, have your trusted mechanic make a complete search for ADs and their compliance as applicable to your individual airplane.


## CLUBS

There are several organizations that support Luscombe airplanes. Some local, and some national in geographical coverage.


### The Luscombe Association

The Luscombe Association states "NO WOOD—NO NAILS—NO GLUE" on their emblem, attesting to their love for the all-metal Luscombe airplanes. The association supports the 8 series and the 11 series Sedans.

The Association says in their membership literature: The Luscombe Association is composed of people who are interested in the Luscombe Corporation, aircraft, and the history and accomplishments of Luscombe aircraft. The Association is a nonprofit organization dedicated to serving the needs of its members around the world. The organization is open to anyone who has an interest in any phase of our Association and is willing to pay dues. There are plenty of activities for members who don't own Luscombes.

The services the Association provides are:

1. Publishes a newsletter, *The Luscombe Association News,* that you can count on every other month. The newsletter covers the following areas:

    A. "Wanted" and "for sale" columns.
    B. Maintenance, modification, and repair techniques and ideas.
    C. Flying stories.
    D. Historical articles.
    E. Reports Luscombe events.

2. Gathers and maintains historical information concerning Luscombe aircraft, the company, and the personnel who manufactured and sold them.

3. Maintains a collection of "paperwork" for Luscombe modifications.

4. Helps members locate aircraft or parts needed.

5. Provides members with sources of technical information, repair, and modifications.

6. Sponsers an annual Luscombe Association forum.

7. Encourages the establishment of regional Luscombe fly-ins.

8. Offers free listings of "wanted" and "for sale" column in the newsletter.

9. Organizes and promotes the National Luscombe Fly-in.

10. Publishes sources for new parts and individuals who specialize in repairs (rebuilding Luscombes).

11. Stationery, decals, patches, etc. are available to members.

12. Establishment of a computerized membership list. Locate Luscombe members in your area, locate members who have modified their aircraft to a special configuration, or simply locate members who have a particular model.

13. Provide back issues of all the Luscombe Newsletters (an index of back issues is available).

The dues for the Association are $7.50 yearly. For further information, contact:

**Luscombe Association**
c/o John Bergeson
6438 W. Millbrook
Remus, MI 49340
Phone: (517) 561-2393


### Continental Luscombe Association

For further information about the Continental Luscombe Association, contact:

**Continental Luscombe Association**
5736 Esmar Rd.
Ceres, CA 95307

## Texas Luscombe Club

For further information about the Texas Luscombe Club, contact:

**Texas Luscombe Club**
Box 579
Lake Jackson, TX 77566

## AN INTERESTING STORY

The following is excerpted from the Luscombe Association Newsletter:

From the front page of the San Fransisco Chronical, 1953:

*Glasgow, Scotland, June 26*—Peter Gluckmann flew his tiny single-engined sports plane into Renfrew Airport here today, completing a 7,000 mile flight from San Mateo, California, in a final nonstop lap from Iceland.

The tall, heavy-set San Francisco watchmaker spanned a continent and an ocean in his peanut-sized plane in just 20 days. The last over-water hop from Reykjavik took him 12 hours.

Gluckmann, who has been flying only four years and never crossed a body of water bigger than Francisco Bay before this jaunt, said his 90-horsepower Luscombe monoplane behaved "just beautifully."

"People say this is a tremendous trip to make," Gluckmann told newsmen here, "but to me it was entirely uneventful and just another flight."

As soon as he arrived he telephoned his parents in London. He had planned the trip as a surprise for them, but they knew all about his impending arrival as British papers carried news of his multi-stop flight.

His journey took him from San Mateo Airport to Arizona, New Mexico, Oklahoma, Michigan, Ontario, Quebec, Labrador, Greenland, and Iceland. Later today he flew south, stopped at Preston, England, for gas, and touched down at Blackpool, on the Irish Sea, to spend the night.

Gluckmann said he was planning to land this morning at Prestwick, near the west coast of Scotland, but the field was fogged in, so he flew on to Edinburg, found fog there, too, and finally landed here.

Gluckmann's plane, with a wingspan of only 35 feet, and a fuel capacity of only 90 gallons, is one of the smallest to cross the Atlantic. He used overleaded Air Force 110 octane gas instead of the usual 80-87 octane.

The big flyer—he's 6 feet 3 inches tall and portly as well—spent a total of 85 hours in the seat of his gold and blue airplane.

At Iceland yesterday, authorities at first refused to let him leave because of bad weather conditions.

"And when I reached the Scottish coast," he said, "I was a little worried what with all that fog. I wasn't sure I'd have enough gas to find a clear field. But it all worked out."

# Chapter 7

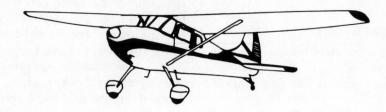

# Piper

There is no other name that is associated with small airplanes more than Piper. Many people refer to all small airplanes as Piper Cubs.

Possibly the most famous is the J3, actually a prewar plane. It was introduced in 1939, and again produced after the war. The Army L-4 was really a J3. At one time J3s were coming out of the factory door at the rate of one every 10 minutes. Production of the J3 ended in 1947, with a total of 14,125 being built (Figs. 7-1 through 7-5).

A simpler flying machine has never been made, and it's the basis for other models right through the Super Cub. It's unique in the fact that all solo flight must be done from the rear seat. Although no Cub is known for great speed, the view from them, and other tandem-seat Cubs, is wonderful. The door is split in half and folds up against the wing, and down along the fuselage, getting out of the way completely.

An interesting side note is the fact some late J3s have aluminum spars in their wings.

The PA-11 Cub Special was introduced in 1947 as an updated version of the J3, allowing the pilot

to solo from the front seat. The engine is completely enclosed by a cowling and could be either a 65-hp or 90-hp engine; 1,428 Specials were built before production stopped in 1949.

The J4 Cub Coupe was built before the war, from 1939 to 1941. The Coupe used many J3 parts, which kept costs of design and production to a minimum. None were built after the war. They seated two side-by-side, and were powered with a 65-hp engine. Many years ago I had one of these birds, and flew it around West Texas. Let me tell you, many are the cars that passed under my wings, beating me in the race with the wind. 1,250 coupes were built (Fig. 7-6).

The J5 Cub Cruiser was introduced just before the war, in 1941, and seated three persons. Like the J4, it shared many J3 parts. The pilot sat in a single bucket seat up front, and there was a bench seat for two to sit—very cozily—in the rear (Fig. 7-7). After the war the J5-C, with a 100-hp engine, was brought out as the Super Cruiser. The PA-12-100 Cruiser followed shortly, as an update to the J5-C, then the PA-12-108 with 108 hp. None

66

Fig. 7-1. The famous "CUB," as found on many restored Piper airplanes.

Fig. 7-2. The J3 Cub in original form.

Fig. 7-3. For low, slow, and enjoyable flight, it's hard to beat a Cub. Notice the exposed cylinders on the engine.

Fig. 7-4. This door opens up to the world. It can be found on the J3, PA-11, and PA-18 models.

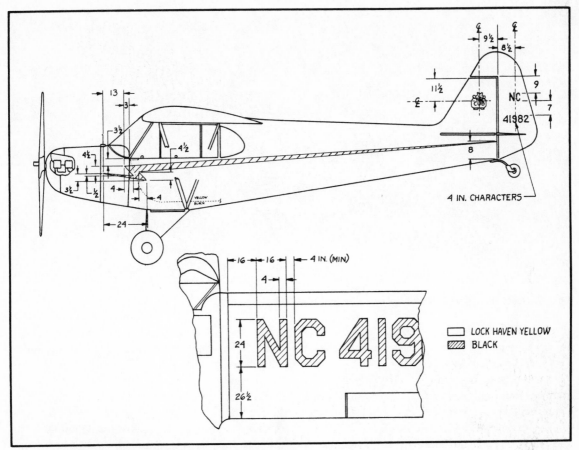

Fig. 7-5. Original paint scheme for the J3. (courtesy Univair)

Fig. 7-6. This J4 used many J3 parts. Piper often used this method of keeping parts development costs down.

Fig. 7-7. Notice the exposed engine cylinders on this 1941 Piper J5A.

of them will fly three adults off the ground on a real hot day unless the original engine has been replaced with something larger (Fig. 7-8).

By the way, the J in the early Piper model numbers indicated Walter C. Jamouneau, Piper's Chief Engineer. Later the PA designator was utilized to indicate Piper Aircraft.

The PA-15 was introduced as the Vagabond in 1948, a very basic airplane. The PA-15 had the Lycoming 0-145 engine, rated at 65 hp, and seated two side-by-side. The main landing gear was solid, with the only shock-absorbing action coming from the finesse of the pilot at landing time.

A short time later the PA-17 (also called the Vagabond) came out; it had more options, such as bungee-type landing gear, floor mats, and the Continental A-65 engine, which is said to have considerably more pep than the Lycoming 0-145. A

Fig. 7-8. PA-12 Super Cruiser. Built in 1946, this three placer has a 115-hp engine.

Fig. 7-9. PA-15 Vagabond. The appearance of this plane is almost identical to the PA-17, also called the Vagabond (courtesy Marion Pyles, Air Pix Aviation Photography)

total of 585 Vagabonds was built (Figs. 7-9 through 7-11).

The Super Cub, PA-18, is basically an airplane whose roots can be traced back to the J3. Although built with a completely redesigned airframe, the PA-18 does outwardly look like a J3 (Fig. 7-12). It's a fun plane to fly; however, it is usually found working for its keep. These planes are utilized in photography, mapping, fish spotting, spraying, glider towing, bush flying, etc.

Starting production in 1949, the PA-18s continued through the early '80s with a total in excess of 9,000 being built. They were available with a variety of engines from 90 to 150 hp.

The last entry of a two-place Piper airplane of tube-and-fabric design was the PA-22-108 Colt. It was really a two-seat, flapless version of the Tri-Pacer, powered with a 108-hp Lycoming engine.

Fig. 7-10. PA-16 Clipper, four-place plane.

Fig. 7-11. The interior of a PA-16 shows sticks for control.

Fig. 7-12. The PA-18 Super Cub is the final model for a design that started in the late 30s, and ended in the mid 80s. Its true Cub heritage is clearly seen (courtesy Marion Pyles, Air Pix Aviation Photography)

The Colt was meant to be used as a trainer, so if you're looking at one, a careful inspection of the airframe should be made. After all, trainers can be treated mighty rough; 1,820 Colts were built between 1961 and 1963.

Piper started production of four-place airplanes with the PA-14 Family Cruiser in 1948. The PA-14 is really a modified PA-12, with an extra seat up front. It was small and underpowered. Only 237 were manufactured before the PA-16 Clipper was introduced in 1949. The Clipper had shorter wings and fuselage than the PA-14, and was really the forerunner of the "short wing" Pipers (PA-20s and 22s). Both the PA-14 and the PA-16 are unique from the standpoint of controls. They have sticks, rather then the control wheels usually associated with four-place airplanes. The original price for a new PA-14 was $3,825. (Figs. 7-10 and 7-11.)

In 1950 the PA-20 Pacer series appeared. Like the PA-14s and 16s, the original PA-20s were fabric-covered and of conventional gear design. They also didn't exhibit very exciting performance numbers. A total of 1,120 Pacers was built.

Evolution of the Pacer saw more powerful engines, and the eventual addition of the nosewheel, the later resulting in the PA-22 Tri-Pacer. Billed as an "anyone can fly it" airplane due to the tri-gear, the PA-22 was sold as an option to the Pacer. However, sales of the Tri-Pacer soared, while those of the Pacer fell. The Pacer was removed from production in 1954. General aviation was demanding easier-to-handle airplanes, and in the Tri-Pacer they found what they wanted.

PA-22s were built from 1951 until 1960 and can be found with 125, 135, 150 and 160-hp engines. The Tri-Pacers are good performers, give fair cruise numbers (even when compared to the modern all-metal designs), and can often be bought cheap—especially if you want to do a restoration job (Figs. 7-13 through 7-18).

I know of no other airplane that can be purchased for less than $3,000, become a family project, rise to a value of $9,000 with mostly labor being invested, and, when done, carry the whole family flying. 7,670 PA-22 Tri-Pacers were built before Piper moved on to all metal airplanes.

## SPECIFICATIONS
### Model: J3C-65
Engine
  Make:      Continental
  Model:     A-65-8
  hp:        65 (at 2300 rpms)
  TBO:       1800

Seats: 2 tandem
Speed
  Max:       87 mph
  Cruise:    73 mph
  Stall:     38 mph

Fig. 7-13. PA-20 Pacer, four-place.

73

Fig. 7-14. PA-22 Tri-Pacer. One of the most economical four-place aircraft ever built.

Fig. 7-15. Tri-Pacer panel.

Fuel Capacity: 12 gal
Fuel Consumption: 4 gph
Rate of Climb: 450 fpm
Transitions
    Takeoff over 50' obs:  730 ft
    Ground run:          370 ft
    Landing over 50' obs:  470 ft
    Ground roll:         290 ft

Weights
  Gross:     1220 lbs
  Empty:     680 lbs
  Baggage:    20 lbs

Dimensions
  Length:   22 ft 4 in
  Height:    6 ft 8 in
  Span:     35 ft 2 in

## Model: J4

Engine
  Make:     Continental
  Model:    A-65
  hp:       65
  TBO:     1800

Seats: 2 side-by-side
Speed
  Max:     95 mph
  Cruise:   80 mph
  Stall:    42 mph

Fuel Capacity: 25 gal
Rate of Climb: 450 fpm
Transitions
    Takeoff over 50' obs:  750 ft
    Ground run:          370 ft

Fig. 7-16. Left rear door is common to all Piper four-place aircraft from the PA-16 thru the PA-22.

Fig. 7-17. PA-22 Colt, the last of the rag-wing Pipers.

Landing over 50' obs:  480 ft
Ground roll:          300 ft

Weights
  Gross:     1301 lbs
  Empty:     650 lbs

Dimensions
  Length:    22 ft  6 in
  Height:    6 ft 10 in
  Span:      36 ft  2 in

## Model: J5
Engine
  Make:    Continental
  Model:   A-75
  hp:      75
  TBO:    1800

Seats: 3
Speed
  Max:     95 mph
  Cruise:   80 mph
  Stall:    43 mph

Fuel Capacity: 25 gal
Rate of Climb: 400 fpm
Transitions
  Takeoff over 50' obs:  1250 ft
  Ground run:        750 ft
  Landing over 50' obs:  900 ft
  Ground roll:        400 ft

Weights
  Gross:     1450 lbs
  Empty:    820 lbs

Dimensions
  Length:    22 ft  6 in
  Height:    6 ft 10 in
  Span:      35 ft  6 in

## Model: J5C
Engine
  Make:    Lycoming
  Model:   0-235-2
  hp:      100
  TBO:    2000

Seats: three
Speed
    Max:      110 mph
    Cruise:   95 mph
    Stall:     45 mph

Fuel Capacity: 20 gal
Rate of Climb: 650 fpm
Transitions
    Takeoff over 50′ obs:   1050 ft
    Ground run:         650 ft
    Landing over 50′ obs:   950 ft
    Ground roll:        450 ft

Weights
    Gross:    1550 lbs
    Empty:    860 lbs

Dimensions
    Length:   22 ft  6 in
    Height:    6 ft 10 in
    Span:     35 ft  6 in

## Model: PA-11-65
Engine
    Make:    Continental
    Model:   A-65

hp:       65
TBO:    1800

Seats: two tandem
Speed
    Max:      100 mph
    Cruise:   87 mph
    Stall:     38 mph

Fuel Capacity: 18 gal
Fuel Consumption: 4.0 gph
Rate of Climb: 514 fpm
Transitions
    Takeoff run:   350 ft
    Landing roll:   290 ft

Weights
    Gross:    1220 lbs
    Empty:    730 lbs
    Baggage:  20 lbs

Dimensions
    Length:   22 ft 4 in
    Height:    6 ft 8 in
    Span:     35 ft 2 in

Fig. 7-18. This PA-22 Colt has been converted to a taildragger.

## Model: PA-11-90
Engine
    Make:     Continental
    Model:    C-90
    hp:       90
    TBO:     1800

Speed
    Max:      112 mph
    Cruise:   100 mph
    Stall:     40 mph

Fuel Capacity: 18 gal
Fuel Consumption: 4.7 gph
Rate of Climb: 900 fpm
Transitions
    Takeoff over 50' obs:   475 ft
    Ground run:         250 ft
    Landing over 50' obs:   550 ft
    Ground roll:        290 ft

Weights
    Gross:    1220 lbs
    Empty:    750 lbs
    Baggage:  20 lbs

Dimensions
    Length:   22 ft 5 in
    Height:   6 ft 8 in
    Span:    35 ft 8 in

## Model: PA-12
Engine
    Make:     Lycoming
    Model:    0-235-C
    hp:       100
    TBO:     2000

Seats: 3
Speed
    Max:      115 mph
    Cruise:   105 mph
    Stall:     49 mph

Fuel Capacity: 38 gal
Fuel Consumption: 6.5 gph

Rate of Climb: 600 fpm
Transitions
    Takeoff over 50' obs:  2190 ft
    Ground run:       720 ft
    Landing over 50' obs:  1400 ft
    Ground roll:       470 ft

Weights
    Gross:    1750 lbs
    Empty:    950 lbs
    Baggage:  41 lbs

Dimensions
    Length:   22 ft 10 in
    Height:   6 ft 10 in
    Span:    35 ft  6 in

## Model: PA-14
Engine
    Make:     Lycoming
    Model:    0-235-C1
    hp:       115
    TBO:     2000

Seats: 4
Speed
    Max:      123 mph
    Cruise:   110 mph
    Stall:     46 mph

Fuel Capacity: 38 gal
Fuel Consumption: 6.2 gph
Rate of Climb: 540 fpm
Transitions
    Takeoff over 50' obs:  1770 ft
    Ground run:       720 ft
    Landing over 50' obs:  1410 ft
    Ground roll:      470 ft

Weights
    Gross:    1850 lbs
    Empty:    1020 lbs
    Baggage:  80 lbs

Dimensions
    Length:   23 ft 2 in

Height:    6 ft 7 in
Span:    35 ft 6 in

## Model: PA-15/17
Engine
    Make:    Lycoming or Continental
    Model:    0-145 or A-65
    hp:    65
    TBO:    2000

Seats: 2 side-by-side
Speed
    Max:    100 mph
    Cruise:    90 mph
    Stall:    45 mph

Fuel Capacity: 12 gal
Rate of Climb: 490 fpm
Transitions
    Takeoff over 50' obs:    1572 ft
    Ground run:    800 ft
    Landing over 50' obs:    1280 ft
    Ground roll:    450 ft

Weights
    Gross:    1100 lbs
    Empty:    630 lbs
    Baggage:    40 lbs

Dimensions
    Length:    18 ft 7 in
    Height:    6 ft
    Span:    29 ft 3 in

## Model: PA-16
## Name: Clipper
Engine
    Make:    Lycoming
    Model:    0-235-C1
    hp:    115
    TBO:    2000

Seats: 4
Speed
    Max:    125 mph
    Cruise:    112 mph
    Stall:    50 mph

Rate of Climb: 580 fpm
Transitions
    Takeoff over 50' obs:    1910 ft
    Ground run:    720 ft
    Landing over 50' obs:    1440 ft
    Ground roll:    600 ft

Weights
    Gross:    1650 lbs
    Empty:    850 lbs
    Baggage:    50 lbs

Dimensions
    Length:    20 ft 1 in
    Height:    6 ft 2 in
    Span:    29 ft 3 in

## Model: PA-18-90 Super Cub
Engine
    Make:    Continental
    Model:    C-90
    hp:    90
    TBO:    1800

Seats: 2 tandem
Speed
    Max:    112 mph
    Cruise:    100 mph
    Stall:    42 mph

Fuel Capacity: 18 gal
Rate of Climb: 700 fpm
Transitions
    Takeoff over 50' obs:    750 ft
    Ground run:    400 ft
    Landing over:    385 ft

Weights
    Gross:    1300 lbs
    Empty:    840 lbs

Dimensions
    Length:    22 ft 5 in
    Height:    6 ft 6 in
    Span:    35 ft 3 in

## Model: PA-18-108 Super Cub
Engine
  Make:     Lycoming
  Model:    0-235-C1
  hp:       108
  TBO:      2000

Seats: 2 tandem
Speed
  Max:      117 mph
  Cruise:   105 mph
  Stall:    42 mph

Fuel Capacity: 18 gal
Fuel Consumption: 6.2 gph
Rate of Climb: 850 fpm
Transitions
  Takeoff over 50' obs:  650 ft
  Ground run:            350 ft
  Landing roll:          385 ft

Weights
  Gross:    1340 lbs
  Empty:     875 lbs

## Model: PA-18-125 Super Cub
Engine
  Make:     Lycoming
  Model:    0-290-D
  hp:       125
  TBO:      2000

Speed
  Max:      125 mph
  Cruise:   110 mph
  Stall:    38 mph

Fuel Capacity: 18 gal
Rate of Climb: 1000 fpm
Transitions
  Takeoff over 50' obs:  510 ft
  Ground run:            210 ft
  Landing over 50' obs:  600 ft
  Ground roll:           300 ft

Weights
  Gross:    1500 lbs
  Empty:     845 lbs

## Model: PA-18-135 Super Cub
Engine
  Make:     Lycoming
  Model:    0-290-D2
  hp:       135
  TBO:      2000

Speed
  Max:      127 mph
  Cruise:   112 mph
  Stall:    38 mph

Fuel Capacity: 36 gal
Rate of Climb: 1050 fpm
Transitions
  Takeoff over 50' obs:  500 ft
  Ground run:            200 ft
  Landing over 50' obs:  600 ft
  Ground roll:           300 ft

Weights
  Gross:    1500 lbs
  Empty:     895 lbs

## Model: PA-18-150 Super Cub
Engine
  Make:     Lycoming
  Model:    0-320-A2A
  hp:       150
  TBO:      2000

Speed
  Max:      130 mph
  Cruise:   115 mph
  Stall:    43 mph

Fuel Capacity: 36 gal
Rate of Climb: 960 fpm
Transitions
  Takeoff over 50' obs:  500 ft
  Ground run:            200 ft
  Landing over 50' obs:  725 ft
  Ground roll:           350 ft

Weights
  Gross:    1750 lbs
  Empty:     930 lbs

## Model: PA-20-125

Engine
- Make: Lycoming
- Model: 0-290-D
- hp: 125
- TBO: 2000

Seats: 4

Speed
- Max: 135 mph
- Cruise: 125 mph
- Stall: 48 mph

Fuel Capacity: 36 gal
Fuel Consumption: 7.7 gph
Rate of Climb: 810 fpm

Transitions
- Takeoff over 50' obs: 1788 ft
- Ground run: 1372 ft
- Landing over 50' obs: 1187 ft
- Ground roll: 500 ft

Weights
- Gross: 1800 lbs
- Empty: 970 lbs
- Baggage: 50 lbs

Dimensions
- Length: 20 ft 4 in
- Height: 6 ft 2 in
- Span: 29 ft 3 in

## Model: PA-20-135

Engine
- Make: Lycoming
- Model: 0-290-D2
- hp: 135
- TBO: 1500

Speed
- Max: 139 mph
- Cruise: 125 mph
- Stall: 48 mph

Fuel Capacity: 36 gal
Fuel Consumption: 7.7 gph
Rate of Climb: 620 fpm

Transitions
- Takeoff over 50' obs: 1600 ft
- Ground run: 1220 ft
- Landing over 50' obs: 1280 ft
- Ground roll: 500 ft

Weights
- Gross: 1950 lbs
- Empty: 1020 lbs
- Baggage: 50 lbs

## Model: PA-22-125

Engine
- Make: Lycoming
- Model: 0-290-D
- hp: 125
- TBO: 2000

Seats: 4

Speed
- Max: 133 mph
- Cruise: 123 mph
- Stall: 48 mph

Fuel Capacity: 36 gal
Fuel Consumption: 7.7 gph
Rate of Climb: 810 fpm

Transitions
- Takeoff over 50' obs: 1788 ft
- Ground run: 1372 ft
- Landing over 50' obs: 1280 ft
- Ground roll: 650 ft

Weights
- Gross: 1800 lbs
- Empty: 1000 lbs
- Baggage: 50 lbs

Dimensions
- Length: 20 ft 4 in
- Height: 8 ft 3 in
- Span: 29 ft 3 in

## Model: PA-22-135

Engine
- Make: Lycoming

Model: 0-290-D2
hp: 135
TBO: 1500

Seats: 4
Speed
  Max: 137 mph
  Cruise: 123 mph
  Stall: 48 mph

Fuel Capacity: 36 gal
Fuel Consumption: 7.7 gph
Rate of Climb: 620 fpm
Transitions
  Takeoff over 50' obs: 1600 ft
  Ground run: 1220 ft
  Landing over 50' obs: 1280 ft
  Ground roll: 500 ft

Weights
  Gross: 1950 lbs
  Empty: 1060 lbs
  Baggage: 50 lbs

## Model: PA-22-150
Engine
  Make: Lycoming
  Model: 0-320-A1A
  hp: 150
  TBO: 1200

Speed
  Max: 139 mph
  Cruise: 123 mph
  Stall: 49 mph

Fuel Capacity: 36 gal
Fuel Consumption: 9.0 gph
Rate of Climb: 725 fpm
Transitions
  Takeoff over 50' obs: 1600 ft
  Ground run: 1220 ft
  Landing over 50' obs: 1280 ft
  Ground roll: 500 ft

Weights
  Gross: 2000 lbs

Empty: 1100 lbs
Baggage: 100 lbs

## Model: PA-22-160
Engine
  Make: Lycoming
  Model: 0-320-B2A
  hp: 160
  TBO: 1200

Speed
  Max: 141 mph
  Cruise: 125 mph
  Stall: 49 mph

Fuel Capacity: 36 gal
Fuel Consumption: 9.0 gph
Rate of Climb: 800 fpm
Transitions
  Takeoff over 50' obs: 1480 ft
  Ground run: 1120 ft
  Landing over 50' obs: 1280 ft
  Ground roll: 500 ft

Weights
  Gross: 2000 lbs
  Empty: 1110 lbs
  Baggage: 100 lbs

## Model: PA-22-108 (Colt)
## Name: Colt
Engine
  Make: Lycoming
  Model: 0-235-C1B
  hp: 108
  TBO: 2000

Seats: 2 side-by-side
Speed
  Max: 120 mph
  Cruise: 108 mph
  Stall: 54 mph

Fuel Capacity: 36 gal
Rate of Climb: 610 fpm

Transitions

| | |
|---|---|
| Takeoff over 50' obs: | 1500 ft |
| Ground run: | 950 ft |
| Landing over 50' obs: | 1250 ft |
| Ground roll: | 500 ft |

Weights

| | |
|---|---|
| Gross: | 1650 lbs |
| Empty: | 940 lbs |

Dimensions

| | |
|---|---|
| Length: | 20 ft |
| Height: | 8 ft 3 in |
| Span: | 30 ft |

## ADs

**77-3-8** is the most widespread and serious AD affecting Piper airplanes. It calls for the inspection/replacement of the wing lift struts on most Piper airplanes. Piper addresses this problem in their Service Bulletin number 528B, of March 10, 1978, which is included here in its entirety courtesy of Univair.

### Service Bulletin no. 528B

**Subject:** Inspection of Wing Lift Strut Assembly

**Reason for Revision:**

1. Revised compliance requirements for factory treated and non-factory treated (re corrosion impedance) lift struts—see Compliance time, below; and

2. Revised identification of field-treated lift struts (i.e., struts having had corrosion impedance measures applied in the field per Piper Service Bulletin No. 528A)—see instruction No. 4.

**Models affected:**

All airplanes incorporating steel lift struts
PA-18 Super Cub   Serial No. 18-1 thru 18-7609035
PA-25 Pawnee   Serial No. 25-1 to 25-7656009

**Compliance time:**

1. Aircraft with NON-FACTORY TREATED lift struts having five (5) years or more time in service: At the next 100 hour inspection or annual inspection, whichever occurs first, and at least every annual inspection thereafter until corrosion impedance measures are applied.

2. Aircraft with FACTORY TREATED (identified per Instruction No. 4, below) lift struts, with less than five (5) years service time: Inspection is required when lift struts reach five (5) years time in service, to be repeated at each subsequent five (5) year interval thereafter.

3. Aircraft with lift struts having had corrosion impedance measures applied IN THE FIELD in compliance with Piper Service Bulletin No. 528 dated October 28, 1976 or No. 528A dated August 16, 1977: Inspection is required at each five (5) year interval (since corrosion-impedance measures accomplished). See NOTE, Instruction No. 4 concerning revised identification of field-treated struts.

**Purpose:** We are advised by the FAA that a campaign to require specific formal inspections of the wing lift strut assemblies on the above referenced aircraft is being finalized. The intended objective of this program is to detect internal lift strut tube corrosion, most likely to occur in the lower lift strut extremity. Since lift struts are closed tubular structures, internal corrosion in most cases may not be readily apparent until corrosion has advanced completely through the tube wall. This Service Release provides an inspection procedure to detect evidence of wing lift strut tube internal corrosion.

**Instructions:**

1. Accomplish inspection per attached Inspection Procedure.

2. Lift strut tubes indicating presence of internal corrosion may either be repaired per FAA Advisory Circular 43.13-1A, pp 81 (Repair of Wing and Tail Brace Struts by an FAA approved repair facility) or replaced; NOTE: see Material Required Section relative to lift strut replacements.

3. Aircraft whose records indicate that lift struts have been switched from one side of the aircraft to the other or which indicate that struts have been interchanged from another aircraft (i.e., inverted from original installation) should have lift struts inspected on both top and bottom surfaces—per attached inspection procedure.

4. Lift Strut assemblies which have been factory treated with corrosion preventive measures by the factory are identified by the installation of a Cherrylock rivet installed at the upper (wing attachment) end.

NOTE:

Lift struts that have had corrosion impedance measures applied in the field (per S.B. 528 or 528A) and have had the NAS1738B4-4 Cherrylock rivet installed on the strut (to signify treated strut) must have the Cherrylock rivet removed and a sheet metal screw installed (see instruction procedure for further details).

5. Alternative preservative materials: In addition to the "Valoil" and "Lionoil" (preservatives) specified in Service Bulletin No. 528, it is permissible to use the following alternate preservatives—Paralketone, linseed oil or any alternate preservatives that satisfy the requirements of Federal Specification TT-S-176D.

**Material Required:**

1. PA-18, PA-22 and PA-25 Series Aircraft: Refer to applicable model parts catalog for part identification information. Replacement Lift Struts may be obtained at owner/operator's discretion, as required, in the normal manner.

NOTE:

Due to limited wing lift strut requirements over the past years, factory stock may—at times—not be able to immediately provide replacement lift struts per this service release. Should this occur, alternate methods of compliance with this service release are denoted in No. 2, below.

2. All other models: Replacement lift struts no longer maintained in factory inventory: Consider (1) repair—per above instructions, (2) fabrication—factory will supply fabrication drawings at no charge on request, or (3) obtain from non-affiliated local aircraft parts supply source.

**Availability of Parts:** See above.

**Effectivity Date:** This service release is effective upon receipt.

**Summary:** This Service Release is submitted to assist above referenced aircraft owner/operators in conducting a positive, universally feasable wing lift strut (corrosion) inspection procedure.

**Inspection Procedure**

1. Securely tape a sheet of 1/4 inch grid graph paper to the lower 11 inches of the bottom surface on all wing lift struts (Fig. 7-19).

2. Using a Maule "Fabric Tester" and

holding tool normal to strut contour, apply pressure at a scale reading of 80 in each of the grid blocks.

3. Remove the paper and inspect the lift struts tubes. A perceptible dent will appear if internal corrosion is present. If any dents are found, be certain the dents are in the metal by carefully removing the paint.

   a. Lift strut tubes indicating the presence of any perceptible dent in the metal must either be repaired per FAA Advisory Circular 43.13-1A by an approved FAA repair facility or replaced with new lift strut assembly before further flight.

   b. If no dents appear in the metal, the lift strut may be considered airworthy.

NOTE

Further internal corrosion may be impeded per the following procedure:

   a. Remove left strut from aircraft.

   b. Inject one quart of Valoil, Lionoil Multi-Purpose L-1, Linseed Oil, Paralketone or any alternate preservative conforming to Federal Specification TT-S-176D, into the bolt hole at the top of the strut.

   c. Plug the bolt holes and slosh oil until interior of the strut is thoroughly coated.

   d. Drain oil from strut (through bolt holes) and install MS51861-44 sheet metal screw, as shown, for future identification.

   e. Reinstall strut to aircraft and rig.

4. Record lift strut inspection in aircraft logbook.

**81-25-5** calls for the replacement of the wing lift strut forks with machined rather then rolled threads.

**STCs AND PARTS**

To install a Lycoming 0-320 150-hp engine in the PA-16 Clipper, contact the Short Wing Piper Club (address elsewhere in this chapter) and ask for information about STC SA805EA.

Univair holds several STCs of interest to the Piper owner; their address is in the back of this book.

STC SA45RM provides for the conversion of

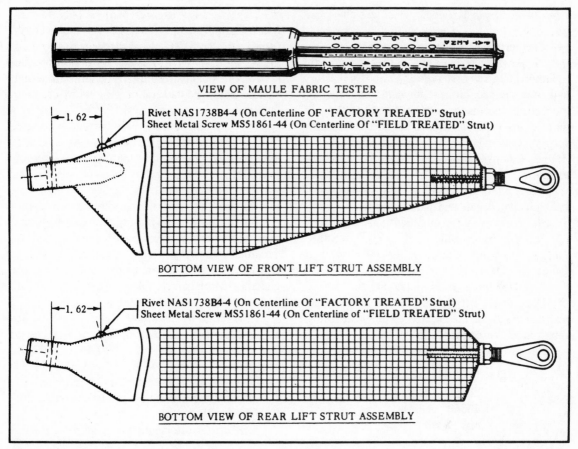

VIEW OF MAULE FABRIC TESTER

Rivet NAS1738B4-4 (On Centerline OF "FACTORY TREATED" Strut)
Sheet Metal Screw MS51861-44 (On Centerline Of "FIELD TREATED" Strut)

BOTTOM VIEW OF FRONT LIFT STRUT ASSEMBLY

Rivet NAS1738B4-4 (On Centerline Of "FACTORY TREATED" Strut)
Sheet Metal Screw MS51861-44 (On Centerline of "FIELD TREATED" Strut)

BOTTOM VIEW OF REAR LIFT STRUT ASSEMBLY

Fig. 7-19. The Maule Fabric Tester and 1/4″ graph paper used in testing for corrosion damage of the wing lift struts. (courtesy Univair)

a PA-22 Tri-Pacer back to a PA-20 Pacer. This is a very popular conversion, as can be seen at any airshow; just look at the number of PA-22/20s you'll see (and probably think they're Pacers). Univair sells all the parts, in a kit, for this particular STC.

Now, if you converted your Tri-Pacer to a Pacer, and want *real* performance, try STC SA181RM. This Univair STC allows a 180-hp Lycoming 0-360 engine to be put on the PA-22/20.

Univair even has an STC for installing a Continental 0-200 engine with an Aeromatic propeller on the J3.

Univair is one of the best sources of information and parts for Piper airplanes. They put out a large number of fact sheets and books about Piper airplanes (as well as most others), including owner's manuals, parts manuals, service manuals, paint schemes, ADs and Service Letters, etc.

## CLUBS

Due to the large number of models within the Piper line, two specialty clubs have formed.

### Cub Club

The Cub Club states its purpose as making available to anyone interested in the Piper J-3, J-4, L-4, J-5, PA-11, PA-12, PA-14, and/or PA-18 an organization whose purpose is to: "Preserve and Promote the Restoration, Maintenance and Use of Cubs."

The Cub Club believes in preserving these

strong and simple airplanes, which are cheap and fun to fly.

The services the club provides are:

1. A newsletter every other month (bi-monthly). The *Cub Club Newsletter* has Cub history, Cub maintenance, rare and unusual Cubs, member stories, and sources for parts. A "For Sale, Wanted, and Trade" section is included. There is no charge for members' ads.

2. Club fly-ins and meetings at major aviation events.

3. Club member T-shirts, caps, note paper, belt buckles, decals and patches, etc.

4. Paperwork for modifications.

5. Computerized mailing list—enables members to locate other members (or aircraft) by geographical area.

6. Back issues of Newsletters.

Dues for the Cub club are $10.00 per year, U.S. and Canada (U.S. funds); $15.00 per year foreign (bank money order for U.S. cash).

For further information, write to:

**Cub Club**
6438 W. Millbrook
Remus, MI 49340
Phone: (517) 561-2393

## Short Wing Piper Club

The Short Wing Piper Club is for persons whose interests are the PA-15, PA-16, PA-17, PA-20, PA-22, and the PA-22 (108).

The SWPC is a large club with several geographical regions, with various regional get-togethers and events. Formally the club was referred to as the Tri-Pacer Owners Club. The *Short Wing Piper News* is their bimonthly newsletter, and is probably the most extensive and largest of all the various club newsletters.

Included in each edition of SWPN are articles and photographs about social events, safety, mechanical difficulties, parts availability, classified ads, general aviation info, etc. Classified ads by members are free.

The SWPC also has a very extensive library that is available to members. Included in this library are Publications involving regulations, Piper Service Bulletins, Lycoming info, parts catalogs, documents showing aircraft specifications, books on Piper aircraft and other information of a more general aviation nature. Tools are available for loan, including the "Bungee Installer."

In addition to the above services, SWPC has a picture album consisting of photographs of Vagabonds, Clippers, Pacers, Tri-Pacers, and Colts contributed by members. This interesting album is available to any member of SWPC, and is mailable.

Membership for the SWPC is $20 yearly ($25 foreign).

For further information, contact:

**Short Wing Piper Club**
c/o Edwin Wach
1412 10th Street
Aurora, NE 68818
Phone: (402) 694-2218

# Chapter 8

# Stinson

Stinson Aircraft Corp, of Detroit, Michigan, owned by AVCO, produced several lightplanes that are considered classics.

The Stinson 108 series airplanes were introduced in 1946. All strong and rugged, many are still in use as bush planes in Canada and Alaska.

Built of tube and fabric, although some have since been metalized (fabric removed and a metal skin installed in its place), these airplanes all had conventional landing gear.

Franklin engines were installed in all models. These engines came in two types: heavy case and light case. Only the heavy case is acceptable, as the light case did not stand up, and is claimed to be almost impossible to rebuild.

The 108 and 108-1 models had the 150-hp engines, and the 180-2 and 3 models had 165 hp.

In late 1948, Piper bought out Stinson and produced a few 108s. A total of 5,259 Stinson 108s was built before production was completely halted.

For the exact year of manufacture, check the serial number. All the Stinson 108s start their serial numbers with 108.

| Serial Numbers | Year |
|---|---|
| 1 through 742 | 1946 |
| 743 through 2249 | 1947 |
| 2250 through 5260 | 1948-49 |

Often when refering to Stinsons, the terms Voyager and Station Wagon will be heard. They are both versions of the 108-2 and 3 airframes. The Voyager cabin is upholstered with cloth and vinyl. When the rear seat is removed a maximum of 350 pounds of cargo may be carried. The Station Wagon is finished in wood and vinyl (similar to the "woody wagons" of the same era) and will carry 600 pounds with the rear seats removed (Figs. 8-1 through 8-6).

## SPECIFICATIONS

**Model: 108**
Engine
    Make:      Franklin
    Model:    6A4-150-B31 or B3 or B4
    hp:        150
    TBO:     1200

Fig. 8-1. The Flying Station Wagon Cabin. (courtesy Univair)

Seats: 4
Speed
    $V_{ne}$:        148 mph
    Cruise:     117 mph
    Flaps:       88 mph
    Stall:        57 mph

Fuel Capacity: 40 gal
Fuel Usage: 8.5 to 11.0 gph
Rate of Climb: 700 fpm
Transitions
    Takeoff over 50' obs:   1750 ft
    Landing over 50' obs:   1610 ft

Weights
    Normal Gross:   2150 lbs
    Utility Gross:   1900 lbs
    Empty:            1200 lbs
    Baggage:           50 lbs

Dimensions
    Length:   24 ft
    Height:    7 ft
    Span:     33 ft 11 in

Serial Numbers
    108-1 thru 108-742 (except 108-11)

**Model: 108-1**
Engine
    Make:     Franklin
    Model:    6A4-150-B31 or B3 or B4
    hp:        150
    TBO:      1200

Seats: 4
Speed
    $V_{ne}$:        148 mph
    Cruise:     117 mph
    Flaps:       88 mph
    Stall:        57 mph

Fuel Capacity: 40 gal
Fuel Usage: 8.5 to 11.0 gph
Rate of Climb: 700 fpm
Transitions
    Takeoff over 50' obs:   1750 ft
    Landing over 50' obs:   1610 ft

Fig. 8-2. The Voyager Cabin. Notice upholstery all around. (courtesy Univair)

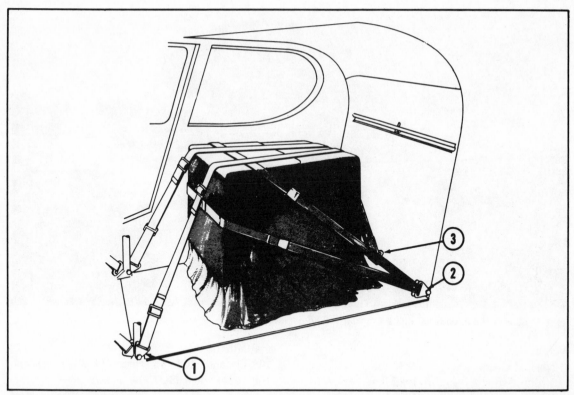

Fig. 8-3. Typical cargo loading in the 108. (1) Outer front seat support; (2) outer rear safety belt lug; (3) center rear safety belt lug. (courtesy Univair)

Fig. 8-4. Stinson 108-1 was built in 1947.

Fig. 8-5. Stinson 108-2, powered with a Franklin 165-hp engine.

Weights
Normal Gross: 2230 lbs
Utility Gross: 1925 lbs
Empty: 1250 lbs
Baggage: 100 lbs

Dimensions
Length: 24 ft
Height: 7 ft
Span: 33 ft 11 in

Serial Numbers
108-11 and 108-743 thru 108-2249 (except 108-1474) and 108-3100

**Model: 108-2**
Engine
Make: Franklin
Model: 6A4-165-B3 or B4
hp: 165
TBO: 1200

Fig. 8-6. Note the large fin on the 108 Series Stinsons. Unfortunately, this specimen has not been moved in many years, as is so with many airplanes.

Speed
  $V_{ne}$:      153 mph
  Cruise:      121 mph
  Flaps:       88 mph
  Stall:        57 mph

Fuel Capacity: 40 gal
Fuel Usage: 9.5 to 13.0 gph
Rate of Climb: 750 fpm
Transitions
  Takeoff over 50' obs:  1400 ft
  Landing over 50' obs:  1640 ft

Weights
  Normal Gross:  2230 lbs
  Utility Gross:  1925 lbs
  Empty:         1250 lbs
  Baggage:        100 lbs
  (Voyager 350 w/o rear seats)
  (Station Wagon 600 w/o rear seats)

Dimensions
  Length: 24 ft
  Height:  7 ft
  Span:   33 ft 11 in

Serial Numbers
  108-1474 and 108-2250 thru 108-3500 (except 108-3100)

## Model: 108-3
Engine
  Make:     Franklin
  Model:    6A4-165-B3 or B4
  hp:       165
  TBO:      1200

Speed
  $V_{ne}$:      158 mph
  Cruise:      126 mph
  Flaps:       88 mph
  Stall:        61 mph

Fuel Capacity: 50 gal
Fuel Usage: 9.6 to 13.0 gph
Rate of Climb: 750 fpm

Transitions
  Takeoff over 50' obs:  1400 ft
  Landing over 50' obs:  1640 ft

Weights
  Normal Gross:  2400 lbs
  Utility Gross:  2000 lbs
  Empty:         1250 lbs
  Baggage:        100 lbs
  (Voyager 350 w/o rear seats)
  (Station Wagon 600 w/o rear seats)

Dimensions
  Length:  25 ft 2 in
  Height:   7 ft 6 in
  Span:    34 ft

Serial Numbers
  108-3501 and up

## ADs

As with all the other classic airplanes, the ADs are old, however, compliance still is required:

**51-15-2:** Inspect the crank case for cracks: 6A4-165-B3 Franklin engine serial numbers 33046 and below. Inspections vary from 50 to 250 hrs depending upon known current cracks, if any. Installation of P/N 18925 (reinforced crankcase) eliminates the need for the inspection. This crankcase has the number 18906 just below the number six cylinder, and 18905 just below the number one cylinder.

## STCs AND PARTS

Due to the difficulty found in maintaining the Franklin engines found in most Stinsons, Univair has developed an STC for conversion to Lycoming engines.

STC SA1552NM for the 108-3 model calls for the use of a Hartzell constant-speed propeller and the Lycoming IO-360-A1A engine.

This 200-hp conversion gives 35 additional horsepower over the 165 Franklin, hence improved performance. Univair claims greater fuel economy also.

At this time Univair also has pending an STC for a 180-hp conversion to the entire 108 series. Write to them for further information; their address is in the back of this book.

## CLUBS
### National Stinson Club

For further information about the National Stinson Club, contact:

**National Stinson Club**
117 Lanford Rd.
Spartanburg, SC 29301
Phone: (803) 576-9698

# Chapter 9

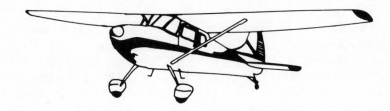

# Taylorcraft

The Taylorcraft airplane started its history as part of Piper Aircraft. Originally C. Gilbert Taylor was in business with William Piper; however, there was a split, and Mr. Taylor set about on his own. Alliance, Ohio, became the site of the first Taylor Aircraft factory. Unfortunately, the Taylor airplanes never enjoyed Piper-like popularity.

In 1939 and 1940 the BL-65, BC-65, and BF-65 planes were produced. They were all alike except for the engines. As indicated by the second letter of their model designator, Lycoming, Continental, and Franklin engines were used. The engines were not fully cowled, and appear similar to the Piper J-3 with the cylinders protruding out each side. In 1940 the price for a Taylorcraft was $1,495 and up.

According to Joseph P. Juptner's book *U.S. Civil Aircraft Vol. 7,* a Taylorcraft BL-65 was the first U.S. aircraft to be fired upon in WWII. This was of course on December 7, 1941, at Pearl Harbor.

In 1941 the BC-12 was introduced; however, it saw short production due to the start of WWII.

After the war, Taylorcraft, like all the other air-craft companies, restarted production. The new plane was the BC-12D, an updated version of the prewar BC-12.

The BC-12D was a tube-and-fabric, side-by-side airplane powered by a Continental 65-hp engine. Even though it was side-by-side and provided a larger cross section to wind resistance than the Piper J3, the Taylorcraft could out distance the Cub by better than 20 miles in an hour.

There were four versions of the BC-12D:

The Ace had a single 12 gallon fuel tank, a single control wheel, and only one door. The Ace sold for $1,995 in December 1946.

The Standard sported dual controls, an upgraded interior, and two doors. It sold for $2,400.

The Custom held 18 gallons for fuel, had a radio, lights, and battery. It sold for $2,500.

The Deluxe had 24 gallons of fuel on board, and sold for $2,600.

The extra fuel was carried in six-gallon wing tanks. The wings had spruce spars and tube steel drag struts. The landing gear was built of steel tub-ing and used shock cord for shock absorption. In the cockpit you found dual control wheels, but brakes only on the pilot's side. The brakes were heel mechanical types. Production of the BC-12D continued through 1950, with better than 3,000 planes delivered.

By late 1950 Taylorcraft Aviation Corp., of Alliance, Ohio, was a thing of the past, and a new company, Taylorcraft Inc., was begun in Conway, PA. This company introduced the model 19.

The model 19, also called the Sportsman, was powered with an 85-hp Continental engine. About 200 were built between 1950 and 1957. A skylight, 24 gallons of fuel, and better brakes were the features of the 19.

When Taylorcraft again folded, the production rights were sold to Univair, of Aurora, Colo. From then until 1965 only parts were produced; no planes were built.

In 1965 Charles and Dorothy Feris purchased the Taylorcraft rights, and returned the production of the Taylorcraft airplane to its original home of Alliance, Ohio. The Feris' had been Taylorcraft dealers before WWII.

In Alliance, production was restarted with the introduction of the F-19 in 1974. The F for Feris, the new model F-19 was powered with the Continental O-200 engine. Other than slight updating, little had changed from the BC-12D airplanes. It really is difficult to improve upon something that is as good, and time-proven, as the postware T-craft airplanes.

Charles Feris passed away in 1976, and his wife, Dorothy, took over and operated the company until it was sold in 1985.

Today you will find Taylorcrafts being built in Lock Haven, PA, in the old Piper plant where the famous Cubs were built.

All the newer Taylorcrafts are covered with Dacron, and most any others you are likely to find will be covered with Dacron also—that is, unless you find a "basket case" to rebuild.

Taylorcrafts are real performers, and the old ones, if in good condition, are about the most efficient (cheap) airplanes you can fly. They use a little over four gallons of fuel per hour in the 65-hp versions.

It should be noted that until the move to Lock Haven, many Taylorcraft employees had experience from the days of C. Gilbert Taylor. At the new production facility similar experience levels prevail, as many of the craftsmen are ex-Piper employees with experience building the Cubs. Of course, Taylorcraft produces all the parts necessary to keep the older models in the air.

Although not true "classics," I have included information on the later Taylorcrafts, as they are built using classic airplane techniques.

The current (1986) price for a new Taylorcraft F-21B is $26,999. Although that price is for a basic airplane with no avionics, it certainly represents a lot of airplane for the money.

In a bid for more of the market, Taylorcraft has introduced the F-22, a tri-geared version of the basic Taylorcraft airframe. It is powered with a 150-hp Lycoming, has flaps (other models did not), and can operate from the most basic of airstrips (Figs. 9-1 through 9-14).

## SPECIFICATIONS

**Model: BC12-65**

Engine

| | |
|---|---|
| Make: | Continental |
| Model: | A-65 |
| hp: | 65 |
| TBO: | 1200 |

Seats: 2 side-by-side

Speed

| | |
|---|---|
| Max: | 112 mph |
| Cruise: | 96 mph |
| Stall: | 38 mph |

Fuel Capacity: 12 gal

Rate of Climb: 500 fpm

Dimensions

| | |
|---|---|
| Length: | 21 ft 9 in |
| Height: | 6 ft 6 in |
| Span: | 36 ft |

**Model: BC-12D**

Engine

| | |
|---|---|
| Make: | Continental |

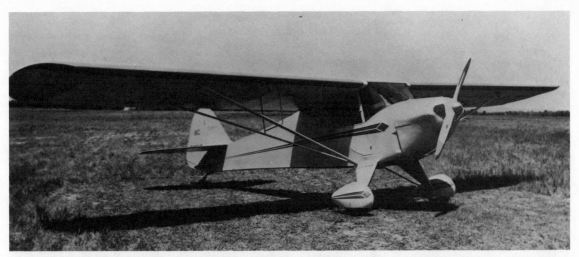

Fig. 9-1. Taylorcraft BC-12D as it looked the day it was new. (courtesy Taylorcraft Owners Club)

INTERIOR VIEW SHOWING
CABIN REFINEMENTS
ROOMY, LUXURIOUS SEATS

Fig. 9-2. The interior of a new BC-12D. (courtesy Taylorcraft Owners Club)

WHEEL OR MODERNIZED STICK CONTROLS
QUICKLY INTERCHANGEABLE

Fig. 9-3. You could fly either by stick or wheel in the Taylorcrafts. (courtesy Taylorcraft Owners Club)

Fig. 9-4. A restored BC-12D as seen in 1984.

Fig. 9-5. This F-21B is a current production airplane. Notice that the basic lines are unchanged. You just cannot improve on something that is perfect. Look at the extra windows. (courtesy Taylorcraft)

Model:     A-65-8A
hp:        65
TBO:       1200

Seats: 2 side-by-side
Speed
    Max:      100 mph
    Cruise:   95 mph
    Stall:    38 mph

Fuel Capacity: 12-24 gal

Fuel Consumption: 4.2 gph
Rate of Climb: 500 fpm
Transitions
    Takeoff run:   350 ft
    Landing roll:  300 ft
Weights
    Gross:    1200 lbs
    Empty:    750 lbs

Dimensions
    Length:    21 ft  9 in

Fig. 9-6. To make the Taylorcraft design compatible with today's pilot a tri-gear version, the F-22, is now available. (courtesy Taylorcraft)

Height:     6 ft 10 in
Span:       36 ft

## Model: 19
Engine
    Make:       Continental
    Model:      C-85
    hp:         85
    TBO:        1800

Seats: 2 side-by-side
Speed
    Max:        120 mph
    Cruise:     110 mph
    Stall:      41 mph

Fuel Capacity: 24 gal
Rate of Climb: 700 fpm
Transitions
    Takeoff over 50' obs:   400 ft
    Ground run:             300 ft
    Landing roll:           300 ft

Weights
    Gross:      1500 lbs
    Empty:      860 lbs

Dimensions
    Length:     22 ft   4 in
    Height:     6 ft 10 in
    Span:       36 ft

## Model: F-19
Engine
    Make:       Continental
    Model:      O-200
    hp:         100
    TBO:        1800

Seats: 2 side-by-side
Speed
    Max:        127 mph
    Cruise:     118 mph
    Stall:      43 mph

Fuel Capacity: 24 gal

Rate of Climb: 775 fpm
Transitions
    Takeoff over 50' obs:   350 ft
    Ground run:             200 ft
    Landing over 50' obs:   350 ft
    Ground roll:            275 ft

Weights
    Gross:      1500 lbs
    Empty:      900 lbs

Dimensions
    Length:     22 ft   1 in
    Height:     6 ft 10 in
    Span:       36 ft

## Model: F-21 and F-21A
Engine
    Make:       Lycoming
    Model:      0-235-L2C
    hp:         118
    TBO:        2000

Speed
    Max:        125 mph
    Cruise:     118-122 mph
    Stall:      43 mph

Fuel Capacity: 24 gal
Fuel Consumption: 6.5 gph
Rate of Climb: 875 fpm
Transitions
    Takeoff over 50' obs:   350 ft
    Ground run:             275 ft
    Landing over 50' obs:   350 ft
    Ground roll:            275 ft

Weights
    Gross:      1500 lbs
    Empty:      990 lbs

Dimensions
    Length:     22 ft 3 in
    Height:     6 ft 6 in
    Span:       36 ft

**Model: F-21B**

Engine
  Make:     Lycoming
  Model:    0-235-L2C
  hp:       118
  TBO:      2000

Speed
  Max:      125 mph
  Cruise:   115 mph
  Stall:    48 mph

Fuel Capacity: 42 gal
Fuel Consumption: 6.0 gph
Range at 75% power: 732 mi
Rate of Climb: 750 fpm
Service Ceiling: 18,000 ft
Transitions
  Takeoff:  450 ft
  Landing:  500 ft

Weights
  Gross:    1750 lbs
  Empty:    1025 lbs

Dimensions
  Length:   22 ft 3 in
  Height:   6 ft 6 in
  Span:     36 ft

## ADs

**75-18-5:** Requires the inspection/replacement of the engine mount bolts on F-19s.

Other than that, there are no ADs of any real consequence. This certainly speaks well for the design and construction of these fine airplanes.

## STCs AND PARTS

For information on an STC for installing a Continental C-85 on your BC-12D, contact:

Jack Gilbert
Box 246
Aliquippa, PA 15881
Phone: (412) 375-5396

Parts are available directly from the Taylorcraft factory and from Univair.

## CLUBS

The Taylorcraft Owners Club, like most other clubs, puts out a newsletter that has everything from club news and happenings to items for sale in it. However, I find the bits of history that are included to be the most interesting.

In particular, I like the way copies of old flyers and information sheets are included. It captures the imagination to see what the sales flyers of a bygone era looked like, to see the "classics" when they were on the showroom floor.

Each year the club sponsers a fly-in at Barber Airport in Alliance, Ohio. This is the very airport that Al Barber once owned. Al Barber was the test pilot for Taylorcraft, and tested well over 3,000 airplanes, right up until the money ran out for Taylorcraft. The airport now belongs to Forrest Barber, Al's son. Forrest, like his father, was a test pilot for Taylorcraft. Barber Airport is where T-Crafts were test flown from.

The club is presided over by Bruce Bixler, who thoughtfully provided much of the material for this chapter.

For further information, contact the Taylorcraft Owners Club at:

**Taylorcraft Owners Club**
12809 Greenbower Rd.
Alliance, OH 44601

# Chapter 10

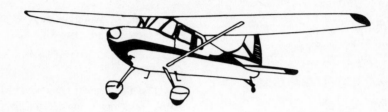

# FARs You Need to Know

The following FARs, and comments about them, are reprinted from the *Stits Poly-fiber Covering and Painting Manual,* by permission of the author, Ray Stits:

Since the early '60s, general aviation has enjoyed a rapid growth, with many new aircraft owners, pilots, and mechanics joining the ranks with the older aviation enthusiasts who had been hoping for just such a growth in popularity and public acceptance since the '30s and '40s.

A large part of the population now enjoying the sport of flying joined our ranks through association with aviation friends and learned to fly or became involved in ownership of aircraft, rebuilding an aircraft, or constructing a sport aircraft and have never found it necessary to become familiar with the FARs (Federal Aviation Regulations).

A brief history note: In the old days, aviation came under the Civil Aeronautics Administration. You will no doubt find reference to this when dealing with classic airplanes.

In early 1959 the name of the Civil Aeronautics

Administration was changed to the Federal Aviation Agency, as a separate government department, and the Civil Air Regulations were then renamed Federal Aviation Regulations (FAR). In early 1967 the name was changed to Federal Aviation Administration, and it became part of the U.S. Department of Transportation (DOT).

Printed here are a few of the FARs, and comments about them.

With the accumulation of experience the regulations governing manufacture, modification and maintenance of aircraft, and mechanic and pilot skills are constantly being rewritten and redefined, generally to the betterment of civil aviation safety. The different areas of regulation are still segregated into "parts," applicable to the particular subject matter; however, all parts of the FARs are intertwined and cross-referenced where applicable.

FAR Part 21 spells out the procedural requirements for the issue of a type certificate necessary for manufacture of an aircraft to be used for commercial purposes in the United States. FAR Part 23 establishes the minimum structural standards and flight characteristic standards for normal, utility, and aerobatic category aircraft, and is the primary basis for the airworthiness certificate for most of the small aircraft manufactured in the United States today. (REF: FAR 21.1, 21.11, 23.1).

## Part 21: Certification Procedures for Products and Parts.
### Subpart A-General
### FAR 21.1 Applicability.

(a) This part prescribes—

(1) Procedural requirements for the issue of type certificates and changes to those certificates; the issue of production certificates; the issue of airworthiness certificates; and the issue of export airworthiness approvals;

(2) Rules governing the holders of any certificate specified in subparagraph (1); and

(3) Procedural requirements for the approval of certain materials, parts, processes, and appliances.

(b) For the purposes of this Part, the word "product" means an aircraft, aircraft engine, or propeller. In addition, for the purposes of Subpart L only, it includes components and parts of aircraft, of aircraft engines, and of propellers; also parts, materials, and appliances, approved under the Technical Standard Order (TSO) system.

### Subpart B-Type Certificates
### FAR 21.11 Applicability.

This subpart prescribes—

(a) Procedural requirements for the issue of type certificates for aircraft, aircraft engines, and propellers; and

(b) Rules governing the holders of these certificates.

## Part 23 Airworthiness Standards
## Normal, Utility, and Acrobatic Category Airplanes
### Subpart A General
### FAR 23.1 Applicability

(a) This Part prescribes airworthiness standards for the issue of type certificates, and changes to those certificates, for small airplanes in the normal, utility, and acrobatic categories that have a passenger seating configuration, excluding pilot seats, of nine seats or less.

(b) Each person who applies under Part 21 for such a certificate or change must show compliance with the applicable requirements of this part.

\*\*\*\*\*\*\*\*\*\*\*\*\*\*\*\*\*\*\*\*\*\*\*\*\*\*\*\*\*\*\*\*\*\*\*\*\*\*\*\*\*\*\*\*\*\*

FAR Part 23 defines the "minimum" standards of structural integrity and flight characteristics considered to be "safe" by current service experience, and some experienced sport plane designers use Part 23 as a guide when designing aircraft to be operated as "amateur built."

When an applicant for a type certificate has satisfactorily complied with all the requirements of Part 23, all the accumulated records, manuals, drawings, flutter and stress reports, information and reports on all materials, processes, drop tests, static tests, flight test reports, etc. become part of the "type design" (REF:FAR 21.31).

\*\*\*\*\*\*\*\*\*\*\*\*\*\*\*\*\*\*\*\*\*\*\*\*\*\*\*\*\*\*\*\*\*\*\*\*\*\*\*\*\*\*\*\*\*\*

### FAR 21.31 Type design

The type design consists of—

(a) The drawings and specifications, and a listing of those drawings and specifications, necessary to define the configuration and the design features of the product shown to comply with the requirements of that part of this subchapter applicable to the product;

(b) Information on dimensions, materials, and processes necessary to define the structural strength of the product;

(c) The Airworthiness Limitations section of the Instructions for Continued Airworthiness as required by Parts 23, 25, 27, 29, 31, 33 and 35 of this chapter; and

(d) Any other data necessary to allow, by comparison, the determination of the airworthiness and noise characteristics (where applicable to later products of the same type).

The quality of all the material specified in the type design must be substantiated by test or compliance with TSO (Technical Standard Order), mil. spec., or other acceptable standards. We can verify from experience (Stits Skycoupe 9A, Type Certificate #4A31) the fact that proof of quality and source of all materials, including the fabric, dope, steel tubing and sheet stock, aluminum sheet, spruce, plywood, rivets, windshields, tires, instruments, baggage compartment, etc. are a part of the design. When a raw material or part such as an automotive fuel gauge (now commonly used on aircraft) does not meet a TSO or mil. spec., the applicant must submit sufficient information to show that the part or material is reliable by service history (millions of cars) and the quality can be maintained.

After a thorough review of all data accumulated during the development and test, and FAA flight tests of a sample aircraft complying with all the data and the type design is found to be in compliance with all regulations, the FAA Administrator, through his "representative," grants a type certificate to the design (REF: FAR 21.21). Thereafter, each aircraft manufactured by the type certificate holder and found to be in exact compliance with the type design on file, will be eligible for an airworthiness certificate (REF: FAR 21.171, 21.173, 21.174).

*******************************************

## Subpart H-Airworthiness Certificates
### FAR 21.171 Applicability.

This subpart prescribes procedural requirements for the issue of airworthiness certificates.

### FAR 21.173 Eligibility.

Any registered owner of a U.S. registered aircraft (or the agent of the owner) may apply for an airworthiness certificate for that aircraft. An application for an airworthiness certificate must be made in a form and manner acceptable to the Administrator, and may be submitted to any FAA office.

### FAR 21.175 Airworthiness certificates: classification.

(a) Standard airworthiness certificates are airworthiness certificates issued for aircraft type certified in the normal, utility, acrobatic or transport category.

(b) Special airworthiness certificates are restricted, limited and provisional airworthiness certificates, special flight permits and experimental certificates.

When the aircraft is repaired using the same type materials as the original, but a different source, the quality of the materials must be at least equal to the original, usually by meeting a mil. spec., TSO, etc. Bolts, nuts, screws, tubing, aluminum sheet, tires, plywood, instruments, control cables, pulleys, etc. fall into this category. When the repairs are made to a damaged aircraft using materials accepted by the Administrator as equal to the original, and the workmanship and repair methods are acceptable to the Administrator and any defects discovered in service, defined as airworthiness directives (AD notes) are corrected, the airworthiness certificate remains in effect (REF: FAR 21.181).

When alterations are made to an aircraft such as installing a different model engine, wing flaps, tanks, larger wheels, or installing a windshield or cowling, etc. from a source other than the original manufacturer, or a different type of material is used to re-cover the aircraft than that specified in the type design, the airworthiness certificate is automatically canceled because that particular aircraft no longer conforms to the type design on file, which was the basis for the granting a type certificate and the airworthiness certificate.

Before an aircraft airworthiness certificate can be renewed a record of the change must be made and approved by the FAA. Modifications to aircraft already in the field are usually handled by an STC or field approval. FAR 21.93 clarifies minor and major changes in the type design.

FAR 21.97 states that in the case of a major change in type design the applicant must submit substantiating data and necessary descriptive data for inclusion in the type design.

## Subpart D-Changes to Type Certificates
### FAR 21.91 Applicability.

This subpart prescribes procedural requirements for the approval of changes to type certificates.

### FAR 21.93 Classification of changes in type design.

(a) In addition to changes in type design specified in paragraph (b) of this section, changes in type design are classified as minor and major. A "minor change" is one that has no appreciable effect on the weight, balance, structural strength, reliability, operational characteristics, or other characteristics affecting the airworthiness of the product. All other changes are "major changes."

**FAR 21.97 Approval of major changes in type design.**

(a) In the case of a major change in the type design, the applicant must submit substantiating data and necessary descriptive data for inclusion in the type design.

(b) Approval of a major change in the type design of an aircraft engine is limited to the specific engine configuration upon which the change is made unless the applicant identifies in the necessary descriptive data for inclusion in the type design the other configurations of the same engine type for which approval is requested and shows the change is compatible with the other configurations.

\* \* \* \* \* \* \* \* \* \* \* \* \* \* \* \* \* \* \* \* \* \* \* \* \* \* \* \* \* \* \* \* \* \* \* \* \* \* \* \* \* \* \* \* \*

There are provisions in the FARs under Part 43 for the obtaining "Field Approval" on individual aircraft when it can be shown the modification from the original design did not degrade the airworthiness and flight characteristics of the aircraft (REF: FAR, Part 43).

\* \* \* \* \* \* \* \* \* \* \* \* \* \* \* \* \* \* \* \* \* \* \* \* \* \* \* \* \* \* \* \* \* \* \* \* \* \* \* \* \* \* \* \* \*

**Part 43-Maintenance, Preventive Maintenance, Rebuilding, and Alteration FAR 43.1 Applicability.**

(a) Except as provided in paragraph (b), this Part prescribes rules governing the maintenance, preventive maintenance, rebuilding, and alteration of any—

(1) Aircraft having a U.S. airworthiness certificate; and

(2) Airframe, aircraft engine, propeller, or appliance of such an aircraft.

(b) This Part does not apply to an aircraft for which an experimental airworthiness certificate has been issued, unless a different kind of airworthiness certificate had previously been issued for that aircraft.

**FAR 43.3 Persons authorized to perform maintenance, preventive maintenance, rebuilding, and alterations.**

(a) Except as provided in this section, no person may maintain, rebuild, alter, or perform preventive maintenance on an aircraft, airframe, aircraft engine, propeller, or appliance to which this Part applies. Those items, the performance of which is a major alteration, a major repair, or preventive maintenance are listed in Appendix A.

(b) The holder of a mechanic certificate may perform maintenance, preventive maintenance, and alterations as provided in Part 65.

(c) The holder of a repairman certificate may perform maintenance and preventive maintenance as provided in Part 65.

(d) A person working under the supervision of a holder of a mechanic or repairman certificate may perform maintenance, preventive maintenance, and alterations that his supervisor is authorized to perform, if the supervisor personally observes the work being done to the extent necessary to ensure that it is being done properly and if the supervisor is readily available, in person, for consultation. However, this paragraph does not authorize the performance of 100-hour or annual inspections, nor inspections performed after a major repair or alteration.

(e) The holder of a repair station certificate may perform maintenance, preventive maintenance, and alterations as provided in Part 145.

(f) An air carrier may perform maintenance, preventive maintenance and alterations as provided in Part 121, 127, or 135 of this chapter, as applicable.

(g) The holder of a commercial operator certificate issued under Part 121 may perform maintenance, preventive maintenance, and alterations as provided in that Part.

(h) The holder of a pilot certificate issued under Part 61 may perform preventive maintenance on any aircraft owned or operated by him that is not used in air carrier service.

(i) A manufacturer may—

(1) Rebuild or alter any aircraft, aircraft engine, propeller, or appliance manufactured by him under a type or production certificate;

(2) Rebuild or alter any appliance or part of aircraft, aircraft engines, propellers, or appliances manufactured by him under a Technical Standard Order Authorization, or Product and Process Specification issued by the Administrator; and

(3) Perform 100-hour, annual, and progressive inspections on an aircraft manufactured by him, while operating under a production certificate or under an approved production inspection system for such aircraft.

## FAR 43.5 Return to service after maintenance, preventive maintenance, rebuilding, or alteration.

(a) No person may return to service any aircraft, airframe, aircraft engine, propeller, or appliance, that has undergone maintenance, preventive maintenance, rebuilding, or alteration unless—

(1) It has been approved for return to service by a person authorized under FAR 43.7;

(2) The maintenance record entry required by FAR 43.9 has been made;

(3) The repair or alteration form authorized by or furnished by the Administrator has been executed in a manner prescribed by the Administrator; and

(4) If a repair or an alteration results in any change in the aircraft operating limitations or flight data contained in the approved aircraft flight manual, those operating limitations or flight data are appropriately revised and set forth as prescribed in FAR 91.31.

(a) This section does not apply to preventive maintenance performed by a certified pilot under FAR 43.3(h). FAR 43.7 Persons authorized to approve aircraft, airframes, aircraft engines, propellers, and appliances for return to service after maintenance, rebuilding, or alteration.

(b) Except as provided in this section, no person, other than the Administrator, may approve any aircraft, airframes, aircraft engines, propellers, and appliances for return to service after it has undergone maintenance, preventive maintenance, rebuilding, or alteration.

(c) The holder of a mechanics certificate or inspection authorization may approve an aircraft, airframe, aircraft engine, propeller, or appliance for return to service as provided in Part 65.

(d) The holder of a repair station certificate may approve an aircraft, airframe, aircraft engine, propeller, or appliance for return to service as provided in Part 145.

(e) A manufacturer may approve for return to service any aircraft, airframe, aircraft engine, propeller, or appliance that he has worked on under FAR 43.3(i). However, except for minor alterations, the work must have been done in accordance with technical data approved by the Administrator.

(f) An air carrier may approve an aircraft, airframe, aircraft engine, propeller, or appliance for return to service as provided in Part 121, 127, or 135 of this chapter, as applicable.

(g) The holder of a commercial operator certificate issued under Part 121 of this chapter may approve an aircraft, airframe, aircraft engine, propeller or appliance for return to service as provided in that Part.

\*\*\*\*\*\*\*\*\*\*\*\*\*\*\*\*\*\*\*\*\*\*\*\*\*\*\*\*\*\*\*\*\*\*\*\*\*\*\*\*\*\*\*\*\*

An engine change in older rare aircraft, different model propeller, additional fuel tanks, larger baggage doors, etc, are usually handled on a "one time" field approval basis, applicable only to that one aircraft, however, if the modification is made with the intent of marketing duplicate kits or parts to be incorporated on another aircraft of the same make/model (as with different covering materials), then it is necessary that the applicant obtain a STC (Supplemental Type Certificate) (REF: FAR 21.111, 21.113, 21.115, 21.117) and the parts or material produced or processed and identified under a PMA (Parts Manufacturer Approval) (REF: FAR 21.301, 21.303).

\*\*\*\*\*\*\*\*\*\*\*\*\*\*\*\*\*\*\*\*\*\*\*\*\*\*\*\*\*\*\*\*\*\*\*\*\*\*\*\*\*\*\*\*\*

## Subpart E Supplemental Type Certificates FAR 21.111 Applicability

This subpart prescribes procedural requirements for the issue of supplemental type certificates.

## FAR 21.113 Requirements of supplemental type certificate.

Any person who alters a product by introducing a major change in type design, not great enough to require a new application for a type certificate under 21.19, shall apply to the Administrator for a supplemental type certificate, except the holder of a type certificate for the product may apply for amendment of the original type certificate. The application must be made in a form and manner prescribed by the administrator.

## FAR 21.115 Applicable requirements.

(a) Each applicant for a supplemental type certificate must show that the altered product meets applicable airworthiness requirements as specified in paragraphs (a) and (b) of FAR 21.101 and, in the case of an acoustical change described in FAR 21.93(b), show compliance with the applicable noise requirements of FAR 36.7 and FAR 36.9 of this chapter.

(b) Each applicant for a supplemental type certificate must meet FAR 21.33 and FAR 21.53 with respect to each change in the type design.

## FAR 21.117 Issue of supplemental type certificates.

(a) An applicant is entitled to a supplemental type certificate if he meets the requirements of FAR 21.113 and FAR 21.115.

(b) A supplemental type certificate consists of—

(1) The approval by the Administrator of a change in the type design of the product; and

(2) The type certificate previously issued for the product.

## FAR 21.119 Privileges

The holder of a supplemental type certificate may—

(a) In the case of aircraft, obtain airworthiness certificates;

(b) In the case of other products, obtain approval for installation on certificated aircraft; and

(c) Obtain a production certificate for the change in the type design that was approved by that supplement type certificate.

## Subpart K Approval of Materials, Parts, Process, and Appliances
## FAR 21.301 Applicability

This subpart prescribes procedural requirements for the approval of certain materials, parts, processes, and appliances.

## FAR 21.303 Replacement and modification parts.

(a) Except as provided in paragraph (b) of this section, no person may produce a modification or replacement part for sale for installation on a type certificated product unless it is produced pursuant to a Parts Manufacturer Approval (PMA) issued under this subpart.

(b) This section does not apply to the following:

(1) Parts produced under a type or production certificate.

(2) Parts produced by an owner or operator for maintaining or altering his own product.

(3) Parts produced under an FAA Technical Standard Order (TSO).

(4) Standard parts (such as bolts and nuts) conforming to established industry or United States specifications.

\*\*\*\*\*\*\*\*\*\*\*\*\*\*\*\*\*\*\*\*\*\*\*\*\*\*\*\*\*\*\*\*\*\*\*\*\*\*\*\*\*\*\*\*\*\*

According to FAR 21.303 it is a violation of regulations when anyone manufactures for sale a part for installation on a type certificated aircraft unless it has been produced under the quality control of a Parts Manufacturers Approval (PMA). Under the provisions of FAR 21.303 and FAR Part 43 for example, a mechanic may purchase 4130 chromoly tubing meeting the approximate mil. spec. from a tubing supplier and build a pair of wing struts or a complete fuselage, etc. for a damaged aircraft and put the aircraft back in service with Form 337, repairs and alterations (REF: FAR 43), without the benefit of an STC and PMA. However, the same mechanic cannot manufacture the same identical wing struts or a fuselage or any part for sale to other aircraft owners or repair shops without an STC or PMA.

When an applicant has gained a Supplemental Type Certificate the data supporting the STC and the data supporting the original type certificate

(REF: FAR 21.41) combined are the basis for issuing a new airworthiness certificate for the particular model of aircraft (REF: FAR 21.117 (b)).

* * * * * * * * * * * * * * * * * * * * * * * * * * * * * * * * * * * * *

## FAR 21.41 Type certificate.

Each type certificate is considered to include the type design, the operating limitations, the certificate data sheet, the applicable regulations of this subchapter with which the Administrator records compliance, and any other conditions or limitations prescribed for the product in this subchapter.

* * * * * * * * * * * * * * * * * * * * * * * * * * * * * * * * * * * * *

When two separate supplemental type certificates have been issued on the same model aircraft, it must be shown that the modifications are compatible when incorporated on the same aircraft, and will not introduce adverse effects or degrade from the original airworthiness.

FAR 43 specifies the minimum requirements when maintaining, rebuilding, or altering an aircraft.

* * * * * * * * * * * * * * * * * * * * * * * * * * * * * * * * * * * * *

## PART 43—Appendix B Recording of Major Repairs and Major Alterations.

(a) Except as provided in paragraphs (b) and (c), each person performing a major repair or major alteration shall—

(1) Execute FAA Form 337 at least in duplicate;

(2) Give a signed copy of that form to the aircraft owner; and

(3) Forward a copy of that form to the local FAA District Office within 48 hours after the aircraft, airframe, aircraft engine, propeller, or appliance is approved for return to service.

(b) For major repairs made in accordance with a manual or specification acceptable to the Administrator, a certificated repair station may, in place of the requirements of paragraph (a)—

(1) Use the customer's work order upon which the repair is recorded;

(2) Give the aircraft owner a signed copy of the work order and retain a duplicate copy for at least 2 years from the date of approval for return to service of the aircraft, airframe, aircraft engine, propeller, or appliance;

(3) Give the aircraft owner a maintenance release signed by the authorized representative of the repair station and incorporating the following information:

(i) Identity of the aircraft, airframe, aircraft engine, propeller, or appliance.

(ii) If an aircraft, the make, model, serial number, nationality and registration marks, and location of the repaired areas.

(iii) If an aircraft, airframe, aircraft engine, propeller, or appliance, give the manufacturer's name, name of the part, model, and serial numbers (if any); and

(4) Include the following or a similarly worded statement—The aircraft, airframe, aircraft engine, propeller, or appliance identified above was repaired and inspected in accordance with current Regulations of the Federal Aviation Administration and is approved for return to service. Pertinent details of the repair are on file at this repair station under:

Order No.......................................................

Date...............................................................

Signed............................................................

Repair Station Name....................................

Address..........................................................

Certificate Number......................................

(c) For a major repair or major alteration made by a person authorized in FAR 43.17, the person who performs the major repair or major alteration and the person authorized by FAR 43.17 to approve that work shall execute FAA Form 337 at least in duplicate. A completed copy of that form shall be—

(1) Given to the aircraft owner; and

(2) Forwarded to the Federal Aviation Administration Aircraft Registration Branch, P.O. Box 25082, Oklahoma City, OK 73125, within 48 hours after the work is inspected.

* * * * * * * * * * * * * * * * * * * * * * * * * * * * * * * * * * * * *

The owner of the aircraft is primarily responsible for maintaining the aircraft in an airworthy condition and the duty falls on the owner or operator to insure that the mechanic is qualified and certificated, has completed the necessary repairs satisfactorily, and recorded the repairs properly before the aircraft is put back into service (REF: FAR Part 91, Subpart C, paragraph 91.161, 91.163, 91.165, 91.167).

\*\*\*\*\*\*\*\*\*\*\*\*\*\*\*\*\*\*\*\*\*\*\*\*\*\*\*\*\*\*\*\*\*\*\*\*\*\*\*\*\*\*

## Subpart C—Maintenance, Preventive Maintenance, and Alterations
### FAR 91.161 Applicability.

(a) This subpart prescribes rules governing the maintenance, preventive maintenance, and alterations of U.S. registered civil aircraft operating within or without the United States.

(b) Sections 91.165, 91.169, 91.170, 91.171, 91.173, and 91.174 of this subpart do not apply to aircraft maintained in accordance with a continuous airworthiness maintenance program as provided in Part 121, 127, or 135 of this chapter.

### FAR 91.163 General.

(a) The owner or operator of an aircraft is primarily responsible for maintaining that aircraft in an airworthy condition, including compliance with Part 39 of this chapter.

(b) No person may perform maintenance, preventive maintenance, or alterations on an aircraft other than as prescribed in this subpart and other applicable regulations, including Part 43.

(c) No person may operate a rotorcraft for which a Rotorcraft Maintenance Manual containing an "Airworthiness Limitations" section has been issued, unless replacement times, inspection intervals, and related procedures specified in that section of the manual are complied with.

### FAR 91.165 Maintenance required.

Each owner or operator of an aircraft shall have that aircraft inspected as prescribed in Subpart D or FAR 91.169 of this Part, as appropriate, and FAR 91.170 of this Part and shall, between required inspections, have defects repaired as prescribed in Part 43 of this chapter. In addition, he shall ensure that maintenance personnel make appropriate entries in the aircraft and maintenance records indicating the aircraft has been released to service.

\*\*\*\*\*\*\*\*\*\*\*\*\*\*\*\*\*\*\*\*\*\*\*\*\*\*\*\*\*\*\*\*\*\*\*\*\*\*\*\*\*\*

The ultimate responsibility for the aircraft being in compliance with all regulations, with all repairs and paperwork in order and the aircraft actually airworthy in all respects, i.e. CG limits, equipment list, proper fuel, markings, etc., falls on the pilot before he lifts off the runway (REF: FAR 91, Paragraph 91.29).

\*\*\*\*\*\*\*\*\*\*\*\*\*\*\*\*\*\*\*\*\*\*\*\*\*\*\*\*\*\*\*\*\*\*\*\*\*\*\*\*\*\*

### FAR 91.29 Civil aircraft airworthiness

(a) No person may operate a civil aircraft unless it is in an airworthy condition.

(b) The pilot in command of a civil aircraft is responsible for determining whether that aircraft is in condition for safe flight. He shall discontinue the flight when unairworthy mechanical or structural conditions occur.

\*\*\*\*\*\*\*\*\*\*\*\*\*\*\*\*\*\*\*\*\*\*\*\*\*\*\*\*\*\*\*\*\*\*\*\*\*\*\*\*\*\*

In reviewing the above material, and Mr. Stits' comments, I think the very last FAR, FAR 91.29, tells it like it is: You are responsible for the airworthiness of the airplane when you are flying it. Here are two questions for you to ponder when you're having your aircraft repaired/altered/maintained:

1. Will the work/inspection be done properly on your airplane?

2. Will the proper parts/replacement parts be utilized?

# Chapter 11

# Maintenance You Can Do

The FARs (Federal Aviation Regulations) specify that preventive maintenance may be performed by pilots/owners of airplanes not utilized in commercial service.

The FARs lists 28 preventive maintenance items in Appendix A of part 43.13. This means that only those operations listed are considered preventive maintenance.

## PREVENTIVE MAINTENANCE ITEMS

**1. Removal, installation and repair of landing gear tires.** When changing/repairing a tire on an airplane, the plane must be jacked up, much like a car. However, particular care must be taken, as improper jacking can damage the airframe. Check your owners manual for the proper jacking procedure.

The actual tire change is quite straightforward. The wheel is removed, the tire deflated, and the bead broken. After the bead is broken on both sides of the wheel, the nuts on the through bolts can be removed, and the wheel split. Installation is just the opposite, except if you are installing a tube, you must be careful not to pinch it between the wheel halves (Fig. 11-1).

**2. Replacing elastic shock-absorber cords on landing gear.** This particular job is difficult at best, due to the tensions required and the tools involved. Talk to your mechanic before you attempt it. You may find that this job is more trouble than it's worth to you. It can very easily result in injury and/or damage to your airplane. I'll leave to your determination which is worse.

**3. Servicing landing-gear struts by adding oil, air or both.** This maintenance procedure is simple, and requires a minimum of tools. The plane must be on jacks. Open strut filler hole carefully, releasing air/oil pressure, then refill with hydraulic oil. Close the filler hole and inflated with air pressure (if required).

**4. Servicing landing-gear wheel bearings, such as cleaning and greasing.** If you are familiar with servicing the bearings on your auto, then this job will present no particular challenge.

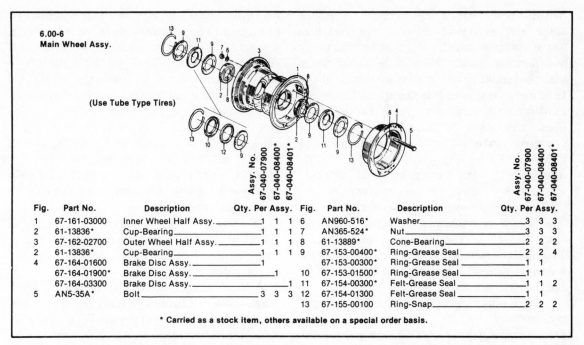

| Fig. | Part No. | Description | 67-040-07900 | 67-040-08400* | 67-040-08401* |
|---|---|---|---|---|---|
| 1 | 67-161-03000 | Inner Wheel Half Assy. | 1 | 1 | 1 |
| 2 | 61-13836* | Cup-Bearing | 1 | 1 | 1 |
| 3 | 67-162-02700 | Outer Wheel Half Assy. | 1 | 1 | 1 |
| 2 | 61-13836* | Cup-Bearing | 1 | 1 | 1 |
| 4 | 67-164-01600 | Brake Disc Assy. | 1 | | |
|  | 67-164-01900* | Brake Disc Assy. | | 1 | |
|  | 67-164-03300 | Brake Disc Assy. | | | 1 |
| 5 | AN5-35A* | Bolt | 3 | 3 | 3 |

| Fig. | Part No. | Description | 67-040-07900 | 67-040-08400* | 67-040-08401* |
|---|---|---|---|---|---|
| 6 | AN960-516* | Washer | 3 | 3 | 3 |
| 7 | AN365-524* | Nut | 3 | 3 | 3 |
| 8 | 61-13889* | Cone-Bearing | 2 | 2 | 2 |
| 9 | 67-153-00400* | Ring-Grease Seal | 2 | 2 | 4 |
|  | 67-153-00300* | Ring-Grease Seal | 1 | 1 | |
| 10 | 67-153-01500* | Ring-Grease Seal | 1 | | |
| 11 | 67-154-00300* | Felt-Grease Seal | 1 | 1 | 2 |
| 12 | 67-154-01300 | Felt-Grease Seal | 1 | | |
| 13 | 67-155-00100 | Ring-Snap | 2 | 2 | 2 |

* Carried as a stock item, others available on a special order basis.

Fig. 11-1. The airplane wheel splits apart for tire changing. Care must be taken during reassembly to prevent the tube from being crushed between the halves. (courtesy Univair)

The wheels are removed as when you change a tire, and the bearings are pulled out. At this point the old grease is cleaned out by use of a solvent. The bearings and their mating surfaces are inspected for damage, then the bearings are repacked with the appropriate grease. Put the bearings back into position, and place the wheel on the axle. Only tighten the wheel nut as is necessary to eliminate any side play. Safety the nut by use of a cotton pin placed through the castellated nut.

**5. Replacing defective safety wiring or cotter pins.** Nuts and bolts are items that must be safety wired. The reason for safetying is to prevent them from becoming loose during flight.

Nuts: Any nuts and bolts that do not move will have nuts locked into place by use of a plastic insert that prevents the nut from moving on the bolt. If the bolt/nut combination can move, then the bolt must be drilled and a castellated nut used. A cotter pin is used as a safety here.

Bolts: Drilled head bolts are most often seen fastening the propeller to the flange on the engine. A safety wire of steel, brass, or stainless steel will be run and twisted thru each of these bolts. The wire will run from one bolt to the next.

The object of the safety wire is to prevent the bolt from turning. The wires are neatly twisted, and must pull on the bolt in the direction of tightening.

**6. Lubrication not requiring disassembly other than removal of nonstructural items such as cover plates, cowlings and fairings.** First check the chart of lubrication requirements for your airplane. Specific types and mounts of grease will be given. In addition, the desired frequency of lubrication will be given. Do not over-lubricate.

**7. Making simple fabric patches not requiring rib stitching or the removal of structural parts or control surfaces.** Due to the wide variety of fabrics and finishes found on airplanes today, I suggest you refer to your airframe log first to determine exactly what process was used in the covering of your airframe. After making this determination, check with the manufacturer for the proper procedure for patching.

**8. Replenishing hydraulic fluid in the hy-**

draulic reservoir. If you have ever filled the brake reservoir of your car with brake fluid, then you are qualified for this job. Just be sure to not overfill, and keep the fluids off of the aircraft finish.

**9. Refinishing decorative coatings of the fuselage, wing, and tail-group surfaces (excluding balanced control surfaces), fairings, cowlings, landing gear, cabin or cockpit interior when removal or disassembly of any primary structure or operating system is not required.** This allows you to make touch-ups to your airplane.

Before you attempt a touch-up, ascertain what type paint you are touching up. You may have enamel, lacquer, acrylic lacquer, or polyurethane. Type must be matched, as well as color, or the job will not be successful, and could even do more damage than you are trying to fix.

The manufacturer of the paint product will supply directions.

**10. Applying preservative or protective material to components when no disassembly of any primary structure or operating system is involved and when such coating is not prohibited or is not contrary to good practices.** Normally this will be more important to seaplane operators; however, anyone near the coast should be interested. The job is merely the application of grease or other proper coating to preclude water/moisture from coming into direct contact with cables, hardware, pulleys, or the inner surfaces of the fuselage.

**11. Repairing upholstery and decorative furnishings of the cabin or cockpit when it does not require disassembly of any primary structure or operating system or affect the primary structure of the aircraft.** This allows the refurbishing of the interior of the airplane. This includes upholstering, replacing side and kick panels, carpets, etc.—just about anything you want to do within the limits of *no structural changes*, such as the seats, seat attachments, changes to the instrument panel, or alterations to (or that would interfere with) the control system.

**12. Making small, simple repairs to fairings, nonstructural cover plates, cowlings** and small patches, and reinforcements not changing the contour so as to interfere with the proper airflow. Since this book is about classics, and they are all old, you will no doubt have stress cracks in the metal cowling.

When these cracks first develop you should drill a small hole at each end. This will stop the spread of the crack. Then the crack must be patched. Patching is accomplished by riveting a small piece of aluminum over the crack.

Should a fiberglass fairing be involved, follow the same procedure in drilling a small hole at the ends of the cracks.

Patching is accomplished by utilizing a fiberglass repair kit, such as can be found in marine supply houses. Just follow the instructions supplied on the patch product.

**13. Replacing side windows where that work does not interfere with the structure or any operating system such as controls and electrical equipment.** Replacement windows are made of an acrylic material. This material can be purchased in bulk from plastic supply houses, or pre-cut windows can be purchased from any number of suppliers (just look in *Trade-A-Plane*).

Installation is simply removal and replacement. Be sure to seal the new window in place with a recommended aircraft sealer. If in doubt, one of the flexible silicone glues will do a good job (Fig. 11-2).

**14. Replacing safety belts.** This is a very simple job. Just remove the old belts and install the new ones. However, there are two areas of caution:

1. Be sure the new belts have TSO-C-22 on all parts.

2. The belts must be installed in their original configuration.

**15. Replacing seats or seat parts with replacement parts approved for the aircraft, not involving disassembly of any primary structure or operating system.** For this to be done properly you may only use direct replacement approved seats. No welding or riveting is allowed.

**16. Troubleshooting and repairing broken landing light wiring circuits.** For any home

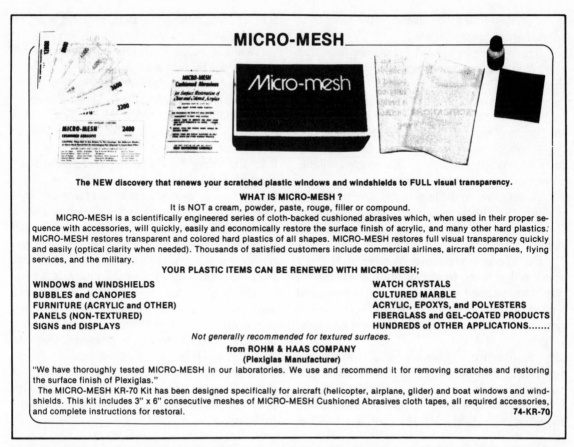

Fig. 11-2. Micro-Mesh is produced by Rohm & Haas, the producers of Plexiglas. Its use can often preclude the purchasing and replacement of windows and windshields. (courtesy Univair)

electrician equipped with a VOM (volt ohm meter), this should be quite easy. First check the bulb, then check to see if there is voltage at the lamp. After that, check at the circuit breaker panel for voltage. Some of the more common places for problems are the connect points at the wing roots and the connect points at the breaker panel. Crimp-on connectors can be used to replace broken original connectors.

**17. Replacing bulbs, reflectors, and lenses of position and landing lights.** The only place you could have a problem with this maintenance item would be in utilizing the wrong bulb. Be sure the proper bulbs are utilized.

**18. Replacing wheels and skis where no weight and balance computation is required.** The best recommendation I can give here is to follow the instructions that came with your skis. Just be sure that the cable is connected that holds the front of the ski up.

**19. Replacing any cowling not requiring removal of the propeller or disconnection of flight controls.** Many cowlings are split into two pieces, and come off quite easily for engine inspection and servicing. Just be careful about tightening the retaining screws. They will only go in and out a limited number of times before the hole becomes enlarged.

**20. Replacing or cleaning spark plugs and setting of spark plug gap clearance.** Before attempting this job solo, I recommend that you have your mechanic do it once with you. However, if you are a competent auto mechanic, you'll have little trouble with this procedure.

Remove the plugs in order, and keep them that way. You're going to inspect them for wear and deposits, and you will want to know what cylinder they came out of. If the same plugs are going back in, put the bottom plugs in the top, and the top in the bottom. This plug rotation will extend plug life.

A special tool is recommended for the adjustment of aviation spark plugs. These are available from most aircraft tools suppliers.

Be sure to torque plugs as per specs when installing them. It's a good idea to use anti-seize on the threads. This will ease their removal at a later date.

For an excellent package of information about spark plugs, write to any of the manufacturers. You'll be rewarded with usage charts, how-tos, and a color chart to compare your plugs. This will assist you with the identification of potential problems (Figs. 11-3, 11-4).

**21. Replacing any hose connection except hydraulic connections.** Most of the hoses that you are allowed to replace are involved with the instrument system. These are either push-on friction fit, or push-on clamp fit. The clamps are either squeeze or screw type. Both may be seen on automobiles.

When replacing hoses be sure to use approved parts. Order by part number.

**22. Replacing prefabricated fuel lines.** This is simply replacing of flexible fuel lines of like part number. One word of caution: Don't over-tighten these lines, as their seal is developed by a tapered thread, not taughtness.

**23. Cleaning fuel and oil strainers.** Fuel: Turn off the fuel to the strainer bowl, then drain the bowl using the quick drain. Cut the safety wire and slide the clip out of the way. This should allow you to pull the bowl off. At this point the strainer screen should drop out. Clean it with solvent and replace it with a new gasket. Put the bowl back into place and fasten the clip. Install new safety wire.

Oil: Your airplane may use an oil screen or an automotive-type canister oil filter. Referring to your engine manual, remove the oil screen and check it for metal flakes, a sure sign of problems. Clean the screen in a solvent, and reinstall same.

A spin-on filter is removed and installed much the same as in a car. For inspectional reasons the filter can will be cut open and inspected for metal particles.

## GENERAL SPARK PLUG CROSS REFERENCE

| AC PLUGS | CHAMPION PLUGS | AC PLUGS | CHAMPION PLUGS |
|---|---|---|---|
| | 14 mm | | 18mm Massive Electrode (Short Reach) |
| SA-43 | REJ38 | A-88 | M41E, M42E |
| A-44 | J43 | S-88 | EM42E |
| SR-47P | REL37W | HS-88 | HM41E |
| | 18 mm Fine Wire (Long Reach) | SR-88 | REM40E |
| 181 | REB36W, REB36P | HSR-88 | RHM40E |
| 281 | RHB36P | SR-87 | REM38E |
| 291 | RHB36W | HSR-87 | RHM38E |
| 283 | RHB32P | SR-86 | REM38E |
| 293 | RHB32W | HSR-86 | RHM-38E |
| 286 | —— | | 18 mm Massive Electrode (Long Reach) |
| | 18 mm Fine Wire (Short Reach) | 171 | REB37E, REB37N |
| SR-83P | REM38P | 271 | RHB37N, RHB37E, RHB38E |
| HSR-83P | RHM38P | 172 | REB87N |
| SR-93 | REM38W | 273 | RHB32N, RHB32E, RHB33E |
| HSR-93 | RHM38W | 175 | REB29N |
| | | 275 | RHB29N, RHB29E |

Fig. 11-3. General spark plug cross reference chart for AC and Champion plugs. (courtesy Univair)

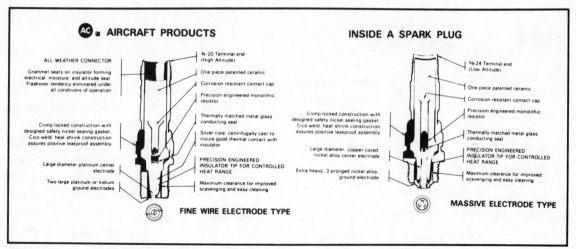

Fig. 11-4. An explanation of the fine wire electrode and massive electrode plugs. (courtesy Univair)

**24. Replacing batteries and checking fluid level and specific gravity.** Just the same as for boats and autos, terminals must remain clean, electrolyte levels must be kept up, and the battery box must be checked for corrosion.

**25. (Gliders only).**

**26. (Balloons only.)**

**27. Replacement or adjustment of nonstructural standard fasteners incidental to operations.** This is the tightening or replacement of screws (etc.) that hold fairings and cowlings in place.

Some airplane owners replace all the old hardware with stainless steel under this section. If you wish to do this, please consult your mechanic first. He no doubt will have some advice.

**28. (Balloons only.)**

## LOGBOOK REQUIREMENTS

Entries must be made in the appropriate logbook whenever preventive maintenance is performed. Without being returned to service with such an entry, the aircraft cannot legally be flown.

A logbook entry must include:

☐ Description of work done.
☐ Date work is completed.
☐ Name of the person doing the work.
☐ Approval for return to service (signature

and certificate number) by the pilot approving the work.

The FARs require that all preventive maintenance work must be done in such a manner, and by use of materials of such quality, that the airframe, engine, propeller, or assembly worked on will be at least equal to its original condition.

I strongly advise that before you undertake any of these allowable preventive maintenance procedures you discuss your plans with a licensed mechanic. The instructions/advice you receive from him may help you avoid making costly mistakes. You may have to pay the mechanic for his time, but it will be money well spent.

In addition to preparation to do your own maintenance by talking with your mechanic, get your own tools. Don't borrow from your friend the mechanic, or he won't be your friend long (Figs. 11-5, 11-6).

Properly performed preventive maintenance gives the pilot/owner a better understanding of his airplane, affords substantial maintenance savings, and give a feeling of accomplishment.

For an in-depth study of preventive maintenance, read *Lightplane Owner's Maintenance Guide* TAB book No. 2244, by Cliff Dossey.

## ANNUAL INSPECTIONS

Although by no means are annual inspections

# AN - GUIDE

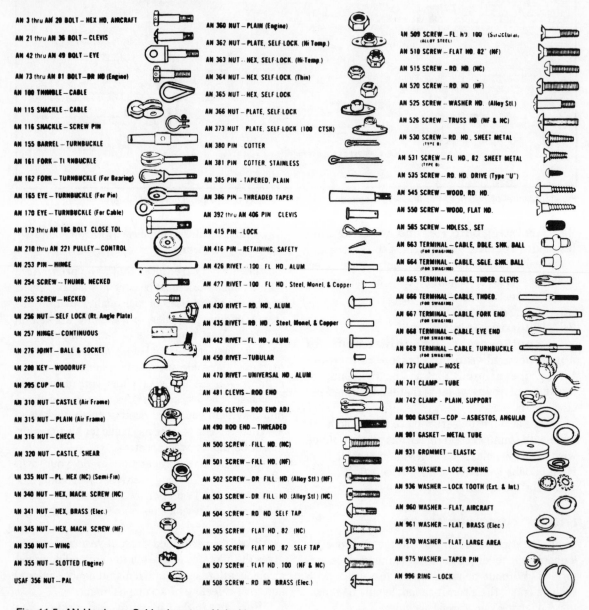

AN 3 thru AN 20 BOLT – HEX HD, AIRCRAFT
AN 21 thru AN 36 BOLT – CLEVIS
AN 42 thru AN 49 BOLT – EYE
AN 73 thru AN 81 BOLT – DR HD (Engine)
AN 100 THIMBLE – CABLE
AN 115 SHACKLE – CABLE
AN 116 SHACKLE – SCREW PIN
AN 155 BARREL – TURNBUCKLE
AN 161 FORK – TURNBUCKLE
AN 162 FORK – TURNBUCKLE (For Bearing)
AN 165 EYE – TURNBUCKLE (For Pin)
AN 170 EYE – TURNBUCKLE (For Cable)
AN 173 thru AN 186 BOLT CLOSE TOL.
AN 210 thru AN 221 PULLEY – CONTROL
AN 253 PIN – HINGE
AN 254 SCREW – THUMB, NECKED
AN 255 SCREW – NECKED
AN 256 NUT – SELF LOCK (Rt. Angle Plate)
AN 257 HINGE – CONTINUOUS
AN 276 JOINT – BALL & SOCKET
AN 280 KEY – WOODRUFF
AN 295 CUP – OIL
AN 310 NUT – CASTLE (Air Frame)
AN 315 NUT – PLAIN (Air Frame)
AN 316 NUT – CHECK
AN 320 NUT – CASTLE, SHEAR
AN 335 NUT – PL. HEX (NC) (Semi-Fin)
AN 340 NUT – HEX, MACH. SCREW (NC)
AN 341 NUT – HEX, BRASS (Elec.)
AN 345 NUT – HEX, MACH. SCREW (NF)
AN 350 NUT – WING
AN 355 NUT – SLOTTED (Engine)
USAF 356 NUT – PAL

AN 360 NUT – PLAIN (Engine)
AN 362 NUT – PLATE, SELF-LOCK (Hi Temp.)
AN 363 NUT – HEX, SELF-LOCK. (Hi-Temp.)
AN 364 NUT – HEX, SELF-LOCK. (Thin)
AN 365 NUT – HEX, SELF LOCK
AN 366 NUT – PLATE, SELF LOCK
AN 373 NUT PLATE, SELF-LOCK (100 CTSK)
AN 380 PIN COTTER
AN 381 PIN COTTER, STAINLESS
AN 385 PIN – TAPERED, PLAIN
AN 386 PIN – THREADED TAPER
AN 392 thru AN 406 PIN CLEVIS
AN 415 PIN – LOCK
AN 416 PIN – RETAINING, SAFETY
AN 426 RIVET – 100 FL HD. ALUM.
AN 477 RIVET – 100 FL HD. Steel, Monel, & Copper
AN 430 RIVET – RD. HD. ALUM.
AN 435 RIVET – RD. HD. Steel, Monel, & Copper
AN 442 RIVET – FL. HD. ALUM.
AN 450 RIVET – TUBULAR
AN 470 RIVET – UNIVERSAL HD. ALUM.
AN 481 CLEVIS – ROD END
AN 486 CLEVIS – ROD END ADJ.
AN 490 ROD END – THREADED
AN 500 SCREW – FILL. HD. (NC)
AN 501 SCREW – FILL. HD. (NF)
AN 502 SCREW – DR FILL. HD. (Alloy Stl.) (NF)
AN 503 SCREW – DR FILL HD. (Alloy Stl.) (NC)
AN 504 SCREW – RD HD SELF TAP
AN 505 SCREW FLAT HD. 82 (NC)
AN 506 SCREW FLAT HD. 82 SELF TAP.
AN 507 SCREW FLAT HD. 100 (NF & NC)
AN 508 SCREW – RD HD BRASS (Elec.)

AN 509 SCREW – FL. HD 100 (Structural, (ALLOY STEEL)
AN 510 SCREW – FLAT HD. 82° (NF)
AN 515 SCREW – RD. HD. (NC)
AN 520 SCREW – RD HD (NF)
AN 525 SCREW – WASHER HD. (Alloy Stl.)
AN 526 SCREW – TRUSS HD (NF & NC)
AN 530 SCREW – RD. HD., SHEET METAL (TYPE B)
AN 531 SCREW – FL. HD., 82 SHEET METAL (TYPE B)
AN 535 SCREW – RD. HD. DRIVE (Type "U")
AN 545 SCREW – WOOD, RD. HD.
AN 550 SCREW – WOOD, FLAT HD.
AN 565 SCREW – HDLESS., SET
AN 663 TERMINAL – CABLE, DBLE. SHK. BALL (FOR SWAGING)
AN 664 TERMINAL – CABLE, SGLE. SHK. BALL (FOR SWAGING)
AN 665 TERMINAL – CABLE, THDED. CLEVIS
AN 666 TERMINAL – CABLE, THDED. (FOR SWAGING)
AN 667 TERMINAL – CABLE, FORK END (FOR SWAGING)
AN 668 TERMINAL – CABLE, EYE END (FOR SWAGING)
AN 669 TERMINAL – CABLE, TURNBUCKLE (FOR SWAGING)
AN 737 CLAMP – HOSE
AN 741 CLAMP – TUBE
AN 742 CLAMP – PLAIN, SUPPORT
AN 900 GASKET – COP – ASBESTOS, ANGULAR
AN 901 GASKET – METAL TUBE
AN 931 GROMMET – ELASTIC
AN 935 WASHER – LOCK, SPRING
AN 936 WASHER – LOCK TOOTH (Ext. & Int.)
AN 960 WASHER – FLAT, AIRCRAFT
AN 961 WASHER – FLAT, BRASS (Elec.)
AN 970 WASHER – FLAT, LARGE AREA
AN 975 WASHER – TAPER PIN
AN 996 RING – LOCK

Fig. 11-5. AN Hardware Guide. (courtesy Univair)

a part of preventive maintenance, included here is a typical list of items that must be inspected during that yearly ritual.

This will assist you in understanding the annual inspection, and perhaps allow you to "get a leg up on it" in cooperation with your mechanic. It also indicates why an annual inspection is expensive.

This particular instruction refers to the Taylor-

# DECIMAL EQUIVALENTS
## OF WIRE, LETTER AND FRACTIONAL SIZE DRILLS

| DRILL SIZE NO. | DECIMAL | DRILL SIZE NO. | DECIMAL | DRILL SIZE NO. | DECIMAL |
|---|---|---|---|---|---|
| 80 | .0135 | 29 | .1360 | 21/64 | .3281 |
| 79 | .0145 | 28 | .1405 | Q | .3320 |
| 1/64 | .0156 | 9/64 | .1406 | R | .3390 |
| 78 | .0160 | 27 | .1440 | 11/32 | .3437 |
| 77 | .0180 | 26 | .1470 | S | .3480 |
| 76 | .0200 | 25 | .1495 | T | .3580 |
| 75 | .0210 | 24 | .1520 | 23/64 | .3594 |
| 74 | .0225 | 23 | .1540 | U | .3680 |
| 73 | .0240 | 5/32 | .1562 | 3/8 | .3750 |
| 72 | .0250 | 22 | .1570 | V | .3770 |
| 71 | .0260 | 21 | .1590 | W | .3860 |
| 70 | .0280 | 20 | .1610 | 25/64 | .3906 |
| 69 | .0292 | 19 | .1660 | X | .3970 |
| 68 | .0310 | 18 | .1695 | Y | .4040 |
| 1/32 | .0313 | 11/64 | .1719 | 13/32 | .4062 |
| 67 | .0320 | 17 | .1730 | Z | .4130 |
| 66 | .0330 | 16 | .1770 | 27/64 | .4219 |
| 65 | .0350 | 15 | .1800 | 7/16 | .4375 |
| 64 | .0360 | 14 | .1820 | 29/64 | .4531 |
| 63 | .0370 | 13 | .1850 | 15/32 | .4687 |
| 62 | .0380 | 3/16 | .1875 | 31/64 | .4843 |
| 61 | .0390 | 12 | .1890 | 1/2 | .5000 |
| 60 | .0400 | 11 | .1910 | 33/64 | .5156 |
| 59 | .0410 | 10 | .1935 | 17/32 | .5313 |
| 58 | .0420 | 9 | .1960 | 35/64 | .5469 |
| 57 | .0430 | 8 | .1990 | 9/16 | .5625 |
| 56 | .0465 | 7 | .2010 | 37/64 | .5781 |
| 3/64 | .0469 | 13/64 | .2031 | 19/32 | .5937 |
| 55 | .0520 | 6 | .2040 | 39/64 | .6094 |
| 54 | .0550 | 5 | .2055 | 5/8 | .6250 |
| 53 | .0595 | 4 | .2090 | 41/64 | .6406 |
| 1/16 | .0625 | 3 | .2130 | 21/32 | .6562 |
| 52 | .0635 | 7/32 | .2187 | 43/64 | .6719 |
| 51 | .0670 | 2 | .2210 | 11/16 | .6875 |
| 50 | .0700 | 1 | .2280 | 45/64 | .7031 |
| 49 | .0730 | A | .2340 | 23/32 | .7187 |
| 48 | .0760 | 15/64 | .2344 | 47/64 | .7344 |
| 5/64 | .0781 | B | .2380 | 3/4 | .7500 |
| 47 | .0785 | C | .2420 | 49/64 | .7656 |
| 46 | .0810 | D | .2460 | 25/32 | .7812 |
| 45 | .0820 | E 1/4 | .2500 | 51/64 | .7969 |
| 44 | .0860 | F | .2570 | 13/16 | .8125 |
| 43 | .0890 | G | .2610 | 53/64 | .8281 |
| 42 | .0935 | 17/64 | .2656 | 27/32 | .8437 |
| 3/32 | .0937 | H | .2660 | 55/64 | .8594 |
| 41 | .0960 | I | .2720 | 7/8 | .8750 |
| 40 | .0980 | J | .2770 | 57/64 | .8906 |
| 39 | .0995 | K | .2811 | 29/32 | .9062 |
| 38 | .1015 | 9/32 | .2812 | 59/64 | .9219 |
| 37 | .1040 | L | .2900 | 15/16 | .9375 |
| 36 | .1065 | M | .2900 | 61/64 | .9531 |
| 7/64 | .1093 | 19/64 | .2968 | 31/32 | .9687 |
| 35 | .1100 | N | .3020 | 63/64 | .9844 |
| 34 | .1110 | 5/16 | .3125 | 1 | 1.0000 |
| 33 | .1130 | O | .3160 | | |
| 32 | .1160 | P | .3230 | | |
| 31 | .1200 | | | | |
| 1/8 | .1250 | | | | |
| 30 | .1285 | | | | |

Fig. 11-6. Quick reference decimal equivalent chart. (courtesy Univair)

craft BC12-D; however, it is similar in scope to the inspections required for all the airplanes covered in this book (Courtesy of Univair).

## Engine Operation:

- ☐ Run engine to minimum 120 degrees oil temperature—check full throttle static rpm (consult specifications for propeller used).
- ☐ Check magnetos 75 rpm drop at 1800 rpm.
- ☐ Check carburetor heat 100 rpm drop at full throttle.
- ☐ Check ignition switch for operation.
- ☐ Check idle rpm 550-600 rpb with carburetor heat off.
- ☐ Oil pressure 10-35 lbs., 30 good.

## Engine Mounts and Attachments:

- ☐ Check engine mount for damage and cracks at gussetts or in corners.
- ☐ Inspect protective finish on mount; sand and touch up bare areas.
- ☐ Inspect rubber shock mounts for rubber deterioration and tension.
- ☐ Engine mount bolts should be tightened to 60-80 inch lbs.
- ☐ Check mount bolts for safety.

## Cowling and Baffles:

- ☐ Clean and inspect engine cowling for dents and cracks at hinges and reinforcement.
- ☐ Check for tension adjustment on cowl door at fasteners.
- ☐ Tension prevents vibration and cowl door at fasteners.
- ☐ Check baffles for cracks and leather installation to prevent chafing.

## Magnetos, Wiring, and Shielding (If Installed):

- ☐ Check magneto for secure attachment.
- ☐ Check breaker point housing for excessive oil.
- ☐ Check points for gap pitting. For correct gap.

- ☐ Check plug wiring connections at magneto and insulation for deterioration and chafing.
- ☐ Check for grommets at baffles and firewall.

## Oil Drain and Safety Plug:

- ☐ Drain oil and check for metal particles.
- ☐ Remove, clean and check oilscreen for metal particles, drain plug and inlet oil temperature housing.
- ☐ Reinstall oil drain plug.
- ☐ Change oil filter if installed and check flexible lines for deterioration.

## Spark Plug Service:

- ☐ Remove plugs, abrasive blast and clean.
- ☐ Plugs with badly burned electrodes should be replaced.
- ☐ Reset gap to .016 on C26 plugs, consult manufacturer's charts for others.
- ☐ Reinstall using thread lubricant and new gaskets to prevent leakage and seizing. Torque to 300 to 360 inch lbs.

## Carburetor and Heater:

- ☐ Check carburetor for mounting security.
- ☐ Inspect carburetor bowl for cracks, particularly at inlet.
- ☐ Drain carburetor float chamber and check inlet finger screen carefully.
- ☐ Operate throttle in cockpit to be sure that throttle arm hits stops in open and closed positions without binding or sticking.
- ☐ Check operation of mixture control (if installed) for binding or sticking and full rich position.
- ☐ Inspect carburetor air box for security and cracks-heater valve for full travel.
- ☐ Check rubber intake hose connections for deterioration and clamp security.
- ☐ Check intake system for leaks and cracks.
- ☐ Clean air filter in kerosene and saturate with #10 oil and allow to drain before installation.

## Fuel Lines and Strainer:

- ☐ Check fuel lines for leaks and hose deterioration.
- ☐ Check hose supports for security and chafing. Drain and clean fuel strainer and resafety.
- ☐ Check for stains around fuel system indicating leaks.
- ☐ Check all connections for tightness.

## Exhaust Stack:

- ☐ Check stack flanges for security, cracks and leaks.
- ☐ Remove all heater shrouds and inspect for corrosion, cracks and leaks that might transfer gas to the cockpit, particularly thru the cabin heater system.
- ☐ Check tail pipe and stacks for security at all clamps and joints.
- ☐ Check cabin heater box and control valve for operation.
- ☐ Check cabin and carburetor heat flexible tubing for security and general condition.

## Engine Controls and Firewall:

- ☐ Check firewall for open holes and gas leaks from engine compartment. (If open holes, use zinc chromate putty or some other recommended commercial brand.)
- ☐ Check all controls for grommets and sealing putty.

## Propeller:

- ☐ Remove spinner and check for cracks or dents in spinner and back plates.
- ☐ Check propeller for separated laminations, cracks, lose metal tipping and protective finish. Blade track within 1/16".
- ☐ Wood propeller hub bolts are to torque from 140 to 150 inch lbs.
- ☐ Metal propeller hub bolts are to torque from 350 to 375 inch lbs.

## Cockpit and Baggage Area:

- ☐ Seats: Check general condition.
- ☐ Check condition of safety belts, Airworthiness Directives on seat belts—if frayed, replace.
- ☐ Check baggage area canvas—if deteriorated, or ripped, replace.

## Windshield:

- ☐ Check weatherstriping for security in channels and for leaks.
- ☐ Check plastic windshield and side windows for cracks, crazing, distortion and discoloration.

## Powerplant Instruments:

- ☐ Check powerplant instruments for mounting security.
- ☐ Check connections and plugs.
- ☐ Check placards and limitation markings.
  Tachometer: Red line—2300 rpm
  Oil pressure: Red line 10 psi and 35 psi
  Oil temperature: Red line—220 degrees F.
  Green arc—120 to 220 degrees F.
  Yellow arc—40 to 120 degrees F.

## Flight Instruments:

- ☐ Check flight instruments for mounting security.
- ☐ Check connections and plugs.
- ☐ Check placards and limitation markings.
  Airspeed: Red line—140 mph Landplane
  129 mph Seaplane

## Door Latch and Hinges:

- ☐ Check door hinge and rivets for looseness.
- ☐ Check door latch plunger for complete extension to prevent doors opening while taxiing.
- ☐ Check door for proper fit or damage resulting from air leaks.

## Engine Controls:

☐ Check mixture control for panel placard and operation smoothness.

☐ Check carburetor heat for panel placard and smoothness of operation.

☐ Check throttle for smooth operation and operation of friction lock.

☐ Check primer for operation and leaks behind the panel.

☐ Check cabin heat for panel placard and full travel of heater butterfly valve.

☐ Check ignition switch for panel and terminal security.

☐ Check for placard—Off, left, right and both.

## Rudder Pedals and Linkage:

☐ Check rudder pedal assemble for play and travel freedom.

☐ Lubricate hinges and torque tube bearings and check for safety.

☐ Check rudder pedal return springs for attachment.

## Cables and Pulleys:

☐ Check all cables for broken strands.

☐ Remove butt fairings and check top deck aileron pulleys for wear and security.

☐ Check aileron pulleys at both ends of panel. Remove floorboards and check pulleys.

## Flight Control Operation:

☐ Check aileron, rudder and elevator controls from cockpit for smooth operation.

☐ Check wheel for neutral position with control surfaces streamlines.

## Trim Tab Controls:

☐ Check stabilizer trim control for smooth operation.

☐ Check indicator against stabilizer for proper position.

## Fuel Selector Valve:

☐ Check fuel valve for smooth operation.

☐ Check placard for "On" and "Off" positions.

☐ Check valve for leaks.

## Landing Gear:

☐ Shock cord—for broken strands and elongation.

## Axles and Wheels:

☐ Remove wheels, wash, check and relubricate bearings.

☐ Check brake shoes for wear and drums for scoring.

☐ Install wheel and axle nut only tight enough to remove end play.

## Tires and Fairings:

☐ Check tires for 20 lbs. of air pressure.

☐ Replace tires that have cord showing.

☐ Check gear fairings for security and chafing.

## Landing Gear:

☐ Hoist aircraft (by engine mount at firewall) and check gear bushings, vee bushings are replaceable if worn.

☐ Check for skin wrinkles indicative of inside damage.

## Wing Fittings:

☐ With wing root fairings removed, inspect wing fittings with a flashlight and magnifying glass for minute cracks in the ears.

☐ Check bolts to be sure there are no threads in bearing, and bolts are properly safetied.

☐ Check wing fitting holes for elongation by having someone pull up and down on wing tips.

## Landing Gear Fittings:

☐ Remove both landing gear fairings and inspect all fittings with flashlight and magnifying glass for signs of cracks or hole elongation.

## Fuselage Structure:

- [ ] Through inspection openings and thru the baggage compartment cover, check the condition of all tubing for rust, damage and protective coating.
- [ ] Check all wood stringers for damage and security.

## Debris Accumulation:

- [ ] Check the bottom of the fuselage and fabric under floorboards for bolts, nuts and other objects that might jam controls or pulleys.
- [ ] Check the rear of fuselage for open drain grommets. If considerable dirt or oil exists on the fuselage bottom use a non-caustic soap and wash out the dirt to prevent fabric rot.

## Control Cables and Pulleys:

- [ ] Check for broken control cable strands by sliding a cloth over the cable in vicinity of fairleads.
- [ ] Check upper and lower elevator turnbuckles for safety and maximum of three threads showing outside of barrel.
- [ ] Check stabilizer control for slippage. Increase tension by tightening nut on idler pulley.

## Fairings:

- [ ] Check all fairings for cracks and missing screws.

## Wings and Ailerons:

- [ ] Wing fabric: Check left and right wing fabric for holes, cracks or checks in the finish and open drain grommets at each rib bay trailing edge. Fabric usually deteriorates on the upper surface of the wing or along the trailing edge.
- [ ] Install inspection grommets at drag wire fitting to inspect drag wires for tension and wing ribs and compression members for damage.

## Struts—Lift:

- [ ] Check right and left wing strut fittings for elongation by having someone lift up and down on the wing.
- [ ] Check bolts for fitting attachment to the spar.
- [ ] Check struts for dents or cracks, also sight down strut trailing edge to ascertain that struts are straight.
- [ ] Check strut end forks and fork lock nut.

## Wing Bolts:

- [ ] Check strut attachment bolts to be sure there are no threads in bearing, that nuts are not bottoming on unthreaded part of bolt and bolts are properly safetied.

## Ailerons:

- [ ] Check both ailerons for wrinkles which are possible sign of structural damage.
- [ ] Check each rib bay for an open drain grommet.
- [ ] Check condition of fabric and finish, refinishing any dope cracks, checks or ringworm.

## Aileron Hinges:

- [ ] Check aileron hinge legs for security at rear spar and false spar.
- [ ] Check hinge pins for wear and safety. Worn or loose pins must be replaced.

## Aileron Controls:

- [ ] Remove inspection covers and check the two cables in each wing for interference and chafing.
- [ ] Check the two pulleys in each wing for condition, wear and safety. Lubricate pulley bearings.
- [ ] Check travel, 23 degrees up, 23 degrees down.
- [ ] Check the four aileron horn bolts, threads in bearing and safety.
- [ ] Check the six turnbuckles in the center top

of fuselage for safety and not more than three threads showing outside the barrel.

☐ To locate broken strands at fairleads or pulleys, slide a cloth over the cable. All cables with broken strands are to be replaced.

## Wing Root Fairings:

☐ Check left and right fairings for tension.

☐ Check all metal screws for security and the fairings for cracks.

## Stabilizer:

☐ Check stabilizer fabric condition and drain grommets for restrictions.

☐ If the fabric strength is suspected a Seybooth tester may be used to accurately test the strength.

☐ Lift up and down on the stabilizer checking for excessive play.

## Fin:

☐ Inspect vertical fin for fabric condition and finish.

☐ Check for wrinkles, dents and signs of internal damage.

## Rudder:

☐ Inspect the fabric cover on the rudder for fabric and dope condition.

☐ Check bottom of rudder for an open drain grommet.

☐ Check rudder for alignment and possible internal damage usually indicated by a wrinkle in the fabric.

☐ Inspect rudder hinge pins for wear and safety.

☐ Check hinge bushings for play. These bushings are pressed in and should be replaced when worn.

☐ Check rudder travel, 26 degrees left, 26 degrees right.

## Elevators:

☐ Check fabric condition and finish on the elevators. Check for open drain grommets along the elevator training edge.

☐ Sight one elevator against the other for alignment.

☐ Check hinge pins and bushing for wear and replace any worn pins or bushings.

☐ Check elevator cable horns for safety, worn bolts and clearance in travel.

☐ Check elevator travel, 27 degrees up, 25 degrees down.

## External Bracing:

☐ Check impennage rigging wires for corrosion and cracks or nicks that might result in failure.

☐ Check fittings for alignment with the wire and check bolts for safety.

☐ Rigging wires should be taut with little hand deflection.

☐ Check each wire to be sure there are no loose fork lock nuts.

## Rudder and Elevator:

☐ Check rudder and elevator horns for worn bolts and safety with no threads in bearing.

☐ Check horns for alignment with the cable and freedom of travel.

☐ Top and bottom cable turnbuckles for safety and a maximum of three threads showing outside the barrel.

☐ Sight the cables through the fuselage for interference and chafing.

## FAA Requirements:

☐ Check all Airworthiness Directives (ADs) for applicability and compliance.

☐ Check for presence of Airworthiness Certificate.

☐ Check for presence of Certificate of Registration.

☐ Check for Operations Limitation/Flight Manual.

☐ Above items are required in cockpit when aircraft is currently licensed.

# Chapter 12

# Re-Covering Your Fabric Airplane

Fabric work is very expensive today; however, most of the expense is in labor. Re-covery of tube-and-fabric airplanes is a form of art, and the only true way to learn is under the direct supervision of a master.

Although many good points are brought out in this chapter about re-covering, it is by no means an exhaustive instruction manual. However, with the following information, and good supervision, anyone can recover an airplane.

## THE DIRTY WORK

The following general instructions for the removal of old fabric coverings and the pre-cover airframe preparations are based upon the *Stits Poly-Fiber Covering and Painting Manual*, by permission of the author, Ray Stits:

Fabric should be removed from the airframe carefully to avoid damaging the structure.

Any screws in wing ribs are removed after spinning a small sharpened tube around the screws or using a razor blade to cut and peel off the finishing tape. Blind rivets through the ribs are removed by carefully drilling in the center to undercut the head with one drill size smaller than the rivet. If a steel mandrel interferes with center drilling it may be recessed with a small drift punch.

Original wire clips should be removed carefully to avoid bending or damage since they will be reused unless replacements can be found. Continuous wire barbs originally designed for the Taylorcraft metal ribs and installed on thin Piper ribs under an STC should be removed very carefully by folding the correct end back to reduce the barb cross section. Any force will split and damage the rib, requiring expensive repair or replacement.

Any oversize rivet holes, screw holes or thin rib caps split during the removal of wire barbs should be tagged immediately for easy location and repair by methods acceptable to FAA before recovery.

After removing all mechanical fasteners the fabric is removed from the wing by carefully cutting just forward of the trailing edge, top and bottom, and peeling the fabric forward and around the wing leading edge. Trying to cut through at the trailing and leading edge with a razor blade or other sharp object will usually result in a deep groove on the metal or plywood surface.

Fabric attached to the wings with lacing cord should be removed by peeling the fabric forward from the trailing edge and cutting the laces progressively, rather than trying to fail the rib lace by jerking the fabric, resulting in broken or bent rib caps.

When removing fabric from a plywood wing leading edge, or other plywood surface, care should be taken not to peel sections of plywood skin with the fabric. If the fabric will not peel easily when folded back 180 degrees it may be soaked with Poly-Fiber reducer to soften the coating bond. If the solvent cannot penetrate through the outside of a solvent resistant finish coat, Poly-Fiber reducer may be applied with a brush along the bond interface to progressively penetrate under the fabric.

Fabric is carefully removed from the fuselage and controls in the same manner as the wings. Avoid damage by not cutting structures under the fabric with a sharp knife or bending/breaking the fabric forming members by trying to rip the fabric off. It is advisable to remove the fabric in large sections, and set it aside for future reference to help establish locations for inspection access holes, drain grommets, and reinforcing tapes.

Old fabric covering is not always a reliable guide to position new inspection access holes. A photo or a sketch should be made of the structures to record those areas which will require and inspection access hole for later maintenance or inspection.

Cellulose-coated fabric removed from an airplane should be considered an extreme fire hazard and not be stored near a flame source or in a residence.

Before installing fabric on the airplane or component, a thorough inspection should be made to assure the structure is ready for covering. Theoretically it will be many years before the fabric is removed as polyester filaments do not deteriorate in any environment in which aircraft,

including AG aircraft, are operated. They deteriorate only when exposed to direct UV radiation. When our (Stits) coating system is used as directed, all UV radiation is blocked.

Old one-component varnish on wood structures that will not be in contact with the fabric should be recoated with EV-400 Epoxy Varnish. One-component varnishes, commonly referred to as "spar varnish" are easily lifted and destroyed when in contact with solvents used in aircraft coatings. The term "spar varnish" refers to a quality recommended for annual application on sailboat spars or masts, not aircraft spars.

Moisture-curing one-component so-called urethane varnishes are also very sensitive to solvents and will wrinkle and lift. Solvent sensitivity tests may be made with Poly-Fiber reducer on a rag, allowing 15 minutes soak time.

Old wood surfaces which will be in contact with the fabric should be dry sanded to remove the majority of the residue of one-component varnishes, wood sealers, or cellulose dope coatings, then sealed with two brush coats of epoxy varnish.

All metal and plywood surfaces which will be covered with fabric are pre-coated with two brush coats of Poly-Brush reduced with equal parts Poly-Fiber Reducer.

Do not coat wood with a metal primer because it does not have the needed flexibility and hides any cracks and decay.

Wood components which will be covered with fabric should never be coated with any solvent soluble lacquer sealers which will absorb and retain solvents from coatings like a sponge and cause bubbles to form or cement seams to slip after the fabric is installed.

Ferrous metal components on which fabric will be cemented on in contact, such as fuselage longerons, tail surface tubes, window and door frames, etc., which are bare or were previously coated with any one component metal primer should be recoated with EP-420 Epoxy Primer. Special attention should be given bottom longeron areas where water may be trapped and cause corrosion. Any one-component metal primer will be softened and penetrated and alkyd types will be wrinkled when in contact with solvents used in aircraft fabric coatings. The damaged primer is not noticed under the fabric until the corrosion stain migrates through the fabric finish surface four or five years later. EP-420 Epoxy Primer will not lift or damage one-component metal primers, therefore there is no purpose in removing old, sound primers before applying epoxy primers.

An asphaltic or rubber base coating should be applied by brush to the structure adjacent and below the battery box for additional protection from the sulfuric acid electrolyte. Control cables routed through the battery box area should be coated with paralketone.

A close inspection should be made of all hardware, clevis pins, jam nuts, screws, rivets, etc. to assure their security and airworthiness. Drag and anti-drag wires should be protected from chafing at the cross point.

All sharp edges which will be in contact with the fabric covering should be taped to smooth the edges and avoid cutting or chafing through the fabric. There are no specifications for the quality or strength of an anti-chafe tape, however I warn against the use of a paper masking tape for this purpose. Paper tape retains moisture and is subject to bacteria degradation. The resin adhesives on paper masking tape, as well as many economical duct tapes, will migrate with age or heat and show as a dark spot through light-colored finishes. Dye on duct tapes may be released by fabric coatings and migrate. We recommend natural white cotton cloth adhesive tape similar in appearance to surgical adhesive tape for anti-chafe purposes.

All wrinkles, dents, repairs, and patches on aluminum fairings which form shapes or contours, such as wing leading edges and turtle decks, will show through the fabric covering when the fabric is bonded directly to the aluminum surface. Rough fabric contouring surfaces may be smoothed and any rivet and screw head protrusions reduced by installing polyester flannel cloth weighing approximately 2.7 oz. per square yard. Flannel available is available at most domestic fabric stores. White is preferred, however the color is not important as long as it is a non-bleeding dye. The flannel is

cemented around the perimeter of the leading edge or turtle deck with Poly-Tak, being careful not to saturate and fill the outside fibers of the flannel. Sufficient adhesive to secure the flannel in position is all that is required.

The use of a flannel cushion on the leading edge eliminates the option of using an overlap cement seam spanwise on the wing. The fabric must wrap around the wing with an overlap cement seam at the trailing edge as a blanket, or an envelope may be used. Flannel cloth provides an escape route for the coating solvent vapors and reduces the possibilities of pinholes through the finish. Flannel cloth may be used on any structure where the bond of the fabric directly to the primary structure is not required as part of the fabric covering procedure. Generally this limits the use of a flannel cushion to convex surfaces such as leading edges and turtle decks and large aluminum fairings at fuselage corners.

Before a component is covered with fabric it must be inspected and the recovery authorized by an FAA representative, certified repair station, or a mechanic authorized by the FAA to conduct the inspection.

*Ed. note:* Reference in the foregoing was made to numerous Stits products. Other, similar, products by other manufacturers may be utilized in a like fashion.

## RE-COVERY SYSTEMS

Originally, the classics were all covered in either cotton or linen. These fabrics do not hold up as well as the new synthetics, but require the same labor to install.

There are four standard covering systems available in today's market. All are advertised in *Trade-A-Plane.*

Each system described here is complete. "Complete" meaning that the installer will use only the items called for in the installation/instruction manual provided by the manufacturer and follow the prescribed methods. The STC for the re-covery of an airframe is issued by the FAA, and is based upon each re-covery job being performed *exactly* as called for in the STC. If you do not comply, the STC is not valid, and neither is your Airworthiness Certificate.

The typical system includes the synthetic material, Dacron or Fiberglass, glues, tapes, and coatings.

## Stits Poly-Fiber

The Stits system is based upon a polyester fabric that can be attached to the airframe by stitching, as in the case of the original cover, or may be glued by use of Poly-Tak, a high strength fabric cement. The latter method is a real time-saver.

After the fabric is in place, it's "heat shrunk" by use of a hot iron. This is the only tautening that will occur, as the Stits system coatings are non-tautening.

The coatings will provide protection from the sun's ultraviolet rays, which are quite destructive to fabrics. The final coats will be color and finish.

## Ceconite

Basically the Ceconite system is similar to Stits; however, the coatings differ. The coatings used in the Ceconite system are tautening (butyrate and nitrate dopes). This, in addition to the thermal shrinking done after attachment of the fabric.

## Razorback Fiberglass

The Razorback method of recovering differs from the first two by use of a different fabric. Fiberglass is utilized, and is considered permanent—so much so that there is no requirement for fabric punch testing at annual time if your plane has been covered with Razorback (Fig. 12-1).

As with the other synthetic systems, seams and attachments are glued, rather than sewed. Initial coatings are made by spraying of butyrate dopes, which cause tautening of the fabric. Other coatings of silver (for protection from ultraviolet rays) and finish coloring are made with non-tautening materials.

## Ceconite 7600

Perhaps this is the most interesting system that

Fig. 12-1. This decal is required by the STC to appear on the tail surface of any aircraft covered with Razorback. It indicates there is no requirement for annual fabric testing. (courtesy Razorback Fabrics)

is currently available for re-covering airplanes. It's the Eonnex system, developed some years ago by Bill Lott. The system is now produced by Ceconite, under the name of Ceconite 7600, and is distributed by Blue River Aviation (address is in the back of this book).

The basic application of the fabric is similar to Stits and Ceconite; however, the coatings are completely different.

Unlike the smelly and flammable coating products utilized in the other systems, the 7600 coatings are water-based and interact with a pre-treatment in the fabric. If you are doing a re-covery project at home, I am sure the wife, family, and neighbors will enjoy the improved atmosphere (lack of smell), and your insurance company will no doubt approve of the non-flammable materials being used. Only the finish coat will produce toxic/flammable fumes.

Other positive points for the 7600 system include the ease of application, as the coatings are applied by use of brushes and/or pads (Figs. 12-2

Fig. 12-2. After the Eonnex fabric has been installed on the airframe it must be heat-shrunk for proper fit. Here the close quarter iron is used to start the tautening process. If you start to tauten over the ribs you will prevent small wrinkles from showing up later. (courtesy Blue River Aircraft)

Fig. 12-3. In this photo, reinforcing tape is being placed over the ribs prior to rib stitching. Notice the rib stitch spacing is marked and the holes punched before centering the tape. (courtesy Blue River Aircraft)

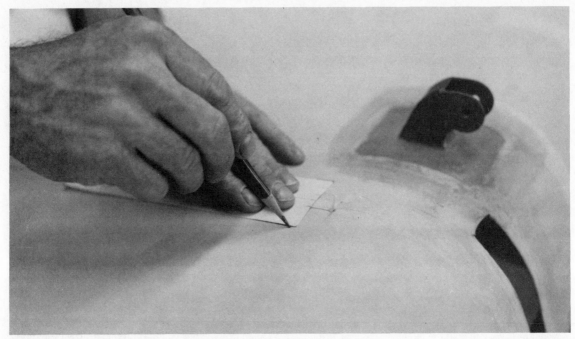

Fig. 12-4. Using a quade made from sandpaper to mark the width of the surface tape prior to applying the cement. This method prevents getting excess cement outside the tape area, and helps apply the tapes in a straight line. (courtesy Blue River Aircraft)

Fig. 12-5. Applying the surface tape cement within the previously marked areas. (courtesy Blue River Aircraft)

Fig. 12-6. Dampening the Eonnex fabric just prior to applying the filler coating. The dampening is being done with a sponge and water. There are no flammable fumes from this process, nor will the smell give you a headache. (courtesy Blue River Aircraft)

Fig. 12-7. Applying the filler coat with a paint pad. The filler coat fills the weave and gives UV protection. (courtesy Blue River Aircraft)

Fig. 12-8. A typical homebuilder's crowded shop. Note the wood stove that is used for heat when there are no explosive vapors present. You won't see stoves in use around other fabric systems. This really points up the safety of the 7600 process. (courtesy Blue River Aircraft)

through 12-8). Additionally, there is the lack of temperature/humidity difficulties encountered with the other systems. 7600 may be applied at all temperatures above freezing.

## ACCEPTED PRACTICES

FAA publication 43.13 is the bible for aircraft maintenance and repair. I recommend that anyone who owns, or thinks about owning, an airplane purchase a copy. Among the heaps of information contained in 43.13 is an entire chapter on fabric covering. Included in this information is instructions for the stitching and attachment of fabric coverings. This reading is *mandatory* for all who plan to re-cover their aircraft.

## TOOLS AND EQUIPMENT

- ☐ 9″ pinking shears.
- ☐ 9″ straight shears.
- ☐ Assorted 3″ to 6″ needles.
- ☐ Long needles, 12″ to 18″ with curved tips.
- ☐ Many T-headed pins.
- ☐ Razor blade knife.
- ☐ Brushes 1″ to 4″ (no nylon bristles).
- ☐ Paint stir sticks.
- ☐ Paint filter cones.
- ☐ Assorted clean tin cans.
- ☐ Several clean/new paint buckets.
- ☐ Paper/cloth towels.
- ☐ Pair of sawhorses (line top with carpets).
- ☐ Tape measure.

# Chapter 13

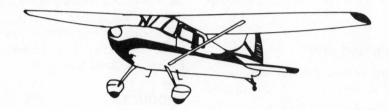

# Care for Your Metal Airplane

Paint applied to the exterior surfaces of alclad aluminum aircraft is not required to qualify for a type certificate or to maintain the airworthiness certificate. The protection provided to the aluminum alloy by the aluminum cladding on the surface is considered adequate to qualify for the initial airworthiness certificate. Cladding is the bonding of a thin overcoat of pure aluminum to the sheet alloy material utilized on an airplane. This cladding resists atmospheric corrosion.

In most cases, leaving the aircraft bare and occasionally washing it to remove airborne particles deposited on the surfaces of unpainted aluminum surfaces will offer adequate corrosion control. This policy seems to work for many airline and military aircraft.

About the only economical justification for painting an aircraft exterior surface is to protect the alloy skins that have lost their aluminum cladding, possibly as a result of age, or by abuse (scrubbing or sanding with extremely abrasive materials will remove the cladding). Painting is also recommended if the aircraft will be stored in a corrosive climate for a long period of time. A corrosive climate refers to salt air, or areas of the country that have heavy industrial pollution.

Pride of ownership no doubt has quite some effect on the appearance of airplanes, and surely results in many of the brightly painted aircraft seen today.

## SUMMARY OF AIRCRAFT FINISHES

Ray Stits states in his *Stits Poly-Fiber Covering and Painting Manual*:

It is our opinion, based upon tests which correspond with many tests conducted by major material suppliers in the U.S. and Germany, the best paint system for metal aircraft is epoxy primers and urethane finish coatings.

Good quality urethane finishes provide two to three times the service life of epoxy finishes. Epoxy finishes are usually about as durable as synthetic enamel finishes, and will chalk in about the same length of time. Epoxy finishes provide far better chemical and solvent resistance than synthetic enamel finishes. Acrylic lacquer rates about the same as synthetic enamel, with no solvent resistance. Catalyzed acrylic enamel provides fair solvent and chemical resistance and rates between epoxy and urethane enamel. Keep the airplane locked in the hangar and all these finishes will still look good in five years. The true test is exposure and operation.

## AIRCRAFT PAINTING COST

As with covering a tube-and-fabric airplane, it's estimated that 85 to 90 percent of the cost of stripping and repainting an airplane is labor. Obtain the best quality materials available, which have been specially formulated for aircraft, along with complete detailed instructions. Don't settle for an inferior product to save a few dollars. The time and effort expended will be the same in either case, but the higher quality materials will result in a better, longer lasting job.

## PAINT SPRAY EQUIPMENT

Spray guns rated by the manufacturer as "all-purpose" or suitable for spraying lacquers, synthetic enamels, and primers are recommended for the application of aircraft finishes. There are three well-known companies that manufacture spraying equipment: DeVilbiss, Binks, and Sharpe.

Further information on spray guns may be obtained from local distributors or by writing to:

**DeVilbiss Company**
Toledo, OH 43692

**Binks Manufacturing Company**
9201 W. Belmont Ave.
Franklin Park, IL 60131

**Sharpe Manufacturing Company**
1224 Wall St.
Los Angeles, CA 90015

## SPRAY OPERATIONS

Follow the instructions that come with the spray gun. Whether a spray gun is purchased new or used, the manufacturer can provide details for the operation, adjustments, dismantling, and cleaning.

Often in reading application instructions you'll see the terms single coat or double coat. A spray "single coat" is applied by overlapping each consecutive pass 50 percent of the fan width. A "double coat" is applied by repeating the coating application in the same direction or at 90 degrees to the first coat (cross coat) before the first coat has flashed off (dried dust free).

## PRODUCTS

There are numerous finishes available on the market today. I have utilized Stits materials in the following instructions; however, similar results should be attained by following the instructions that apply to any of the current manufacturers' products.

Most of the manufacturers, or their distributors, advertise in *Trade-A-Plane*, and are glad to send you literature about their products.

## REFINISHING AN AIRPLANE

The following instructions give the basics of refinishing a metal airplane. For more detailed instructions read *Refinishing Metal Aircraft* by Joe Christy (TAB book No. 2291). Two notes of caution: First, read and follow the manufacturer's instructions that are given on the products you utilize. Second, never mix products from different suppliers, as they may fail to function as planned.

### Stripping the Airframe

Mask any area that may be damaged by paint stripper by using polypropylene or cloth masking tape and polypropylene plastic sheet or equivalent material. Methylene chloride will damage polymethyl methacrylate, a transparent polymer—better known by a Rohm and Haas trade name, "Plexiglass."

Stripper is best applied with a brush. After the old paint has softened, spray the area with cold water to remove the residue. The person(s) performing this operation should wear rubber gloves and eye protection.

After the stripping has been completed, there will no doubt be areas of old paint that failed to cooperate. These may be removed with "soft" tools such as plastic scrapers, Scotch Brite pads, or the like. Don't use hard tools, as they will damage the cladding. In addition, *never* use steel wool, as microscopic particles will be left that will later cause corrosion. Aluminum wool is an adequate replacement for steel wool.

## Corrosion

Corrosion discovered during the stripping procedure should be cleaned with Aluma-Dyne E-2311 Phosphoric Acid Etch and Brightener.

The remainder of the aircraft, where no corrosion has been seen, is given a complete scrubbing with Scotch Brite pads and 310 Alkaline Cleaner. The scrubbing action gives a clean yet rough surface—a surface with teeth for greater adhesion of the primer coating. An acid etch of the entire craft is optional at this point; however, if done, the craft must be well-rinsed afterwards.

Within eight hours, the freshly scrubbed surfaces must be treated with Aluma-Dyne E-2300 Chromic Etch Conversion. Application is made with a brush or sponge. Be sure to protect your hands and eyes from these chemicals.

A complete water rinse is again made to remove the conversion coating materials. Left behind will be a thin oxide film on the aluminum surface.

## Priming

Before proceeding with the priming, wipe all surfaces down with clean towels wetted with C-2200 Metl-Sol cleaner. Be sure not to use "shop rags" that come from a supplier, as they may be contaminated, even though clean. If they are contaminated they will leave a residue that could cause a poor finish job.

The EP-420 Epoxy Primer is applied, first with a wet tack coat, then two medium coats at 30 minute intervals. The primer should be applied within 24 hours of the conversion coating.

At this point you are able to perform any "body" work that is necessary. Utilizing Micro-Putty, fill in and sand any dents in the leading edges. After sanding, apply primer over the repaired area.

## Finish

The finish coat must be applied within 48 hours of the primer. If more time than that has elapsed, a complete sanding of the primed surfaces will be required. If the surface is not sanded, it will not provide good "teeth" for the finish coat to adhere to.

Any fingerprints or oily spots must be removed with C-2210 Paint Surface Cleaner.

Go over the entire airplane with a good quality tack rag, then following all directions supplied, mix and reduce the Aluma-Thane.

The first coat should be a wet tack coat, followed by two heavier coats at 15 to 20 minute intervals. Allow sufficient time between applications to prevent runs and sags.

## Interior Surfaces

Interior surfaces or airplanes are normally painted only for cosmetic reasons. Since they are not exposed to the elements of nature, their preparation is quite simple. Cleaning can be accomplished with C-2200 Metl-Sol, followed by priming. The color coating can be the same as the exterior, or an inexpensive automotive lacquer spray may be utilized. Remember, these are cosmetic coatings only.

## Refinishing Old Paint

If you have a plane that has sound acrylic lacquer, epoxy paint, or synthetic enamel, you may be able to apply a new finish over it.

Clean the old surface with 310 Alkaline Cleaner and sand it smooth. Be sure that oils, waxes, and silicones are removed from the old finish.

After the above preparations have been made you can coat it with Aero-Thane Enamel.

## FINISHING TIPS

1. Do not use wax-coated paper cups for

measuring, transferring, or storing the various liquids. Solvents in the coatings may dissolve the wax and contaminate the material in the cup.

2. Do not intermix coatings, reducers, cleaners, or solvents from one brand to another. Although similar in nature, they may not mix well, causing a poor paint job.

3. Do not force urethane finishes to dry with heat, or even sunlight for that matter. The heat will cause blistering.

4. Unless the urethane has been given at least 12 hours of cure, do not put it outside in dampness. The result could be a flat finish.

5. Excessive humidity can cause the urethane finish to blush, and dry with no gloss.

6. Apply your coats of urethane within 30 minutes of one another, not several days apart. Fresh solvents from new paint applied to partially cured urethane can lift the paint, resulting in a real mess.

7. Should you touch your face or hair, you will transmit body oils to whatever else you touch. Keep your oily fingers off the airplane during the painting process. If you suspect you may have touched something, wipe that area with solvent.

8. Pay attention to the "pot-life" of your two-part paints.

9. Use a proper respirator when spraying. The fumes are not good for you, can make you ill immediately, and may have cumulative effects after long periods of exposure.

## POLISHING AN AIRPLANE

The following appeared in the Luscombe Association newsletter, and is reprinted here with their permission:

For all those who are considering polishing a metal airplane, I have some advice: *Don't*. But since I know you will not listen to me about that, I hope you will listen to me about how to polish it.

The first step is to remove all the paint. This will take several gallons of good paint remover and lots of time. Do not use any kind of metal scraper, steel wool, or sandpaper on the metal skin. This will leave marks impossible to polish out. Use only

a scraper made of some material such as micarda. Micarda is a material similar to the material used in the pulleys for controls on the Luscombe.

After the paint is removed, you will see that the skin has a rather dull, milky look to it. This look is caused by the metal surface being etched before it was painted. This etching was necessary to make the paint adhere properly to the skin. At this point you need a good electric buffer of some kind. Any automotive type buffer will work, but the best one to use is the one sold by the Swift Association. This machine leaves no swirl marks such as you get from the rotating disc type. It is called the #5 Cyclo Polisher. Write Box 644, Athens, TN 37303 for more information.

You will also need some sort of polishing compound to use with the polisher. The best thing to use seems to be a hand rubbing compound of the type intended to be used on automotive paints. I like Dupont #606S. This is a good fast-cutting compound that will not cut too fast and will leave a good fine polish job. You might also want to use a dusting of corn starch to help remove the last of the film left by the polishing compound. (The #606S is cheaper by the gallon).

Now that you have polished the aircraft, you will notice that there is some black powder scattered around by the polishing. It is on the aircraft as well as the person who does the polishing. Wash both the aircraft and the polisher with good soap to remove the black powder. Dry the aircraft thoroughly with soft cloths. Old diapers or T-shirts or towels work well.

It is time now to put the finishing touches on the polish job. I like Met-All polish. It is a bit finer polish than 606S and it will be all you need to keep the shine up. The more you polish, the better the shine will get. You must keep polishing since any kind of moisture is now your enemy. It is nice to live in a hot, dry climate, or at least to keep the aircraft in a dry warm hangar. You can follow the polishing with any good automotive wax.

After you complete polishing, you will notice that some panels will not shine as well as others. The drawn panels, such as the cowl nose piece, 'D' window panels, lower cowl, cowl top panel and others are made of a different alloy than the rest of the skins. The alloy for these parts cannot be of the same hard type alloys since they must be soft enough to be drawn and formed. These soft alloys were never given the final coating of pure aluminum that the other skins were. This final coat is the one that shines so well. So be prepared to see a rather dark film look to these panels. Also, if you polish the other panels too vigorously you will polish this film away and these panels will also look dark and not shine as well. Once this film is gone, it is gone forever, so be careful as you polish.

To the best of my knowledge there is nothing you can do to keep the shine except polish. There is no 'miracle' polish to keep the shine forever. Nor will any type of clear lacquer, varnish, or plastic coating work—only good honest elbow grease.

Hope this information helps you.

Richard Lawrence
Lincoln Park, MI

# Chapter 14

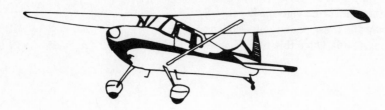

# Engines Found in Classics

You are completely dependent on the integrity of your airplane's engine for your life, and the lives of your passengers. The more you know about it the better.

## DEFINITIONS

Here are a few definitions to help you understand engines better:

**remanufacture**—The disassembly, repair, alteration, and inspection of an engine. It includes bringing all specifications back to new limits. A factory remanufactured engine comes with new logs and zero time.

**new limits**—The dimensions/specifications used when constructing a new engine. These parts will normally reach TBO (time between overhaul) with no further attention, save for routine maintenance.

**overhaul**—The disassembly, inspection, cleaning, repair, and reassembly of the engine. The work may be done to new limits or to "service limits."

**service limits**—The dimensions/specifications below which use is forbidden. Many used parts will fit into this category; however, they are unlikely to last the full TBO as they are already partially worn.

**top overhaul**—The rebuilding of the head assemblies, but not of the entire engine. In other words, the case of the engine is not split, only the cylinders are pulled. Top overhauls are utilized to bring oil burning and/or low compression engines within specifications. It is a method of stretching the life of an otherwise sound engine. A top overhaul is not necessarily an indicator of a poor engine. Its need may have been brought on by such things as pilot abuse, lack of care, lack of use of the engine, or plain abuse (i.e., hard climbs and fast letdowns). An interesting note: The term top overhaul does not indicate the extent of the rebuild job (i.e., number of cylinders rebuilt or the completeness of the job).

**TBO (time between overhaul)**—The manufacturer's recommended maximum engine life. It has no legal bearing on airplanes not used in commercial service. It's only an indicator. Many well-cared-for engines last hundreds of hours beyond TBO—*but not all*.

**nitriding**—A method of hardening cylinder barrels and crankshafts. The purpose is to reduce wear, thereby extending the useful life of the part.

**chrome plating**—Used to bring the internal dimensions of the cylinders back to specifications. It produces a hard, machineable, and long-lasting surface. There is one major drawback of chrome plating: longer break-in times. However, an advantage of the chrome plating is its resistance to destructive oxidation within combustion chambers.

**Magnaflux/Magnaglow**—Terms associated with methods of detecting invisible defects in ferrous metals (i.e., cracks). Parts normally Magnafluxed/Magnaglowed are crankshafts, camshafts, piston pins, rocker arms, etc.

## ENGINE MODEL CODE

The model number of an aircraft engine will usually describe either the horsepower:

Continental C-85 (85 hp)
Continental A-65 (65 hp)

. . . or the number will indicate the cubic inch displacement of the engine rounded off to the nearest number divisible by 5:

Lycoming O-235 (233 cubic inch displacement)

The O that appears as part of many airplane engine model numbers merely indicates that the engine is horizontally opposed in configuration—the only type that you will find in the classics.

Suffix codes describe individual models of engines (magnetos, timing, balancing, etc.). Example: O-235-L2C—opposed cylinder engine of 235 cubic inch displacement, L2C model (which in this case is the 118-hp version which burns low-lead fuel).

## CYLINDER COLOR CODES

Cylinder color codes are applied via paint, or by banding part of the lower cylinder.

Orange indicates a chrome-plated cylinder barrel.

Blue indicates a nitrided cylinder barrel.

Green means that the cylinder barrel is .010 oversize.

Yellow is used for .020 oversize.

## SPARK PLUG COLOR CODES

Spark plug color codes identify the reach length of the required plugs. The color will be seen in the fin area of the cylinder between the plug and the rocker box.

Grey or unpainted indicates short-reach plugs.

Yellow indicates long-reach plugs.

## USED ENGINES

Unless you're purchasing an airplane with a brand-new engine on it, you'll need to concern yourself with various phrases and facts.

Many airplane ads proudly state the hours on the engine (i.e., 876 SMOH). Basically this means that there have been 876 hours of use since the engine was overhauled. *Not* stated is *how* it was used or *how completely* it was overhauled. There are few standards.

## TIME vs VALUE

The time (hours) since new or overhaul is an important factor when placing a value on an airplane. The recommended TBO, less the hours currently on the engine, is the time remaining. This is the span you will have to live in.

Three basic terms are usually used when referring to time on an airplane engine:

☐ Low Time—first 1/3 of TBO
☐ Mid Time—second 1/3 of TBO
☐ High Time—last 1/3 of TBO

Naturally, other variables come into play when referring to TBO: Are the hours on the engine since new, rebuild, or overhaul? What type of flying has the engine seen? Was it flown on a regular basis? Lastly, what kind of maintenance did the engine get? The logbook should be of some help in determining any questions about maintenance.

Airplanes that have not been flown on a regular basis—and maintained in a like fashion—will never reach full TBO (time between overhaul). Manufacturers refer to regular usage as 20 to 40 hours monthly. However, there are few privately owned airplanes meeting the upper limits of this requirement. Let's face it, most of us don't have the time or money required for such constant use. This 20 to 40 hours monthly equates to 240 to 480 hours yearly. That's a lot of flying.

When an engine isn't run, acids and moisture in the oil will oxidize (rust) engine components. In addition, lack of lubrication movement will cause the seals to dry out. Left long enough, the engine will seize and no longer be operable.

Just as hard on engines as no use is abuse. Hard climbing and fast descents, causing abnormal heating and cooling conditions, are extremely destructive to air cooled engines. Trainer aircraft often exhibit this trait, due to their type of usage (i.e., takeoff and landing practice).

Naturally, preventive maintenance should have been accomplished and logged throughout the engine's life (i.e., oil changes, plug changes, etc.). All maintenance must be logged, so says the FARs.

Beware of the engine that has just a few hours on it since an overhaul. Perhaps something is not right with the overhaul, or it was a very cheap job, just to make the plane more salable.

When it comes to overhauls/rebuilds I always recommend the large shops that specialize in aircraft engine rebuilding. I'm not saying that the local FBO can't do a good job. I just feel that the large organizations, specializing in this work, have more experience and better equipment with which to work.

Engines are expensive to rebuild/overhaul; even a Continental C-series, found on many of the smaller classics, will cost $2000 to $3000. And it is the rule to spend $4000 and up on engines from larger four-placers.

## AVIATION FUELS YOU WILL USE

The following information is reprinted by permission of AVCO Lycoming, as found in their "Key Reprints" (Key Reprints are available by writing to AVCO Lycoming):

We have received many inquiries from the field expressing concern over the limited availability of 80/87 grade fuel, and the associated questions about the use of higher leaded fuel in engines rated for grade 80/87 fuel. The leading fuel suppliers indicate that in some areas 80/87 grade aviation fuel is not available. It is further indicated that the trend is toward phase-out of 80/87 aviation grade fuel. The low lead 100 LL Avgas, blue color, which is limited to 2ml tetraethyl lead per gallon will gradually become the only fuel available for piston engines. Whenever 80/87 is not available you should use the lowest lead 100 grade fuel available. Automotive fuels should never be used as a substitute for aviation fuel in aircraft engines.

The continuous use, more than 25 percent of the operating time, with the higher leaded fuels in engines certified for 80 octane fuel can result in increased engine deposits both in the combustion chamber and in the engine oil. It may require increased spark plug maintenance and more frequent oil changes. The frequency of spark plug maintenance and oil drain periods will be governed by the amount of lead per gallon and the type of operation. Operation at full rich mixture requires more frequent maintenance periods; therefore it is important to use properly approved mixture leaning procedures.

To reduce or keep engine deposits at a minimum when using the higher leaded fuels, 100 LL Avgas blue, or 100 green, it is essential that the following four conditions of operation and maintenance are applied.

A. Fuel management required in all modes of flight operation. (See A, General Rules.)

B. Prior to engine shutdown run up to 1200 rpm for one minute to clean out any unburned fuel after taxiing in. (See B, Engine Shut Down.)

C. Replace lubricating oil and filters each 50 hours of operation, under normal environmental conditions. (See C, Lubrication Recommendations.)

D. Proper selection of spark plug types and good maintenance are necessary. (See D, Spark Plugs.)

The use of economy cruise engine leaning whenever possible will keep deposits to a minimum. Pertinent portions of the manual leaning procedures as recommended in Avco Lycoming Service Instruction No. 1094 are reprinted here for reference.

## A. General Rules

1. Never lean the mixture from full rich during takeoff, climb or high-performance cruise operation unless the airplane owner's manual advises otherwise. However, during takeoff from high elevation airports or during climb at higher altitudes, roughness or reduction of power may occur at full rich mixtures. In such a case the mixture may be adjusted only enough to obtain smooth engine operation. Careful observation of temperature instruments should be practiced.

2. Operate the engine at maximum power mixture for performance cruise powers and at best economy mixture for economy cruise power, unless otherwise specified in the airplane owner's manual.

3. Always return the mixture to full rich before increasing power settings.

4. During let-down and reduced power flight operations it may be necessary to manually lean or leave the mixture setting at cruise position prior to landing. During the landing sequence the mixture control should then be placed in the full rich position, unless landing at high elevation fields where leaning may be necessary.

5. Methods for manually setting maximum power or best economy mixture.

    a. Engine tachometer—Airspeed Indicator Method: The tachometer and/or the airspeed indicator may be used to locate, approximately, maximum power and best economy mixture ranges. When a fixed-pitch propeller is used, either or both instruments are useful indicators. If the airplane uses a constant-speed propeller, the airspeed indicator is useful. Regardless of the propeller type, set the controls for the desired cruise power as shown in the owner's manual. Gradually lean the mixture from full rich until either the tachometer or the airspeed indicator are reading peaks. At peak indication the engine is operating in the maximum power range.

    b. For Cruise Power: Where best economy operation is allowed by the manufacturer, the mixture is first leaned from full rich to maximum power, then leaning slowly continued until engine operation becomes rough or until engine power is rapidly diminishing as noted by an undesirable decrease in airspeed. When either condition occurs, enrich the mixture sufficiently to obtain an evenly firing engine or the regain of most of the lost airspeed or engine rpm. Some slight engine power and airspeed must be sacrificed to gain best economy mixture setting.

    c. Exhaust Gas Temperature Method (EGT): Refer to Service Instruction No. 1094 for procedure.

Recommended fuel management—Manual leaning, will not only result in less engine deposits and reduced maintenance cost, but will provide more economical operation and fuel saving.

## B. Engine Shutdown

The deposit formation rate can be greatly retarded by controlling ground operation to minimize separation of the non-volatile components of the higher leaded aviation fuels. This rate can be accelerated by (1) Low mixture temperatures and (2) Excessively rich fuel/air mixtures associated with the idling and taxiing operations. Therefore, it is important that engine idling speeds should be set at their proper 600 to 650 rpm range with the idle mixture adjusted properly to provide smooth idling operation. Shut down procedure recommends setting rpm at 1200 for one minute prior to shut down.

## C. Lubrication Recommendations

Many of the engine deposits formed by the use of the higher leaded fuel are in suspension within the engine oil and are not removed by a full flow filter. When sufficient amounts of these contaminants in the oil reach high temperature area of the engine then can be baked out, resulting in possible malfunctions such as in exhaust valve guides, causing sticking valves. When using the higher leaded fuels, the recommended oil drain period of 50 hours should not be extended, and if occurrences of valve sticking is noted, all guides should be reamed using the procedures as stated in Service Instruction No. 1116, and a reduction in the oil drain periods and oil filter replacement used.

## D. Spark Plugs

Spark plugs should be rotated from the top to bottom on a 50 hour basis, and should be serviced on a 100 hour basis. If excessive spark plug lead fouling occurs, the selection of a hotter plug from the approved list in Service Instruction No. 1042 may be necessary. However, depending on the type of lead deposit formed, a colder plug from the approved list may better resolve the problem. Depending on the lead content of the fuel and the type of operation, more frequent cleaning of the spark plugs may be necessary. Where the majority of operation is at low power, such as patrol, a hotter plug would be advantageous. If the majority of operation is at high cruise power, a colder plug is recommended.

## COLOR CODING OF AVGAS

Red: 80 Octane containing .50ml lead/gal.
Blue: 100 Octane containing 2ml lead/gal.
Green: 100 Octane containing 3ml lead/gal.

## A WORD FROM THE FAA

In April 1977 the use of Tricresyl Phosphate (TCP) was approved for use in Lycoming and Continental engines that do not incorporate turbosuperchargers.

Prior to that date approval had been given for use in Franklin engines.

TCP is a fuel additive that is available from:

Alcor, Inc.
10130 Jones-Maltsberger Rd.
Box 32516
San Antonio, TX 73284

and from most FBOs.

## A FEW OTHER WORDS

There have been some valve modifications made to some Continental engines that you should watch for. These changes are to relieve the valve erosion problems encountered when using 100 LL AVgas.

**A-65/A-75:** Replace the intake valves with part #639661, and the exhaust valves with part #639662. **C-75/C-85/C-90/C-145/O-200/O-300:** Replace the intake valves with part #641792, and intake valve seats with part #641793.

There are similar modifications available for the AVCO Lycoming engines. These modifications will be noted in the engine log. Check for them.

Fine wire spark plugs, if approved for your engine, are claimed to be less prone to lead fouling.

## AUTO FUELS

Recently there has been considerable controversy and discussion about the use of auto fuels in certified aircraft engines. There are pros and cons for both sides; however, I feel that it is up to the individual pilot to make his own choice about the use of non-aviation fuels in his airplane.

Among the pros:

☐ One will always hear economy. Unleaded auto fuel is certainly less expensive than 100LL.

☐ Auto fuel does appear to operate well in the older engines that require 80 octane fuel.

☐ If you have a private gas tank/pump, it might be advantageous to utilize auto fuel. It'll be far easier to locate a jobber willing to keep an auto fuel tank filled than it will be to find an avgas supplier willing to make small deliveries.

Among the cons:

☐ Lack of consistency among the various gasolines and their additives. In particular, many low lead auto fuels have alcohol in them. Alcohol is destructive to some parts in the typical aircraft fuel system.

☐ Most FBOs are reluctant to make auto fuels available for reasons such as product liability, less profit, and the possibility of a supply cutoff by a displeased avgas distributor.

☐ The engine manufacturers claim the use of auto fuel will void warranty service.

If you desire further information about the legal use of auto fuels in your airplane, contact the EAA (Experimental Aircraft Association), who have an ongoing program of testing airplanes and obtaining STCs for the use of auto fuel. The address for the EAA may be found in the back of this book.

These STCs are available from the EAA for a minimal fee, based upon engine horsepower. The EAA is constantly expanding the list of airplanes and engines for which auto fuel are available.

Here is a partial list indicating makes/models with STCs available.

## Engines
### Continental

A-65
A-75
C-75
C-85
C-90
C-125
C-145
E-165
E-185
E-225
O-200
O-300
GO-300

### AVCO Lycoming
O-320-A,C,E

## Airframes
### Aeronca

7AC
7BCM
7CCM
7DC
7EC
11AC
11BC
11CC

### Alon

A-2
A-2A

### Cessna
120
140
140A
170
170A
170B

### Champion
7EC
7FC

### Ercoupe
415-C
415-D
415-E
415-G
415-C/D

### Forney
F-1
F-1A

### Luscombe
8
8A
8C
8D
8E
8F

### Piper
J3
J3C-65
J4
J4A
J4E
J5A
PA-11
PA-17
PA-18

**Taylorcraft**
- BC-65
- BC12-D
- BC12D-85
- 19
- F19

## ENGINE APPLICATIONS/SPECIFICATIONS

The following is a chart that includes model numbers, hp, fuel required, takeoff rpm, recommended TBO, and the airplanes they were originally installed in (Figs. 14-1 through 14-6).

**Continental**

| Model | hp | Fuel | T/O rpm | TBO | Acft |
|---|---|---|---|---|---|
| A65 | 65 | 80 | 2300 | 1800 | Aeronca |
| | | | | | Ercoupe |
| | | | | | Luscombe |
| | | | | | Piper |
| | | | | | Taylorcraft |
| A75 | 75 | 80 | 2600 | 1800 | Luscombe |
| | | | | | Piper |
| C75 | 75 | 80 | 2275 | 1800 | Ercoupe |
| C85 | 85 | 80 | 2575 | 1800 | Aeronca |
| | | | | | Alon |
| | | | | | Cessna |
| | | | | | Taylorcraft |
| C90-8F | 95 | 80 | 2625 | 1800 | Piper |
| C90-12F | 95 | 80 | 2625 | 1800 | Alon |
| | | | | | Cessna |
| | | | | | Luscombe |
| | | | | | Piper |

Fig. 14-1. This Continental 65-hp engine is mounted on a Piper J3 Cub. Notice the magneto on the rear of the engine, the unshielded spark plugs, exhaust pipes, and how the engine mounts are attached.

Fig. 14-2. Continental 0-200 engine, popular replacement engine for those desiring more power and performance. (courtesy Teledyne Continental)

| Model | hp | Fuel | T/O rpm | TBO | Acft |
|---|---|---|---|---|---|
| C90-14F | 95 | 80 | 2625 | 1800 | Cessna |
| C90-16F | 95 | 80 | 2625 | 1800 | Alon |
| | | | | | Cessna |
| C145-2 | 125 | 80 | 2700 | 1800 | Cessna |
| O-200A | 100 | 80 | 2750 | 1800 | Taylorcraft |
| O-300A | 145 | 80 | 2700 | 1800 | Cessna |

## Franklin

| Model | hp | Fuel | T/O rpm | TBO | Acft |
|---|---|---|---|---|---|
| 2A-120B | 60 | 80 | N/A | 1500 | Ch 7-ACA |
| 6A4-150 | 150 | 80 | 2600 | 1200 | Stinson |
| 6A4-165 | 165 | 80 | 2800 | 1200 | Stinson |

## Lycoming

| Model | hp | Fuel | T/O rpm | TBO | Acft |
|---|---|---|---|---|---|
| O-235-C1B | 115 | 80 | 2800 | 2000 | J5C |
| | | | | | PA-12 |
| | | | | | PA-11 |
| | | | | | PA-14 |
| | | | | | PA-16 |
| | | | | | PA-18 |
| O-235-C2 | 115 | 80 | 2800 | 2000 | PA-18 |
| | | | | | PA-22 |
| O-235-L2C | 118 | 100 | 2800 | 2000 | F-21 |
| O-290-D | 130 | 80 | 2800 | 2000 | PA-18 |
| | | | | | PA-20 |
| | | | | | PA-22 |

| Model | hp | Fuel | T/O rpm | TBO | Acft |
|-------|-----|------|---------|------|------|
| O-290-D2 | 140 | 80 | 2800 | 1500 | PA-18 |
| | | | | | PA-20 |
| | | | | | PA-22 |
| O-320-A1A | 150 | 80 | 2700 | 1200 | PA-22 |
| O-320-A2A | 150 | 80 | 2700 | 1200 | PA-18 |
| | | | | | PA-22 |
| O-320-A1B | 150 | 80 | 2700 | 1200 | PA-22 |
| O-320-A2B | 150 | 80 | 2700 | 1200 | PA-18 |
| | | | | | PA-22 |
| O-320-B2A | 160 | 91 | 2700 | 1200 | PA-22 |

*O-320 series engines may have the TBO extended to 2000 hrs by installing 1/2 inch exhaust valves.

## STORAGE OF ENGINES

The following information is provided courtesy of Teledyne Continental. It applies to all aircraft engines, and shows to what extent you must go to care for your engine investment.

### General

Engines in aircraft that are flown only occasionally tend to exhibit cylinder wall corrosion more than engines in aircraft that are flown frequently.

Of particular concern are new engines or engines with new or freshly honed cylinders after a top or major overhaul. In areas of high humidity, there have been instances where corrosion has been found in cylinders after an inactive period of only a few days. When cylinders have been operated for approximately 50 hours, the varnish deposited on the cylinder walls offers some protection against corrosion.

Obviously, proper steps must be taken on

Fig. 14-3. Continental C-85 85-hp engine. (courtesy Teledyne Continental)

Fig. 14-4. Lycoming 0-235 engine. (courtesy AVCO Lycoming)

engines used infrequently to lessen the possibility of corrosion. This is especially true if the aircraft is based near the sea coast or in areas of high humidity and flown less than once a week.

In all geographical areas the best method of preventing corrosion of the cylinders and other internal parts of the engine is to fly the aircraft at least once a week long enough to reach normal operating temperatures which will vaporize moisture and other by-products of combustion. Aircraft engine storage recommendations are broken down into the following categories:

☐ Flyable Storage (7 to 30 days).
☐ Temporary Storage (up to 90 days).
☐ Indefinite Storage.

## Flyable Storage (7 to 30 days)

a. Service aircraft per normal airframe manufacturer's instructions.

b. Each seven days during flyable storage, the propeller should be rotated by hand without running the engine. Rotate the engine six revolutions, stop the propeller 45 to 90 degrees from the original position. For maximum safety, accomplish engine rotation as follows:

(1) Verify magneto switches are "OFF."
(2) Throttle position "CLOSED."
(3) Mixture control "IDLE CUT-OFF."
(4) Set brakes and block aircraft wheels.
(5) Leave aircraft tiedowns installed and verify that the cabin door latch is open.
(6) Do not stand within the arc of the propeller.

c. If at the end of thirty (30) days the aircraft is not removed from storage, the aircraft should be

Fig. 14-5. Lycoming 0-320 engine. (courtesy AVCO Lycoming)

flown for thirty (30) minutes, reaching, but not exceeding, normal oil and cylinder temperatures. If the aircraft cannot be flown it should be represerved in accordance with "B" (Temporary Storage) or "C" (Indefinite Storage).

**Temporary Storage (up to 90 Days)**

a. Preparation for Storage

1. Remove the top spark plug and spray atomized preservative oil (Lubrication Oil-Contact and Volatile Corrosion-Inhibited, MIL-L-46002, Grade 1) at room temperature, through upper spark plug hole of each cylinder with the piston in approximately the bottom dead center position. Rotate crankshaft as each pair of opposite cylinders is sprayed. Stop crankshaft with no piston at top dead center.

NOTE

Shown below are some approved preservative oils recommended for use in Teledyne Continental engines for temporary and indefinite storage: MIL-L-46002, Grade 1 Oils:

**NOX RUST VCI-105**
Daubert Chemical Co.
4700 S. Central Ave.
Chicago, IL 60600

**TECTYL 859A**
Ashland Oil, Inc.
1401 Winchester Ave.
Ashland, KY 41101

2. Re-spray each cylinder without rotating

crank, to thoroughly cover all surfaces of the cylinder interior, move the nozzle or spray gun from the top to the bottom of the cylinder.

3. Reinstall spark plugs.

4. Apply preservative to engine interior by spraying the above specified oil (approximately two ounces) through the oil filler tube.

5. Seal all engine openings exposed to the atmosphere using suitable plugs, or moisture resistant tape, and attach red streamers at each point.

6. Engines, with propellers installed, that are preserved for storage in accordance with this section should have a tag affixed to the propeller in a conspicuous place with the following notation on the tag: "DO NOT TURN PROPELLER—ENGINE PRESERVED."

b. Removal From Storage

1. Remove seals, tape, paper and streamers from all openings.

2. With bottom spark plugs removed from the cylinders, hand turn propeller several revolutions to clear excess preservative oil, then reinstall spark plugs.

3. Conduct normal start-up procedure.

4. Give the aircraft a thorough cleaning and visual inspection. A test flight is recommended.

**Indefinite Storage**

a. Preparation for storage

1. Drain the engine oil and refill with MIL-C-6529 type 2. Start engine and run until normal oil and cylinder head temperatures are reached. The preferred method would be to fly the aircraft for thirty minutes. Allow engine to cool to ambient temperature. Accomplish steps a. in Flyable Storage and a. 1 through 6 in Temporary Storage.

Fig. 14-6. Lycoming 0-320 installed in a Piper Tri-Pacer. Notice the baffles that control the air flow around the engine. Lower left is the alternator, lower center is the oil cooler, lower right is the starter.

MIL-C-6527 type 2 may be formulated by thoroughly mixing one part compound MIL-C-6529 type 1 (ESSO Rust-Ban 628, Cosmoline No. 1223 or equivalent) with three parts new lubricating oil of the grade recommended for service (all at room temperature).

2. Apply preservative to engine interior by spraying MIL-L-46002, grade 1 oil (approximately two ounces) through the oil filler tube.

b. Install dehydrator plugs MS27215-2, in each of the top spark plug holes, making sure that each plug is blue in color when installed. Protect and support the spark plug leads with AN-4060 protectors.

c. If the carburetor is removed from the engine place a bag of desiccant in the throat of the carburetor air adaptor. Seal the adaptor with moisture resistant paper and tape or a cover plate.

d. Place a bag of desiccant in the exhaust pipes and seal the openings with moisture resistant tape.

e. Seal the cold air inlet to the heater muff with moisture-resistant tape to exclude moisture and foreign objects.

f. Seal the engine breather by inserting a dehydrator MS27215-2 plug in the breather hose and clamping in place.

g. Attach a red streamer to each place on the engine where bags of desiccant are placed. Either attach red streamers outside the sealed area with tape or to the inside of the sealed area with safety wire to prevent wicking of moisture into the sealed area.

h. Engines with propellers installed that are preserved for storage in accordance with this section should have each propeller tagged in a conspicuous place with the following notation on the tag: "DO NOT TURN PROPELLER—ENGINE PRESERVED."

As an alternative method of indefinite storage, the aircraft may be serviced in accordance with the procedures under Temporary Storage providing the airplane is run up at maximum intervals of 90 days and then re-serviced per the temporary storage requirements.

Procedures necessary for returning an aircraft to service are as follows:

a. Remove the cylinder dehydrator plugs and all paper, tape, dessiccant bags, and streamers used to preserve the engine.

b. Drain the corrosion preventative mixture and reservice with recommended lubricating oil.

## WARNING

*When returning the aircraft to service do not use the corrosion preventive oil referenced in Indefinite Storage a.1. for more than 25 hours.*

c. With bottom plugs removed rotate propeller to clear excess preservative oil from cylinders.

d. Reinstall the spark plugs and rotate the propeller by hand through the compression strokes of all the cylinders to check for possible liquid lock. Start the engine in the normal manner.

e. Give the aircraft a thorough cleaning, visual inspection and test flight per airframe manufacturers instructions.

Aircraft stored in accordance with the indefinite storage procedures should be inspected per the following instructions:

a. Aircraft prepared for indefinite storage should have the cylinder dehydrator plugs visually inspected every 30 days. The plugs should be changed as soon as their color indicates unsafe conditions of storage. If the dehydrator plugs have changed color in one-half or more of the cylinders, all desiccant material on the engine should be replaced.

b. The cylinder bores of all engines prepared for indefinite storage should be resprayed with corrosion preventative mixture every six months, or more frequently if bore inspection indicates corrosion has started earlier than six months. Replace all desiccant and dehydrator plugs. Before spraying, the engine should be inspected for corrosion as follows: Inspect the interior of at least one cylinder on each engine through the spark plug hole. If cylinder shows start of rust, spray cylinder corrosion preventative oil and turn prop six times, then respray all cylinders. Remove at least one rocker box cover from each engine and inspect the valve mechanism.

# Chapter 15

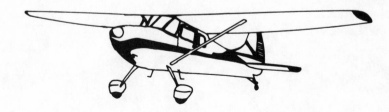

# Installation
# and Care of Propellers

Your connection with the air you move in is the propeller. Without it you have no means of transforming the power from the engine into motion. In short, without it, you don't fly. The propellers you will see on classic airplanes are either metal or wood, with most being fixed-pitch.

The following information is provided courtesy of Sensenich Corp. Look for their name on the propellers of classics. More often than not, the prop you see will be a Sensenich product; they have been around since the 1930s (Fig. 15-1).

## TECHNICAL DEFINITIONS

**pitch, geometric**—The geometrical pitch of an element of a propeller is the distance which the element would advance along a helix of slope equal to its blade angle. The nominal or standard pitch of our propellers is the geometric pitch as determined at 75 percent of the radius.

**pitch, effective**—The effective pitch of a propeller is the distance an aircraft actually advances along its flight path in one revolution of the propeller.

**rotation**—The rotation of the propeller is determined when viewing the propeller from the slipstream, A right-hand propeller is one which rotates clockwise when viewed from the slipstream, that is, from the cockpit in a tractor installation. A left-hand propeller is one which rotates counterclockwise when viewed in the same manner.

## WOODEN PROPELLERS

Your Sensenich wood propeller was manufactured from aircraft-quality selected lumber. The laminations are bonded with high strength waterproof resorcinal glue, and were assembled under closely controlled factory conditions. Propeller balance was strictly maintained during manufacture and verified before shipment from the factory. Assembly of the Type Certificated propeller/engine/aircraft must be accomplished by personnel holding the appropriate FAA license (Fig. 15-2).

Fig. 15-1. The Sensenich factory as it appeared in the days of the classics. (courtesy Sensenich)

## Installation

The propellers covered by these instructions are all of the two-blade, fixed-pitch type constructed of laminated birch wood. They have metal leading edge strips which protect the wood against abrasion. The metal strips are attached to the wood with wood screws and rivets. In addition to the metal strips, 10 to 15 inches of the outer area of each blade is covered with sturdy fabric as further protection against damage from stones during takeoff or landing.

Some of the propellers covered by these instructions have integral spinners constructed of molded plywood.

## Installation of Hub

1. Make sure the threads on the bolts are free from metal chips and other foreign matter.

2. Coat the threads with light engine oil.

3. Insert the bolts in holes so that nuts will be on front face of propellers. On some flange mounted installations it may be necessary to install the bolts with heads on front face of propeller. Use a soft headed hammer, if necessary, to drive the bolts through the hub.

4. Put on the hub bolt nuts and draw up

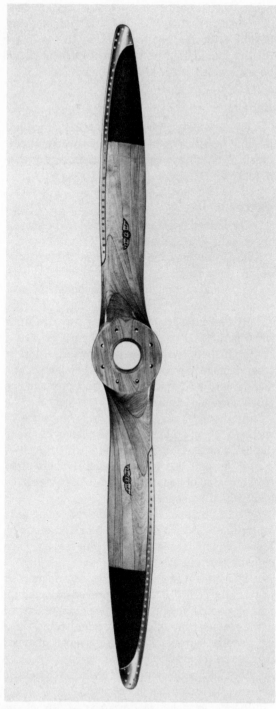

Fig. 15-2. An original wood prop, as appeared on many classics. These propellers are still available from the Sensenich Company. (courtesy Sensenich)

evenly, a little at a time, moving back and forth across the hub from one bolt to another. this will help prevent throwing the propeller out of track and pitch.

5. Use a torque wrench to tighten the nuts to a torque reading as recommended in the table below. A tolerance of plus or minus 25 inch pounds can be allowed on these values. It is important that the nuts are not tightened beyond the recommended values, in order that the surface of the wood propeller will not be fractured. Any fracture of the wood will allow moisture to enter the wood, thus leading to checking of the wood and consequent early rejection from service.

| Bolt Diameter | Recommended Torque |
| --- | --- |
| 3/8  inch | 200 inch-pounds |
| 7/16 inch | 250 inch-pounds |
| 1/2  inch | 300 inch-pounds |

### Track

1. After the hub has been installed, the complete assembly should be placed on a conventional checking stand and checked to determine if the blades track within 1/16 of each other.

2. If the blades do not track; the hub bolts should be loosened and hard paper, pasteboard, or thin metal shims placed between the fixed hub flange and the propeller hub face, so as to bring the tips of the blades into alignment within 1/16 inch of each other. Tighten the hub bolt nuts with the recommended torque when checking the track.

### Balance

All propellers should be checked for balance before installation on an engine. This is especially true of propellers coming from spare propeller stocks. Propellers that have been in stock any length of time may have lost their balance and, therefore, should be checked and corrected before installation on an engine.

### Installation on Engine

1. General—After balance has been corrected and cotter pins or safety wire installed through the

hub bolts, the propeller is ready for installation on the engine.

2. Pre-Installation Operations

Observe where applicable, the following operations:

(a) Recheck entire surface of propeller including fabric covering and tipping.

(b) Clean shaft threads and splines thoroughly, removing all nicks, burns, and galls from the shaft.

(c) In the case of spline shaft installations, clean the rear cone and place it on shaft.

(d) Clean thoroughly and coat the threads of the propeller shaft and nut with an approved antiseize compound.

(e) Locate propeller on the shaft, being careful not to damage the shaft, shaft threads, or rear cone seat.

(f) On spline shaft installations make certain the halves of the front cone are mates. Place them on the nut. If the cone is new it may come in one piece, in which case it will be necessary to saw the halves apart and carefully remove the metal left in the split.

(g) Carefully start the nut on the threads of the engine shaft. Tighten the nut by means of a three-foot bar placed through the holes in the nut. This applies to the No. 20 shaft only . On the No. 0 taper shaft and the No. 10 splines shaft use an 18-inch bar. *Caution:* Hammering on the bar should be avoided.

(h) Install the snap ring and safety the shaft nut in the manner provided on the particular hub being used.

(i) When installing propellers on the integral hub flange shafts, place the propeller on the stub shaft, insert bolts in the flange and tighten, as explained previously.

## Storage

If the propeller does not go into service immediately after repair, it should be stored in a horizontal position, supported by the hub and not at the blades. Propellers should never be allowed to stand against a wall, or be stored in such a manner that the weight is taken by the blades. Pro-

pellers should not be stored where they are close to, or in a direct line with, the flow of air from any heating or cooling equipment. If at all possible, a relative humidity of from 30 to 60 percent should be maintained in the storage room.

## Repairs

We strongly recommend that propellers needing repairs be sent only to approved propeller repair stations or propeller manufacturers or their branches.

## Operating Tips

The following practices will add to the service life of your wood propeller:

(1) Do not use the propeller as a tow-bar to move your aircraft.

(2) Avoid running-up in areas containing loose stones and gravel.

(3) Place the propeller in a horizontal position when parked.

(4) Inspect frequently for bruises, scars, or other damage to wood and blade leading-edge protection. It is good practice to conduct preflight and post-flight inspections.

(5) Protect your propeller from moisture by waxing with an automotive type paste wax. Keep the drain holes in metal tipping open.

(6) Assume that your propeller is unairworthy after any kind of impact until it has been inspected by qualified personnel.

(7) Inspect and check propeller attaching bolts for tightness at least every 100 hours or annually. More frequent inspection may be necessary when climatic changes are extreme.

(8) All wood and metal tipping repairs must be made at the factory or by an approved propeller repair station. If your propeller was manufactured with recessed synthetic leading edge protection, a kit is available from the factory for repair of minor damage to the plastic material.

(9) Check propeller balance whenever there is evidence of roughness in operation.

If your propeller begins to show any of the following damage, it should be retired from service:

(a) Cracks in hub bore.

(b) A deep cut across the wood grain.

(c) A long, wide, or deep crack parallel to the grain.

(d) A separated lamination.

(e) Oversize or elongated hub bore or bolt holes.

(f) An appreciable warp (discovered by inspection or through rough operation).

(g) An appreciable portion of wood missing.

(h) Obvious damage or wear beyond economical repair.

## Wood Propeller Model Numbers

Sensenich Simplified Model or Part Number system can be explained by use of the following examples:

(a) 86C-67

(b) 86CA-67

(c) 86CASP-72

(d) 86CS-72

(e) 86CAL-67

The first two figures, 86, indicate the propeller diameter in inches. The following letter, C, designates one basic blade design selected from a group applicable to the particular diameter. All of the above listed propellers have the same basic blade design.

A letter other than L or S following the first letter in the Model designation indicates a variation in hub dimensions from another Model having the same diameter and same basic blade design.

The letter L following in any position after the first letter in the Model designation indicates a left-hand rotating propeller. All other propellers are right-hand rotation. Example (e) is the same as example (b) except that it is left-handed.

The letter S following in any position after the first letter in the Model designation indicates that the propeller has a built-in spinner. If the letter S is followed by the letter P the spinner is constructed of plywood. Example (c) is of the same basic blade design, fits the same hub and differs from example (b) only in so far as it has an integral spinner constructed of plywood. If the letter P does not follow the letter S then the integral spinner is of solid wood construction as in example (d).

The last two numbers indicate the pitch of the propeller in inches. Examples (a), (b), and (e) have a pitch of 67 inches. Examples (c) and (d) each have a pitch of 72 inches. this is the geometric pitch measured at 75 percent of the radius.

If the Model number is preceded by the letter W, the propeller was manufactured after April 25, 1968.

## Applications

| Model | Engine | Propeller |
|---|---|---|
| **Aeronca** | | |
| 7AC | Cont A-65 | 72CK42 |
| 11AC | Cont A-65 | 72CK42 |
| 7BCM | Cont C-85 | 72GK50 |
| 7CC | Cont C-90 | 72GK48 |
| 7DC | Cont C-85 | 72GK44 |
| 7EC | Cont C-90 | 72GK48 |
| 15AC | Cont C-145 | 73BR44 |
| | | |
| **Cessna** | | |
| 120,140 | Cont C-85 | 74FK49 |
| 140 | Cont C-90 | 74FK51 |
| 170,170A | Cont C-145 | 73BR50 |
| | | |
| **Champion** | | |
| 7EC | Cont C-90 | 72GK48 |
| | | |
| **Ercoupe** | | |
| 415C | Cont A-65 | 72CK44 |
| 415C-G | Cont C-75 | 72FKT48 |
| | | |
| **Luscombe** | | |
| 8A | Cont A-65 | 76CK44 |
| 8B | Lyco O-145B | 70LY38 |
| 8C,D | Cont A-75 | 72GK46 |
| 8E | Cont C-85 | 72GK50 |
| 8F | Cont C-90 | 72GK52 |
| 11A | Cont E-165 | 80EY80 |
| | | |
| **Piper** | | |
| J3C-65 | Cont A-65 | 72CK42 |
| J3L-65 | Lyco O-145B | 70LY34 |
| J4 | Cont A-65 | 72CK42 |
| J5 | Cont A-75 | 70D40 |

| | | |
|---|---|---|
| J5C | Lyco O-235 | 74FE46 |
| PA-11 | Cont A-65 | 72CK42 |
| PA-11 | Cont C-90 | 72GK50 |
| PA-12 | Lyco O-235C | 76RM44 |
| PA-14 | Lyco O-235C1 | 74FM52 |
| PA-15 | Lyco O-145B | 70LY36 |
| PA-16 | Lyco O-235C1 | 74FM52 |
| PA-17 | Cont A-65 | 72CK42 |
| PA-18 | Cont C-90 | 72GK50 |
| PA-18 | Lyco O-235C1 | 74FM52 |
| PA-18 | Lyco O-290D | 74FM52 |
| PA-20 | Lyco O-290D | 74FM57 |

**Stinson**

| | | |
|---|---|---|
| 108 | Frank 6A4-150 | 76JA53 |
| 108-1 | Frank 6A4-150 | 76JR53 |
| 108-2,3 | Frank 6A4-165 | 76JR53 |

**Taylorcraft**

| | | |
|---|---|---|
| BC12D | Cont A-65 | 72CK44 |
| 19 | Cont C-85 | 72GK46 |

## METAL PROPELLERS

Your Sensenich propeller has been manufactured under closely controlled conditions to the approved design in accordance with the applicable FAA Regulations. Stamped on the propeller hub face are the Model and Serial Numbers, the Type Certificate Number, and the Production Certificate Number (Sensenich Corp. P.C. No.1).

### Metal Propeller Model Numbers

The Sensenich Metal Propeller Designation System, is a coded means of telling all about a particular propeller.

The number 74DM6S5-2-60 is broken down as:

74—Basic propeller diameter
D —Blade design
M6—Propeller hub design
C  SAE ARP-502 flange
K  SAE No. 1 flange
M6 SAE No. 2 flange with 6/16″ bolts
M7 SAE No. 2 flange with 7/16″ bolts
M8 SAE No. 2 flange with 8/16″ bolts
R  SAE No. 3 flange
S5—Integral doweled spacer

Spacer length is given in 1/4 inch units
–2 —Allowable reduction (inches) from basic diameter
60—Blade pitch at 75 percent radius

**Do**

1. Have your propeller installed by an A&P mechanic. For convenience, the proper installation bolt torque is shown on the blade decal near the hub. Always have the blade track checked after the hub bolts are tightened. Note: Every propeller is accurately balanced at the factory. If the propeller-engine combination feels rough in flight, ask your mechanic to remove the propeller, rotate it 180 degrees on the engine crankshaft flange, and reinstall. Again check the blade track. If the blades track, this will verify trueness of the crankshaft flange.

2. Inspect the blades of your propeller before each flight for nicks, cuts, and stone bruises. Have the minor repairs promptly performed by an A&P mechanic. If a crack is discovered, *the propeller must be immediately removed from service.*

3. Have major repairs performed by an FAA Certified Propeller Repair Station or by the factory.

4. Conform to applicable rpm limitations and periodically have your tachometer checked for accuracy.

5. Frequently wipe the propeller blades clean with an oily rag. This oily wipe off will remove corrosive substances, and the oily residue will repel water and corrosives.

6. The recommended flight time between reconditioning for your Sensenich fixed-pitch metal propeller is 1000 hours *provided it has not received prior damage requiring immediate attention.* This accomplishes the removal of fatigued surface metal and the accumulation of small nicks and cuts too numerous to be repaired individually.

**Do Not**

1. Permit installation of a propeller unless it is the model approved under the Aircraft type Certificate and has been obtained from a reliable source. Beware of a propeller of unknown service history.

2. Push or pull on the propeller when moving the aircraft by hand.

3. Run up your engine/propeller over loose stones or gravel.

4. Paint over corroded or damaged blades. This hides the defect and may deter needed repair.

5. Permit repair of blade damage by peening or welding. These practices will lead to early blade failure.

6. Fly your aircraft under any circumstances before a thorough inspection by qualified personnel if the propeller has been subject to impact.

7. Have your propeller straightened except by an FAA Certified Propeller Repair Station or the factory. Even partial straightening of blades for convenience of shipping to a repair station may cause hidden damage which, if not detected, could result in the return to service of a non-airworthy propeller. Report anything of this nature before repair is initiated.

**minor repair**—Rounding out a shallow nick or cut, as long as the strength, weight, and stiffness of the blade is not materially affected.

**major repair**—Includes diameter reduction to repair tip damage, repairs to deep cuts and nicks, and straightening of bent blades.

## Applications

| Model | Engine | Propeller |
|-------|--------|-----------|
| **Aeronca** | | |
| 7AC | Cont A-65 | 74CK-0-46 |
| 11AC | Cont A-65 | 74CK-0-46 |
| 11CC | Cont C-85 | 74CK-2-44 |
| | | |
| **Cessna** | | |
| 120,140 | Cont C-85 | 76AK-2-44 |
| | | |
| **Ercoupe** | | |
| 415C,D | Cont C-75 | 76AK-2-48 |
| 415C-G | Cont C-85 | 76AK-2-46 |
| | | |
| **Piper** | | |
| J3C | Cont A-65 | 74CK-0-46 |
| J4 | Cont A-65 | 74CK-0-46 |
| PA-11 | Cont A-65 | 74CK-0-46 |
| PA-11 | Cont C-90 | 76AK-2-42 |
| PA-11 | Lyco O-235C | 76AM6-2-46 |
| PA-12 | Lyco O-235C | 76AM6-2-46 |
| PA-12 | Lyco O-235C1 | 76AM6-2-48 |
| PA-14 | Lyco O-235C1 | 76AM6-2-48 |
| PA-16 | Lyco O-235C1 | 76AM6-2-50 |
| PA-17 | Cont A-65 | 74CK-2-48 |
| PA-18 | Cont C-90 | 76AK-2-42 |
| PA-18 | Lyco O-235C1 | 76AM6-2-48 |
| PA-18 | Lyco O-290D | 74DM6-0-50 |
| PA-18 | Lyco O-290D2 | 74DM6-0-52 |
| PA-18 | Lyco O-320 | 74DM6-0-56 |
| PA-20 | Lyco O-235C1 | 76AM6-2-50 |
| PA-20 | Lyco O-235C1 | 76AM6-2-50 |
| PA-20 | Lyco O-290D | 74DM6-0-56 |
| PA-20 | Lyco O-290D2 | 74DM6-0-57 |
| PA-22C | Lyco O-235C1B | 76AM6-2-48 |
| PA-22 | Lyco O-320 | 74DM6-0-60 |
| | | |
| **Taylorcraft** | | |
| BC12D | Cont A-65 | 74CK-0-48 |
| F21 | Lyco O-235L2C | 72CK-0-50 |

## Standard/Climb/Cruise

When referring to propellers, you often hear the terms *climb prop* or *cruise prop*. Usually the terms will be accompanied by "better" performance than is afforded with the standard propeller. The tables seen in this chapter give only standard propellers. However it is easy to convert from standard to optional:

Cruise—Add 2 inches of pitch
Climb—Reduce the pitch by 2 inches.

When climb/cruise propellers are recommended, the lower pitch (climb propeller) can be expected to offer better takeoff, climb, and high-altitude performance. The higher pitch (cruise) propeller should be chosen only if takeoff and climb are not critical.

# Chapter 16

# New Avionics in Old Planes

Back in the Introduction I mentioned the "classic" style of flying. VFR navigation was all done by pilotage, looking out the window to see where you were. But, alas, times have changed.

Today's modern airway system requires at least a minimum of avionics on board to freely travel where we want to go.

Although you may not need it at your home base, a good COMM radio will allow you to land at most controlled airports. Without it, you will be relegated to operating only from uncontrolled airports, and won't even be able to use UNICOM at those. A COMM radio does offer additional safety.

If you do very much cross-country a NAV radio would be nice; after all, those VOR signals are already out there, so why not put them to use—at least as a backup to pilotage.

There is one other electronic box that is needed to give complete flexibility in your operations. This is the transponder. The transponder enhances your image on the FAA Air Traffic Controller's radar screen, and can identify your airplane by digital means. If you have altitude reporting capabilities

on your transponder, it will even tell the controller that too.

I have not included much information relative to IFR flying, as there are few "classics" doing that —although it is completely possible, if the airplane is equipped for such operations. However, you will find some very well-equipped classics around, and find that they are flown in IFR weather on a regular basis.

## DEFINITIONS

**A-panel**—Audio Panel. Allows centralized control of all radio equipment.

**ADF**—Automatic Direction Finder.

**CDI**—A panel-mounted device that gives visual output of the NAV radio.

**COMM**—VHF transceiver for voice radio communications.

**ELT**—Emergency Locator Transmitter (required by FARs for all but local flying).

**LOC/GS**—Localizer/Glideslope. Visual output is via a CDI, with the addition of a horizontal indicator.

Fig. 16-1. King KY 92 COMM transceiver. (courtesy King Avionics)

**MBR**—Marker Beacon Receiver.

**NAV**—VHF navigation receiver for utilizing VORs.

**NAV/COMM**—Combination of COMM and NAV in one unit.

**XPNDR**—Transponder (may or may not have altitude encoding).

## NEEDS

It all costs money—money to purchase the equipment, and money to maintain it. It's quite easy to spend more for avionics than you originally spent for your classic.

Now let's examine your flying needs/habits and apply them to avionics.

If you are a casual flier, and do little or no cross-country flying, then you can get by with a minimum of equipment:

☐ ELT.

If you do some VFR cross-country flying you'll need a little more equipment just for convenience,

KY 92 COMM TRANSCEIVER INTERIOR VIEW

Fig. 16-2. Inside the King KY 92. This unit is entirely solid state, therefore is cool running, and uses little electrical power. (courtesy King Avionics)

Fig. 16-3. King KX 170B NAV COMM. This particular radio is one of the most popular NAV COMMs ever built. (courtesy King Avionics)

Fig. 16-4. Narco MK 12D NAV COMM. This unit has digital readout, and by a flick of the active/standby switch instant frequency change is possible. (courtesy Narco Avionics)

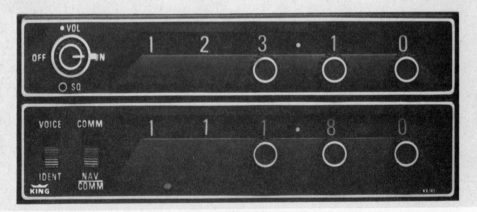

Fig. 16-5. King KX 145 NAV COMM. (courtesy King Avionics)

Fig. 16-6. CDIs by King. The KI 208 is for VOR only, and the KI 209 displays VOR and glideslope. (courtesy King Avionics)

and to utilize those electronic airways our tax money goes for:

- [ ] NAV/COMM.
- [ ] XPNDR.
- [ ] ELT.

Fig. 16-7. Narco Escort II. This unit fits a standard 3″ panel hole, and weighs only 3 pounds (width 3.25″, height 3.25″, depth 10.75″). Its key features are: Automatic Omni, Digital RMI, Electronic Course Deviation Indicator, Digital OBS, High visibility display, 5 watt transmitter, small size; saves panel space and electric power. (courtesy Narco Avionics)

Should you be flying all over the country on extensive trips, you might want to add an extra NAV/COMM just as a backup.

If you fly occasional IFR, you'll need still more equipment:

- [ ] Dual NAV/COMM.
- [ ] LOC/GS/MBR.
- [ ] ADF.
- [ ] XPNDR.
- [ ] ELT.

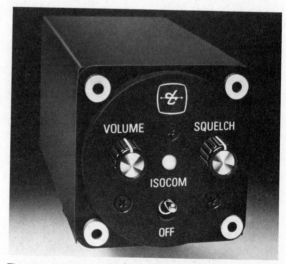

Fig. 16-8. Intercom unit allows pilot and passenger to converse via headphones. (courtesy David Clark Co.)

Fig. 16-9. Narco CP 136 audio panel used to control several radio devices. (courtesy Narco Avionics)

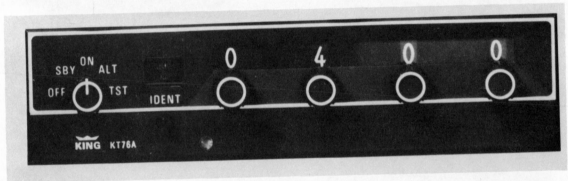

Fig. 16-10. King KT 76A transponder. (courtesy King Avionics)

Fig. 16-11. Narco AT 150 transponder. (courtesy Narco Avionics)

Some of the classics don't have electrical systems, so you may wonder what you do in that case for electric power. Really, it's quite simple: A wind generator is installed under the fuselage to supply power to a small battery.

A wind generator has a small propeller on it that is mounted directly to the armature shaft. As you move forward, the propeller turns the shaft,

### New Equipment

New equipment is state-of-the-art, offering the newest innovations, best reliability, smallest size, lowest power requirements, and—best of all—a warranty.

New avionics can be purchased from your local avionics dealer, or thru a discount house (many advertise in *Trade-A-Plane*).

You can visit your local avionics dealer and purchase all the equipment you want, and have him install it. Of course, this will be the most expensive method. However, you'll have new equipment, expert installation, and service backup.

The discount house will save you money at the time of the initial purchase, but you may be left out when the need for warranty service arises. Some manufacturers won't honor warranty service requests unless the equipment was purchased from and installed by an authorized dealer. This may not seem fair to the consumer, but it is an effective method of protecting the authorized dealers.

### Used Equipment

Used avionics may be purchased from dealers or individuals. The aviation magazines and *Trade-A-Plane* are good sources of used equipment.

A few words of advice for those contemplating the purchase of used avionics:

- ☐ Purchase nothing with tubes in it.
- ☐ Purchase nothing more than six years old.
- ☐ Purchase nothing made by a defunct manufacturer.
- ☐ Purchase nothing "as is."
- ☐ Purchase nothing "working when removed."

Used equipment can be a wise investment, but it is very risky unless you happen to be an avionics technician, or have access to one. I recommend against the purchase of used avionics unless you are *very* familiar with the source.

There are a few purists who will purchase and completely rebuild vintage equipment for their classic. This is for cosmetic reasons only, and

Fig. 16-12. Narco HT 800 COMM. This handheld COMM is the answer for the pilot flying a plane with no electrical system. (courtesy Narco Avionics)

and electricity is generated. Wind generators used to power only a single COMM radio. Remember, when that original radio was built it had vacuum tubes in it, and drew lots of power. It was all the wind generator system could handle. However, with today's new solid-state electronics, you could power an amazing amount of avionics with a simple system such as this.

By the way, there is a wind generator system on the ultra-modern Boeing 767 airliner. It deploys in case of electrical failure, and provides the power necessary for a safe landing.

### FILLING THE PANEL

There are several ways of going about filling those vacant spots on your instrument panel.

Fig. 16-13. The panel of this 1941 J5A shows an easy mix of new and old.

## Reconditioned Equipment

unless you are going after prizes at airshows, I recommend against this. Even when completely rebuilt, the equipment is very limited, and often unreliable (as was often the case when new).

## Reconditioned Equipment

There are several companies that advertise reconditioned avionics at bargain (or at least low) prices.

This equipment has been removed from service and completely checked out by an avionics shop. Parts that have failed, are near failure, or are likely to fail, will have been replaced.

These radios offer a fair buy for the airplane owner, and are normally warrantied by the seller for a specified period of time.

However, reconditioned is not new. Everything in the unit has been used but not everything will be replaced during reconditioning. You will have some new parts, and some old parts.

## Radio Kits

Now enter the latest method of purchasing avionics. Buy kits and build them yourself.

Radio Systems Technology offers a limited line of avionics from audio panels to a 720 channel NAV/COMM in kit form.

For certification purposes, you build it, then ship it back to the manufacturer for checkout and certification. By building it you will save money and learn about the inside of these complex boxes (so says the kit manufacturers). RST will also service it at a later date, should you need it. This is certainly an interesting way for the budget-minded individual to acquire avionics.

Fig. 16-14. Many "classic" airplanes have no electrical system. However, with a wind-driven generator such as this, a modern NAV/COMM can be operated from a small rechargeable battery. The unit is only a few inches across.

## SUMMARY

I have many years of experience in electronics and strongly recommend that when contemplating the purchase of avionics, *save your money until you can purchase new equipment.*

If you have equipment on board that is currently working properly, keep it and save your money. Above all, if it works, *don't fix it.* As soon as someone gets into these boxes to realign, or just to "touch up" the tuning, the box thinks it's found a new Mama, and will holler for her at all inconvenient times. If you decide to replace your older equipment, either keep the stuff as a second system, spares, or make an outright sale. You won't get real dollar value on a trade, and dual systems are nice to have.

Recommended reading: *Upgrading Your Airplane's Avionics,* TAB book No. 2301, by Timothy R.V. Foster.

# Chapter 17

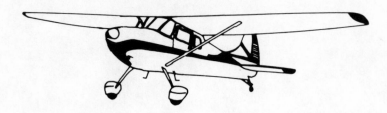

# A New Classic You Can Build

If the idea of a classic airplane appeals to you, but you don't care to fly an airplane that is approaching 40 years of age, there is an alternative—build an airplane based upon the classics.

Building an airplane is lots of work; however, the rewards are plenty, and there are certain side benefits. You have the pride of your work, and a plane that is custom built *for* and *by* you. You can maintain it, including giving the annual inspections, and make any changes or repairs to it.

## WAG-AERO SPORT TRAINER

The following is reprinted by permission of Wag-Aero:

You, as a builder, can now reproduce the most nostalgic, reliable, and economical plane of all time—a classic design of proven performance and serviceability. To aid your project, you have at your disposal 15 sheets of detailed drawings, plus isometrics, full-sized patterns, and references to part numbers; individual material kits which allow

ease of purchasing and considerable savings; many pre-assembled parts, allowing speedy completion and minimum tool investment. Availability of parts is vast. For those of you who have some earlier Piper parts at your disposal, your project is already started, as all earlier parts are directly interchangeable on the Sport Trainer. All of these advantages put together a unique program to aid you in constructing the airplanes that is every pilot's dream.

Build an authentic replica and relive the 1930s with a Sport Trainer that is brand new—rigged correctly, trimmed right, and perfect to the touch, or improvise your best ideas on an already proven design. View the countryside with a wide range of engines—make and hp to suit your taste and budget. Plan cross-countries utilizing the 13 1/2 gallon auxiliary wing tank kit. Install the arctic heater and extend your fun flying throughout the year. Replace the wheels with skis, and you'll look forward to the first snowfall. Teach your son or daughter the basics of flying in the best trainer ever. And don't forget—the Sport Trainer will take off in 375 feet and land in less, and is extremely maneuverable in the air. The Sport Trainer is truly everybody's airplane.

The kits available have been engineered by Wag-Aero to allow the customer the least amount of effort in locating the necessary items to build the Sport Trainer, and at the same time allowing a considerable savings from individual purchase price. Materials are conveniently divided into distinct kits, allowing separate purchases as the project is completed, and allowing purchase of only needed items at a reasonable cost. Wag-Aero has had many years of experience in Sport Trainer components, and also in the marketing of material kits for homebuilt aircraft. The Sport Trainer material kits and engineered drawings are a culmination of this past experience, along with a genuine interest among aircraft enthusiasts for the classic design of the Sport Trainer.

The Sport Trainer is a fun airplane—interesting to build and fun to fly. You can feel the pleasure and accomplishment of not only building, but owning the finest two-place utility aircraft.

## Specifications

| | | |
|---|---:|---|
| Top Speed | 102 | mph |
| Cruise Speed | 94 | mph |
| Stall Speed | 39 | mph |
| Rate of Climb | 490 | fpm |
| Range (std) | 220 | mi |
| (aux) | 455 | mi |
| Svc Ceiling | 12,000 | ft |
| Glide Ratio | 10:1 | |
| Empty Weight | 720 | lbs |
| Useful Load | 680 | lbs |
| Gross Weight | 1400 | lbs |
| Fuel Cap (std) | 12 | gal |
| (aux) | 26 | gal |
| Fuel Consump. | 4.8 | gph |
| Length | 22 ft 2 3/4 | in |
| Wing Span | 35 ft 2 1/2 | in |
| Height | 6 ft 8 | in |
| Engine | 65 hp through 125 hp | |

## WAG-AERO SPORTSMAN 2 + 2

The following is reprinted by permission of Wag-Aero:

A true four-place amateur-built aircraft, designed for the recreational pilot, the Sportsman combines many great characteristics, providing roominess for four, and versatility such as extra baggage area and additional fuel. With all the improvements, the Sportsman still retains the docile maneuverability and short field capabilities of the Sport Trainer. Wide-stance landing gear and slow-speed characteristics make it an ideal trainer for you or your family. For the sport recreational pilot, it offers superior floatplane performance and easy accessibility with its unique doors and optional turtledeck entry. The Sportsman utilizes large tires for off-airport operation, and has instrument panel layout to accommodate full IFR radio and gyro group.

Building of the aircraft is a pleasure with the most comprehensive set of drawings furnished to date. Convenient builder material kits are available, with many preformed, pre-bent, and finished parts, for ease and speed of construction. The Sportsman will accept standard wings from Piper PA-12, PA-14, PA-18, or use our convenient kit and construct your own.

Now is the time! You will be pleasantly surprised with the in-depth detail of the drawings. You will appreciate the availability of the material kits. You will relish the versatility of the airplane. Experience the satisfaction of building and owning this great utilitarian airplane!

## Specifications

| | | |
|---|---:|---|
| Top Speed | 129 | mph |
| Cruise Speed | 124 | mph |
| Stall Speed | 38 | mph |
| Rate of Climb | 800 | fpm |
| Range | 670 | mi |
| Svc Ceiling | 14,800 | ft |
| Glide Ratio | 11:1 | |
| Empty Weight | 1080 | lbs |
| Useful Load | 1120 | lbs |
| Gross Weight | 2200 | lbs |
| Fuel Cap | 39 | gal |
| Length | 23 ft 4 1/2 | in |
| Wing Span | 35 ft 9 | in |

Fig. 17-1. The Wag-Aero Sport Trainer. (courtesy Wag-Aero)

Fig. 17-2. The basic superstructure of the Sport Trainer. Notice the similarity to the Piper J3. (photo by Lee Fray of the Sport Aviation Association, courtesy Wag-Aero)

Fig. 17-3. The Sportsman 2+2. (courtesy Wag-Aero)

| Height | 6 ft 7 1/2 in |
| Engine | 125 hp through 200 hp |

## KIT COSTS

The basic prices (1986) for these airplane kits are:

| Wag-Aero Trainer | $9942.00 |
| Wag-Aero Sportsman 2+2 | $9014.50 |

This is a materials kit and includes no prewelded structures, engine, propeller, or the finishing color coating. Wag-Aero does make available some jig welded assemblies, including complete fuselages (Figs. 17-1 through 17-5).

For further information about these airplanes, contact Wag-Aero. The address is in Appendix A.

Fig. 17-4. The basic superstructure of the Sportsman 2+2. Notice the optional hinged turtledeck. (courtesy Wag-Aero)

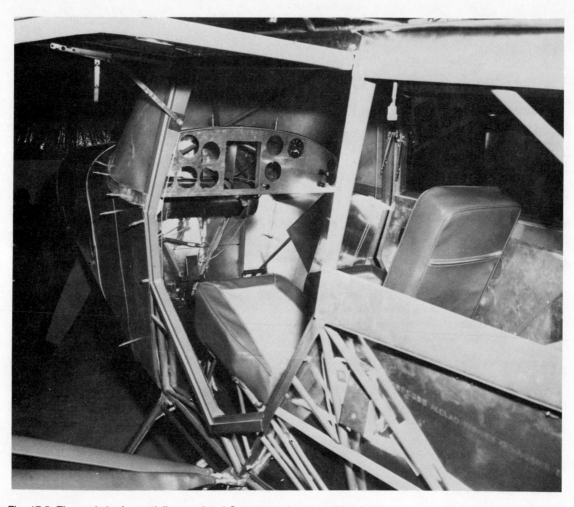

Fig. 17-5. The cockpit of a partially completed Sportsman. (courtesy Wag-Aero)

# Appendix A

# Manufacturers and Suppliers

The following is a list of addresses of manufacturers and suppliers of parts and equipment for classic airplanes.

**Airtex Products Inc.** *(interiors/coverings)*
259 Lower Morrisville Rd.
Fallsington, PA 19054
Phone: (215) 295-4115

**Avco Lycoming**
Williamsport, PA 17701

**Blue River Aircraft Supply** *(Ceconite 7600)*
Box 91
Harvard, NE 68944
Phone: (402) 772-3651

**Ceconite Co.**
4677 Worth St.
Los Angeles, CA 90063
Phone: (213) 266-2793

**Cessna Aircraft Co.**
Box 1521
Wichita, KS 67201
Phone: (316) 685-9111

**Continental Teledyne**
Box 90
Mobile, AL 36601

**David Clark Co.** *(headsets)*
376 Franklin St.
Worcester, MA 01604
Phone: (617) 756-6216

**King Radio Corp.**
400 N. Rogers Rd.
Olathe, KS 66062
Phone: (913) 782-0400

**Narco Avionics**
270 Commerce Dr.
Ft. Washington, PA 19034
Phone: (215) 643-2900

**Radio Systems Technology, Inc.**
13281-T Grass Valley Ave.
Grass Valley, CA 95945
Phone: (916) 272-2203

**Razorback Fabrics, Inc.**
Manila, AR 72442
Phone: (501) 561-4447

**Sensenich Corp.**
Box 4187
Lancaster, PA 17604
Phone: (717) 569-0435

**Skyport Aircoupe Svcs.** *(Ercoupe parts)*
1340 Francis St.
Jackson, MI 49203

**Stits Poly-Fiber Aircraft Coatings**
Box 3084
Riverside, CA 92519
Phone: (714) 684-4280

**Taylorcraft Aviation Corporation**
P.O. Box 947
820 E. Bald Eagle St.
Lock Haven, PA 17745
Phone: (717) 748-6712

**Univair** *(parts)*
2500 Himalaya Rd.
Aurora, CO 80011
Phone: (303) 364-7661

**Wag-Aero Inc.** *(parts)*
Box 181
Lyons, WI 53148
Phone: (414) 763-9586

# Appendix B

# General Aviation District Offices

FAA GADO (General Aviation District Offices) and FSDO (Flight Standards District Offices) are listed here by state. For assistance, call the office nearest you.

## Alabama
**GADO 2**
6500 43rd Avenue, North
Birmingham, AL 35206
Phone: (205) 254-1393

## Alaska
**GADO 1**
1515 East 13th Avenue
Anchorage, AK 99501
Phone: (907) 272-1324 and 279-5231

**FSDO 61**
3788 University Avenue
Fairbanks, AK 99701
Phone: (907) 452-1276

**FSDO 62**
Post Office Box 2118
Juneau, AK 99701
Phone: (907) 586-3700

## Arizona
**GADO 9**
15041 North Airport Drive
Scottsdale, AZ 85260
Phone: (602) 241-2561

## Arkansas
**GADO 6**
FAA NWS Building, Room 201
Adams Field
Little Rock, AR 72202
Phone: (501) 372-3437

## California
**GADO 1**
7120 Hayvenhurst Avenue, Suite 316
Van Nuys, CA 91406
Phone: (213) 997-3191

**GADO 2**
1387 Airport Boulevard
San Jose, CA 95110
Phone: (408) 275-7681

**GADO 3**
3750 John J. Montgomery Drive
San Diego, CA 95110
Phone: (714) 293-5280

**GADO 4**
Fresno Air Terminal
2401 North Ashley
Fresno, CA 93727
Phone: (209) 487-5306

**GADO**
Santa Monica Municipal Airport
3200 Airport Avenue, Suite 3
Santa Monica, CA 90405
Phone: (213) 391-6701

**GADO 8**
Riverside Municipal Airport
6961 Flight Road
Riverside, CA 92504
Phone: (714) 787-1245

**GADO 12**
Executive Airport
Sacramento, CA 95822
Phone: (916) 440-3169

**FSDO 64**
P.O. Box 2397
Airport Station
Oakland, CA 94614
Phone: (415) 273-7155

**FSDO 65**
2815 East Spring Street
Long Beach, CA 90806
Phone: (213) 426-7134

**Colorado**
**GADO 3**
Jefferson County Airport
Building 1
Broomfield, CO 80020
Phone: (303) 466-7326

**GADO 3S**
764 Horizon Drive
Grand Junction, CO 81501
Phone: (303) 243-9518

**Connecticut**
**GADO 19**
(*See* Massachusetts)

**Delaware**
**GADO 9**
North Philadelphia Airport
Philadelphia, PA 19114
Phone: (215) 597-9708

**District of Columbia**
**FSDO 62**
GT Bldg., Suite 112
Box 17325
Dulles International Airport
Washington, D.C. 20041
Phone: (703) 557-5360

**Florida**
**GADO 5**
Building 121
Opa Locka Airport
Opa Locka, FL 33054
Phone: (305) 681-7431

**GADO 7**
FAA Building
Craig Field
855 Saint John's Bluff Road
Jacksonville, FL 32211
Phone: (904) 641-7311

**FSDO 64**
Saint Petersburg/Clearwater Airport
Clearwater, FL 33520
Phone: (813) 531-1434

**Georgia**
**GADO 1**
FAA Building
Fulton County Airport
Atlanta, GA 30336
Phone: (404) 221-6481

**Hawaii**
**FSDO 61**
218 Lagoon Drive
Room 215
Honolulu, HI 96819
Phone: (808) 836-0615

**Idaho**
**GADO 1**
3975 Rickenbacker Street
Boise, ID 83705
Phone: (203) 334-1238

**Illinois**
**GADO 3**
Post Office Box H
DuPage County Airport
West Chicago, IL 60185
Phone: (312) 584-4490

**GADO 19**
Capitol Airport
Springfield, IL 62708
Phone: (217) 525-4238

**Indiana**
**GADO 10**
Indianapolis International Airport
Box 41525
Indianapolis, IN 46241
Phone: (317) 247-2491

**GADO 18**
1843 Commerce Drive
South Bend, IN 46628
Phone: (219) 232-5843

**Iowa**
**GADO 4**
3021 Army Post Road
Des Moines, IA 50321
Phone: (515) 284-4094

**Kansas**
**GADO 11**
Administration Building
Fairfax Municipal Airport
Kansas City, KS 66115
Phone: (913) 281-3491

**GADO 22**
Flight Standards Building
Mid-Continent Airport
Wichita, KS 67209
Phone: (316) 943-3244

**Kentucky**
**GADO 13**
FAA Building
Bowman Field
Louisville, KY 40205
Phone: (502) 582-6116

**Louisiana**
**GADO 8**
FAA Building
Lakefront Airport
New Orleans, LA 70126
Phone: (504) 241-2506

**GADO 8 South**
FAA Office
Lafayette Airport
Lafayette, LA 70508
Phone: (318) 234-2321

## GADO 11
Terminal Building
Room 137
Downtown Airport
Shreveport, LA 71107
Phone: (318) 226-5379

## Maine
## GADO 15
Portland International Jetport
Portland, ME 04102
Phone: (207) 774-4484

## Maryland
## GADO 21
Elm Road
BWI International Airport
Baltimore, MD 21240
Phone: (301) 761-2610

## Massachusetts
## GADO 13
Norwood Municipal Airport
Norwood, MA 02062
Phone: (617) 762-2436

## GADO 19
Barnes Municipal Airport
Westfield, MA 01085
Phone: (413) 568-3121

## Michigan
## GADO 8
Kent County International Airport
5500 44th Street SE
Grand Rapids, MI 49508
Phone: (616) 456-2427

## GADO 20
Flight Standards Building
Willow Run Airport
Box 860
Ypsilanti, MI 48197
Phone: (313) 485-2550

## Minnesota
## GADO 14
6201 34th Avenue South
Minneapolis, MN 55450
Phone: (612) 725-3341

## Mississippi
## GADO 4
FAA Building Municipal Airport
Box 6273
Pearl Branch
Jackson, MS 39208
Phone: (601) 969-4633

## Missouri
## FSDO 62
9275 Jenaire Drive
Burkley, MO 63134
Phone: (314) 425-7100

## Montana
## FSDO 61
Administration Building
Room 216
Billings Logan International Airport
Billings, MT 59101
Phone: (406) 245-6179

## FSDO 65
FAA Building
Room 3
Helena Airport
Helena, MT 59601
Phone: (406) 499-5270

## Nebraska
## GADO 12
General Aviation Building
Lincoln Municipal Airport
Lincoln, NE 68521
Phone: (402) 471-5485

## Nevada

**GADO 11**
601 South Rock Blvd.
Suite 102
Reno, NV 89502
Phone: (702) 784-5321

**FSDO 66**
5700 C South Haven
Las Vegas, NV 89119
Phone: (702) 736-0666

## New Hampshire

**GADO 15**
(*See* Maine)

## New Jersey

**FSDO 61**
150 Riser Road
Teterboro Airport
Teterboro, NJ 07608
Phone: (201) 288-1745

## New Mexico

**GADO 1**
2402 Kirtland Drive, SE
Albuquerque, NM 87106
Phone: (505) 247-0156

## New York

**GADO 1**
Albany County Airport
Albany, NY 12211
Phone: (518) 869-8482

**GADO 11**
Building 53
Republic Airport
Farmingdale, NY 11735
Phone: (516) 694-5530

**GADO 17**
Rochester-Monroe Airport
Rochester, NY 14624
Phone: (716) 263-5880

## North Carolina

**GADO 3**
FAA Building
Municipal Airport
Box 27005
Charlotte, NC 28219
Phone: (704) 392-3214

**GADO 11**
Route 1, Box 486A
Morrisville, NC 27560
Phone: (919) 755-4240

## North Dakota

**FSDO 64**
Box 5496
Fargo, ND 58105
Phone: (701) 232-8949

## Ohio

**GADO 5**
4242 Airport Road
Lunken Executive Building
Cincinnati, OH 45226
Phone: (513) 684-2183

**GADO 6**
Federal Facilities Building
Cleveland Hopkins International Airport
Cleveland, OH 44135
Phone: (216) 267-0220

**GADO 7**
4393 East 17th Avenue
Port Columbus International Airport
Columbus, OH 43219
Phone: (614) 469-7476

## Oklahoma

**GADO 9**
FAA Building
Wiley Post Airport
Bethany, OK 73008
Phone: (405) 789-5220

**FSDO 65**
General Aviation Terminal Building
Room 103
Tulsa International Airport
6501 E Apache
Tulsa, OK 74115
Phone: (918) 835-2378

## Oregon
**GADO 2**
Mahlon Sweet Airport
90606 Greenhill Road
Eugene, OR 97402
Phone: (503) 688-9721

**GADO 3**
Portland/Hillsboro Airport
3355 NE Cornell Road
Hillsboro, OR 97123
Phone: (503) 221-2104

## Pennsylvania
**GADO 3**
Allentown-Bethlehem-Easton Airport
Allentown, PA 18103
Phone: (215) 264-2888

**GADO 9**
North Philadelphia Airport
Philadelphia, PA 19114
Phone: (215) 597-9708

**GADO 10**
Room 201
Administration Building
Capitol City Airport
New Cumberland, PA 17070
Phone: (717) 782-4528

**GADO 14**
Allegheny County Airport
West Mifflin, PA 15122
Phone: (412) 462-5507

## Rhode Island
**GADO 13**
(*See* Massachusetts)

## South Carolina
**GADO 9**
Columbia Metropolitan Airport
West Columbia, SC 29169
Phone: (803) 765-5931

## South Dakota
**FSDO 66**
Rural Route 2, Box 633B
Rapids City, SD 57701
Phone: (605) 343-2403

## Tennessee
**FSDO 62**
322 Knapp Blvd.
Room 101
Nashville Metropolitan Airport
Nashville, TN 37217
Phone: (615) 251-5661

**FSDO 63**
2488 Winchester
Room 137
Memphis, TN 38116
Phone: (901) 345-0600

## Texas
**GADO 2**
8032 Aviation Place
Love Field Airport
Dallas, TX 75235
Phone: (214) 357-0142

**GADO 3**
FAA NWS Building
Room 202
6795 Convair Road
El Paso, TX 79925
Phone: (915) 778-6389

**FSDO 61**
Administration Building
Room 240
Meacham Field
Fort Worth, TX 76106
Phone: (817) 624-4911

**FSDO 62**
8800 Paul B Koonce Drive
Room 224
Houston, TX 77061
Phone: (713) 645-6628

**GADO 7**
Route 3, Box 51
Lubbock, TX 79401
Phone: (806) 762-0335

**FSDO 64**
1115 Paul Wilkins Road
Room 201
San Antonio, TX 78216
Phone: (512) 824-9535

## Utah
**FSDO 67**
116 North 2400 West
Salt Lake City, UT 84116
Phone: (801) 524-4247

## Vermont
**GADO 15**
(*See* Maine)

## Virginia
**GADO 16**
Byrd Field
Sandstone, VA 23150
Phone: (804) 222-7494

**FSDO 62**
GT Building, Suite 112
Box 17325
Dulles International Airport
Washington, D.C. 20041
Phone: (703) 557-5360

## Washington
**GADO 5**
5620 East Rutter Avenue
Spokane, WA 99206
Phone: (509) 456-4618

**FSDO 61**
FAA Building
Boeing Field
Seattle, WA 98108
Phone: (206) 767-2724

## West Virginia
**GADO 22**
301 Eagle Mountain Road
Room 144
Kanawha Airport
Charleston, WV 25311
Phone: (304) 343-4689

## Wisconsin
**FSDO 61**
General Mitchell Field
FAA/WB Building
Milwaukee, WI 53207
Phone: (414) 747-5531

## Wyoming
**FSDO 62**
Natrona County International Airport
FAA/WB Building
Casper, WY 82601
Phone: (307) 234-8959

# Appendix C

# Prices of Classics

It is difficult to place exact values on *any* airplane, and the classic airplanes are even more difficult than most.

The reasons for this difficulty is the differences among the various examples found on the market. Among these variables are:

- ☐ Total usage.
- ☐ Engine condition.
- ☐ Fabric/metal skin condition.
- ☐ Corrosion.
- ☐ Avionics.
- ☐ Interior condition.
- ☐ Damage history.
- ☐ Quality of recent work.
- ☐ Availability of parts.
- ☐ Insurability.

And the list could go on; however, these are among the more common variables you must consider when purchasing a classic airplane.

## PRICE GUIDE

The following is a list of various classics by make and model, and given is an average value. This value must be adjusted up/down depending on the above variables. Additionally, prices vary proportionately with the buyer's desire to purchase and the seller's wish to market. *Buyer beware*.

| *Make* | *Model* | *$Value* |
|---|---|---|
| **Aeronca** | 7AC | 5,500 |
| | 7BCC | 5,700 |
| | 7CCM | 5,700 |
| | 7DC | 5,800 |
| | 7EC | 6,600 |
| **(Champion)** | 7EC | 7,000 |
| | 7FC | 7,000 |
| | 7ACA | 5,000 |
| **Cessna** | 120 | 6,600 |
| | 140 | 6,800 |
| | 140A | 7,700 |
| | 170 | 9,000 |

| | | | | | |
|---|---|---|---|---|---|
| | 170A | 10,500 | | PA-14 | 8,000 |
| | 170B | 12,000 | | PA-15 | 6,000 |
| **Ercoupe** | 415C | 5,500 | | PA-16 | 8,000 |
| | 415D | 5,500 | | PA-17 | 6,500 |
| | 415E | 6,000 | | PA-18/90 | 8,000 |
| **(Forney)** | | 6,400 | | PA-18/150 | 12-15,000 |
| **(Alon)** | | 7,200 | | PA-20 | 8,000 |
| **(Mooney)** | | 9,000 | | PA-22/125 | 6,000 |
| **Luscombe** | 8A,B | 7,000 | | PA-22/150 | 7,000 |
| | 8C,D | 7,200 | | PA-22/Colt | 5,000 |
| | 8E | 7,500 | **Stinson** | 108 | 7,000 |
| | 8F | 8,000 | | 108-1 | 7,200 |
| **Piper** | J3 | 9,000 | | 108-2,3 | 8,500 |
| | J4 | 7,000 | **Taylorcraft** | BC12-D | 5,000 |
| | J5 | 8,500 | | 19 | 8,000 |
| | J5C | 8,900 | | F-19 | 9,500 |
| | PA-11 | 7,000 | | F-21 | 19,000 |
| | PA-12 | 9,500 | | | |

# Index

Edited by Steven H. Mesner

# Other Bestsellers From TAB

☐ **LIGHTPLANE REFURBISHING TECHNIQUES—Joe Christy**

Discover how you can save up to 80 percent of the cost of refurbishing a lightplane using the new FAA-approved aircraft recovering, painting, and interior refurbishing materials that were introduced in the early 1980's—lightweight Dacrons with special finishes, the water-based Ceconite 7600 system, and new plastic beads which can strip old paint from aluminum alloy aircraft skins without damaging the aluminum coating. 160 pp., 160 illus.

**Paper $12.95**            **Hard $18.95**
**Book No. 2437**

☐ **THE CESSNA 172—Bill Clarke**

If you're the owner of a Cessna 172, a prospective owner, pilot, dealer, service or maintenance person, or anyone else who needs a quick reference to Cessnas . . . you'll find all the information you need conveniently gathered together and clearly presented in this buyer's guide. It supplies all the background knowledge on these airplanes that you need to make a wise purchase, new or used, to improve the performance and comfort of your Cessna, to make sure it meets all the FAA requirements, and to keep it running safely and smoothly for years. 320 pp., 113 illus.

**Paper $12.95**            **Hard $19.95**
**Book No. 2412**

☐ **THE ILLUSTRATED HANDBOOK OF AVIATION AND AEROSPACE FACTS—Joe Christy**

A complete look at American aviation—civil and military. All the political, social, economic, and personality factors that have influenced the state of U.S. military airpower, the boom-and-bust cycles in Civil aviation, America's manned and unmanned space flights, and little-known facts on the flights, and little-known facts on the birth of modern rocketry, it's all here in this complete sourcebook! 480 pp., 486 illus.

**Paper $28.95**            **Book No. 2397**

☐ **FLYING A FLOATPLANE—Marin Faure**

Generously laced with illustrations and photos to provide fascinating insight on every facet of this unique breed of flight—from the history of floatplanes and a look at currently available aircraft to what it's like to fly one, unique takeoff and landing characteristics, taxiing, docking, maintenance tips, even emergency procedures. Plus, there's an invaluable section covering both American and Canadian floatplane regulations. 256 pp., 135 illus.

**Paper $16.95**            **Book No. 2379**

☐ **PILOT'S CROSS-COUNTRY GUIDE TO NATIONAL PARKS AND HISTORICAL MONUMENTS—Vici and Warren DeHaan**

This book catalogs historical national landmarks, monuments, and parks located throughout the United States. Specific information is supplied on the sites' access to airports, restaurants, lodging, ground transportation, and more. The authors, who have visited all the landmarks and parks included in this guide, offer firsthand advice on both sightseeing and area accommodations. 192 pp., 128 illus.

**Paper $14.95**            **Book No. 2413**

☐ **WINGS OF THE WEIRD AND WONDERFUL—Captain Eric Brown**

*The Guinness Book of Records* lists Captain Eric "Winkle" Brown, the former Chief Naval Test Pilot and Commanding Officer of Great Britain's Aerodynamic Flight at the Royal Aircraft Establishment, as having flown more types of aircraft than any other pilot in the world! Though his test and naval flying writings are already internationally known, he has once more opened his flying logbooks to reveal some of the more unusual types of aircraft. 176 pp., 77 illus.

**Paper $12.95**            **Hard $19.95**
**Book No. 2404**

☐ **UNCONVENTIONAL AIRCRAFT—Peter M. Bowers**

Here's a pictorial account of over 75 years of "far-out" flying machines—probably the largest collection of unconventional aircraft information ever assembled! Examine the biplane/monoplane, flying automobiles and convertaplanes, the ambulance planes, the special seaplanes and the "what-is-its." You'll find amazing and unusual planes that are tailless, rotary propelled, that move in the air, on land and water. 288 pp., 352 illus.

**Paper $17.95**            **Book No. 2384**

☐ **FLY LIKE A PRO—Donald J. Clausing**

This is a handbook that should be required reading for every pilot—aspiring professional or private IFR or VFR pilot. It's your opportunity to learn professional flying techniques by flying co-pilot with a senior captain—a learning experience that all professional pilots go through but one that few private pilots ever encounter. The author gives indepth coverage of all the things that make up advanced, no-nonsense airmanship. 252 pp., 18 illus.

**Paper $13.95**            **Book No. 2378**

# Other Bestsellers From TAB

☐ **THE ILLUSTRATED BUYER'S GUIDE TO USED AIRPLANES—Clarke**

Includes invaluable time- and money-saving tips on purchasing a used aircraft including plane specs and a current price guide to Two-Placers, Four-Place Easy Fliers, Complex Airplanes. Heavy Haulers, and Affordable Twins. Designed to help you side-step this many pitfalls of the used aircraft market, this time- and money-saving guide has been compiled with input from many knowledgeable sources, plus the author's years of aviation experience. 288 pp., 167 illus.
**Paper  $16.95**                              **Book No. 2372**

☐ **HOW TO MAKE $10,000 A MONTH AG FLYING—Ward**

Imagine! You can earn big money in a field that offers a potentially lucrative, recession-proof business! So, chart your course and get ready to "take off" in an exciting career. You can be in the pilot's seat in less than 90 days! Guiding you through every phase of what is required of an Ag pilot it discusses such topics as: What does an Ag pilot do? Flying an Ag plane. The equipment. The chemicals. How to land that first job . . . and more! 210 pp., 12 illus.
**Paper  $12.95**                              **Book No. 2330**

☐ **FLYING WITH LORAN C—Bill Givens**

Now, for the first time, an experienced private pilot gives you all the facts on the Loran (long-range navigation) system originally developed for use by boats and ships . . . and the new amazingly lightweight and affordable, microprocessor-based Loran C equipment that can be easily installed in any lightplane, even homebuilts and ultralights! It's an essential sourcebook for every VFR private pilot looking for an efficient, low-cost navigational aid! 208 pp., 95 illus.
**Paper  $15.95**                              **Book No. 2370**

☐ **MAKE YOUR AIRPLANE LAST FOREVER—Nicholas E. Silitch**

Expensive aircraft repair bills can become a thing of the past with this easy-to-use handbook! All it takes to steer clear of budget-wrenching emergency repairs is simple preventive maintenance—troubleshooting techniques that will extend the operating life of your plane and increase its safety, dependability, and flying efficiency. You'll fly longer and safer—in a plane that looks and flies in tip-top shape! 160 pp., 83 illus.
**Paper  $10.95**                              **Book No. 2328**

*Prices subject to change without notice.

To purchase these or any other books from TAB, visit your local bookstore, return this coupon, or call toll-free 1-800-233-1128 (In PA and AK call 1-717-794-2191).

| Product No. | Hard or Paper | Title | Quantity | Price |
|---|---|---|---|---|
|  |  |  |  |  |
|  |  |  |  |  |
|  |  |  |  |  |

☐ Check or money order enclosed made payable to TAB BOOKS Inc.

Charge my  ☐ VISA  ☐ MasterCard  ☐ American Express

Acct. No. _____  Exp. _____

Signature _____

Please Print
Name _____

Company _____

Address _____

City _____

State _____  Zip _____

| | |
|---|---|
| Subtotal | |
| Postage/Handling ($5.00 outside U.S.A. and Canada) | $2.50 |
| In PA add 6% sales tax | |
| TOTAL | |

Mail coupon to:
**TAB BOOKS Inc.**
Blue Ridge Summit
PA 17294-0840                    BC